Border Cinema

Global Media and Race

Series Editor: Frederick Luis Aldama, The Ohio State University

Global Media and Race is a series focused on scholarly books that examine race and global media culture. Titles focus on constructions of race in media, including digital platforms, webisodes, multilingual media, mobile media, vlogs, and other social media, film, radio, and television. The series considers how race—and intersectional identities generally—is constructed in front of the camera and behind, attending to issues of representation and consumption as well as the making of racialized and antiracist media phenomena from script to production and policy.

Monica Hanna and Rebecca A. Sheehan, eds., *Border Cinema: Reimagining Identity through Aesthetics*

Border Cinema

Reimagining Identity through Aesthetics

EDITED BY MONICA HANNA
AND REBECCA A. SHEEHAN

Rutgers University Press
New Brunswick, Camden, and Newark, New Jersey, and London

Library of Congress Cataloging-in-Publication Data

Names: Hanna, Monica, editor of compilation. | Sheehan, Rebecca A., 1979– editor of compilation.
Title: Border cinema : reimagining identity through aesthetics / edited by Monica Hanna and Rebecca A. Sheehan.
Description: New Brunswick, N.J. : Rutgers University Press, [2019] | Series: Global media and race | Includes bibliographical references and index.
Identifiers: LCCN 2018027678| ISBN 9781978803169 (cloth) | ISBN 9781978803152 (pbk.)
Subjects: LCSH: Boundaries in motion pictures. | Identity (Psychology) in motion pictures. | Motion pictures—Aesthetics. | Digital cinematography.
Classification: LCC PN1995.9.B67 B665 2019 | DDC 791.43—dc23
LC record available at https://lccn.loc.gov/2018027678

A British Cataloging-in-Publication record for this book is available from the British Library.

∞ The paper used in this publication meets the requirements of the American National Standard for Information Sciences—Permanence of Paper for Printed Library Materials, ANSI Z39.48-1992.

www.rutgersuniversitypress.org

Manufactured in the United States of America

Contents

Border Cinema

1

Introduction

Moving Images: Contesting Global Borders in the Digital Age

MONICA HANNA AND
REBECCA A. SHEEHAN

The rise of digital media and the intensification of globalization since the 1990s have significantly transformed the form and content of global cinema. The coincidence of digitalization and globalization has produced what this book helps to define and describe as a flourishing border cinema: a cinema whose aesthetics reflect, construct, intervene in, denature, and reconfigure geopolitical borders. The chapters in this collection demonstrate how contemporary border cinema collectively resists border fortification processes and shows how cinematic media have functioned technologically and aesthetically to engender contemporary shifts in national and individual identities while imagining a way out of the limitations of current political rhetoric and ideologies. Industrial and aesthetic turns toward the digital have permitted both a spike in cinema's global distribution and formal innovations and experiments. These innovations have been particularly rich in the area of cinema's empathic uses of sound and image as part of what this volume identifies as a haptic border aesthetics—one that communicates unique individual experiences through a universal language of images, sound, affective and embodied responses to generic tropes, and tactility capable of crossing cultural borders.[1] Along with focusing on the various kinds of cinematic narratives that have registered contemporary border crises, this collection is interested in how recent shifts in cinematic aesthetics brought about by digital filmmaking formally reflect and mediate evolving conceptions of individual and collective identities in relation to global borders.

Film theorists have long understood (or misunderstood) the digital as rupturing analog filmmaking's photochemical index, its ontologically privileged relationship to the real. This apparent crisis occasioned by technological shifts in film production from the analog to the digital echoes disruptions caused by economic and political globalization that have led to an unfixing and reordering of indexes defining national identities. Political scientists and cultural theorists have in various ways registered how globalization's demands for transnational flows of labor and capital have contested the economic and political sovereignty of the modern nation-state. This movement from local to transnational economic, political, social, and individual identity formations is manifested in the rise of multilateral economic and political agreements, including entities like the European Union (EU), agreements like the North American Free Trade Agreement (NAFTA), and economic forums like the G20. The dislocation of the local, meanwhile, is reflected in the rising numbers of refugees and migrants across the globe, whose movements have been prompted by the high stakes of global capitalism.

This move toward the transnational has been further facilitated by technologies of the digital age. We see this in the rise of digital border crossings through social media, blogs, short messaging services, virtual private networks, and the like, used for purposes ranging from resistance and protest movements (the Arab Spring, Dakota Access Pipeline Resistance, the Me Too Movement, Occupy Wall Street, the Umbrella Movement in Hong Kong, and Yo Soy 132), to "alt" government Facebook and Twitter accounts that emerged following U.S. president Donald Trump's inauguration (Alt EPA, Alt National Park Service, Alt White House, and Rogue POTUS Staff), to the web-based deployment of political propaganda to influence the political process (Russia's intervention in the 2016 U.S. presidential election and various European elections); to recruitment efforts on the part of ideologically extremist groups (ranging from white supremacist and white nationalist organizations like the Ku Klux Klan and neo-Nazis to al-Qaeda and the Islamic State of Iraq and the Levant, commonly known as ISIS).

Perhaps nothing bears witness to these shifts more clearly than the current backlash against them evident in contemporary politics throughout Europe and the United States and articulated through various ideological positions, from populism and protectionism to antiglobalization. This backlash is typified by Trump's 2016 presidential campaign slogans and subsequent policy proposals, which have focused on bans and wall building, often using what Ian Haney López refers to as "dog whistle politics" to stoke racial animus, particularly against Arabs and Latinos. A similar backlash was manifested in Britain's "Brexit" vote, which was fueled by anti-immigrant, racist, and nationalist rhetoric.[2] A backlash against globalization and transnationalism has also been articulated through anticapitalist rather than xenophobic rhetoric, particularly by socialist political candidates in the West (from Jeremy Corbyn in the United Kingdom to Bernie Sanders in the United States) who have assumed similar antitrade and protectionist stances popular with both Trump and Brexit supporters.

Political theorist Wendy Brown reads the rise of wall building as a response to globalization perceived as a threat to national sovereignty.[3] The chapters in this volume variously read in cinematic terms the postglobalization backlash Brown puts her finger on as attempts to refix indexical relationships between nation and geography, skin color and religion, accent and citizenship—relationships that have been challenged in a world increasingly globalized by trade and technology. Though her book *Walled States, Waning Sovereignty* was published in 2010, the theories Brown presents are relevant to more recent political developments including the proposed U.S.-Mexican border wall and the effective wall that Brexit creates between the United Kingdom and European countries. Brown explores the paradoxes of Western countries extolling the tearing down of certain walls (notably, the Berlin Wall) and the opening of economic borders while constructing fences and walls at their own national borders. She links this national desire for walls, despite their demonstrated inefficacy and high cost, to unease with the nation-state's waning sovereignty as the perceived "price" of globalized capitalism's successes, arguing that these walls are meant to provide a visual testimony to sovereignty that is belied by their very existence. Brown's theorization of borders is essential for thinking about the relationship between the virtual and the real, ideology and spectacle, and how images both reflect and produce the world they inhabit. *Walled States, Waning Sovereignty* reminds us that these physical walls serve most importantly as spectacles rather than pragmatically as effective measures against real twenty-first-century threats to national security like cyberterrorism, which cannot be contained by walls. In these instances, the virtual qualities of the digital realize potent physical powers to transgress borders that render *real* physical borders into impotent but materially large (and expensive) spectacles whose power is limited and determined by their function as images circulated by the media in the service of various political agendas, from the production of xenophobia to the scapegoating of immigrants for the failures of late capitalism. The ideological power of the image has never been greater.

Along with *Walled States, Waning Sovereignty*, another important reference point for our work in this collection is Gloria E. Anzaldúa's seminal poetic and theoretical investigation of borders, *Borderlands/La Frontera: The New Mestiza*.

In this work Anzaldúa, like Wendy Brown after her, investigates the function of borders as spectacles of power and imposed demarcations of difference. For Anzaldúa, borders function as lines that both divide and connect. Significantly, Anzaldúa's interest in borders begins with the U.S.-Mexican national border, which is the setting for her family history in southern Texas, though she then applies her analysis to a broader conception of borders as the manifestation of binary epistemologies surrounding identity categories. Rejecting this binary thinking, she proposes the concept of a "borderlands" where these borders are muddled and binaries break down. The applicability of Anzaldúa's work goes far beyond the work of scholars thinking about the U.S.-Mexican border; it is invoked by scholars of transnational and marginalized communities more broadly. Taking a cue, then, from Anzaldúa, whose work informs many of the following chapters, our volume brings together investigations of border cinemas from the Americas, Asia, Europe, and the Middle East. While the chapters are by no means exhaustive or representative of the full spectrum of border cinema being produced around the globe, we have brought them together intentionally as works that speak to similar concerns and possibilities at this particular technological and political moment. The connections across these chapters demonstrate significant similarities and productive differences in how border cinemas across regions investigate the roles of borders and push the ways in which cinema can contest those very borders through aesthetic means afforded by novel technologies.

Border Cinema expands the parameters of what we understand by the terms that make up its title—*border* and *cinema*—and charts the implications for their ongoing intersections. As analog aesthetics give way to digital worlds, live-action images to computer-generated imagery (CGI), the passive spectator to the active user, and as age-old genres and tropes of national cinemas undergo recombination, cinema's expansions bear the imprint of and act as a metaphor for the expanded conceptions of geopolitical borders in a digital age. Cinema's expansions have involved multiple transitions. One of these is from the singular to the multiple, evident in the complexity and hypertextual tendencies of mainstream narrative cinema. A second transition is from the passive to the active, evident in recombinatory mechanisms that challenge linear narrative with hypertextual and contingent relations between images, from poetic aesthetics to video game adaptations, online fan communities, and virtual reality that transform spectators into users. A third transition is from the localized to the globalized, evident in the rise of the global distribution and consumption of cinema, along with cinema's new multiplatform saturation, with ubiquitous exhibition on screens as small as smartphones and as large as those found in theater megaplexes. The transitions marking cinema's expansions are also transitions that mark expanding concepts of borders. Border subjects now may mediate local situations through global media platforms, especially the new media of the internet, which has contested the geographic underpinnings for communities and identities by bringing subjects together who are physically worlds apart. Through an examination of expanded definitions of *border* and *cinema*, this collection updates the work of Ella Shohat and Robert Stam's groundbreaking collection *Multiculturalism, Postcoloniality, and Transnational Media*. Drawing in part on the Third Cinema movement, Shohat and Stam contend that "axes of identity" (nation, gender, race, sexuality, and ethnicity, among others) cannot be separated from the critical study of media and political power given "the global nature of the colonizing process [including neocolonial and neoimperialist processes], and the global reach of the contemporary media."[4] While *Border Cinema* stages a similarly interdisciplinary conversation, its focus on how the evolution of cinema's aesthetics have particularly reflected and participated in the figure of the border, a physical anathema to globalization's goals and digital technology's reach, allows for a more nuanced discussion about the relationship between aesthetics and identity.

Border Cinema also expands and updates the conversations of Hamid Naficy's collection *Home, Exile, Homeland: Film, Media, and the Politics of Place* and Jim Pines and Paul Willemen's *Questions of Third Cinema*, both of which were published at a globally momentous time that witnessed the reconfiguration of the former Soviet Union, Tiananmen Square and the transformations of post-Mao China, the release of Nelson Mandela, and other historical events that signaled a major shift in global borders and politics. This era marks the beginning of the era of globalization (and digital media) on which *Border Cinema* focuses its attention. Similarly to these earlier collections, *Border Cinema* registers a shift in global politics borne out by cinema at the crossroads of another major shift in global politics, this one characterized by both a backlash against the globalized economy loosed in the late 1980s and a recent surge of transgressions against the borders of identities (defined by the "axes" Stam and Shohat laid out: nation, gender, race, sexuality, and ethnicity) through a globe-crossing cultural and personal interactions enabled by digital technology.

At the same time that this volume explores the expanding notions of *border* and *cinema*, it also seeks to continue the conversation started by the major theorists of Third Cinema about the intertwined relationship between aesthetics and politics. For instance, Fernando Solanas and Octavio Getino's seminal essay "Toward a Third Cinema" called for a "cinema of subversion" to advance a "culture of subversion" that would combat the greatest weapon of neocolonialism, Hollywood. The cinema Solanas and Getino envisioned had to be subversive not only in its content but also in its visual and auditory aesthetics, in its very *form*. As Solanas and Getino open their 1968 film *La hora de los hornos* (The hour of the furnaces) with rapid-cut editing, they mimic their view of cinema as a weapon, the camera acting as a gun shooting down colonial narratives and the acceptance of the West's cultural imperialism. Similarly, Julio García Espinosa called for an "imperfect cinema" whose aesthetics of roughness, on-location filming, unpolished camerawork, and imperfect editing would counter Hollywood's aesthetics of high-budget visual perfection. These "imperfect" aesthetics worked against the cultural imperialism Hollywood was able to advance with shiny images of consumption. They also democratized filmmaking by making low-budget productions not only palatable but popular with Latin American audiences, opening an exhibition space for anyone who wanted to make movies, not just the wealthy of the First World. *Border Cinema* expands on the intersections between aesthetics and politics defined by Third Cinema proponents in the 1960s and 1970s and reimagined by film theorists of the 1980s. By focusing on the figure (and reconfigurations) of the border in the age of globalization, the application of cinema's aesthetics to politics has necessarily shifted from the Marxist concerns of Third Cinema at the height of Western imperialism to concerns about how digital aesthetics and expanded cinema impact and reflect identity (and its transformations) at a later stage of global capitalism. *Border Cinema* explores this critical shift.

Focusing on the intersection of contemporary cinematic aesthetics and borders, this collection intervenes in cinema studies and border studies in several essential ways. First, it considers how CGI, hypertext, and interactive aesthetics have been used to challenge essential, hegemonic, and homogeneous notions of identity and nationality. These techniques intervene in traditional conceptions of the power and unidirectionality of the cinematic image, from the screen's influence on the spectator to the assumed privilege of cinema's photographic index of reality. These digital shifts reveal that reality to be often a well-concealed construction, making the premise of the image as document just as suspect as the notion of the passive spectator. A recognition of the constructed nature of the cinematic image (and its correspondent ability to construct reality rather than simply reflect it), as well as the active potential of the spectator, have both been elevated in the postdigital age through hypertextual aesthetics and radical transformations in genre and national cinematic conventions. Several films analyzed in this collection use aesthetics to challenge homogeneous notions of identity through recombinatory mechanisms that challenge linear narrative processes by replacing the spectator with the user, the passive with the active, and the stable or fixed with the performative and changing, implying the self-determination of the individual as a challenge to the fixed identities and referents upon which borders depend.

Second, this volume explores how recent films and film cycles have innovated aesthetically and generically in order to raise challenges to traditional tropes that organize and define borders through the histories of national cinemas and traditional genre conventions. Several chapters investigate how interventions in and interruptions to the authority of the documentary image have been widely performed by aesthetic modes borrowed from subversive genres (animation, experimental cinema, television, and the music video) and used as figurative challenges to the authority of national borders and traditionally essentialized identifiers (race, gender, ethnicity, and class). Others explore how diverse challenges to traditional cinematic aesthetics have unsettled audience expectations when it comes to genre and film form (plot structure, editing, and mise-en-scène).

Finally, the volume examines how the ever increasing possibilities of digital production expand cinema's reach beyond sound and vision to the haptic, imagining novel avenues for empathic connection between radically different subjects, both on- and offscreen. Thus, the haptic promises an uncharted territory for sensing the other, challenging vision's primacy and its weakness as a sense quick to judge by appearances: the color of the other's skin, the other's gender, the other's class. It is thus no wonder that vision is the sense most traditionally associated with injustice. "Justice" is an allegorical figure who is necessarily "blind," and Plato depicts the deception of truth in the realm of vision: the shadowy underworld of the cave is the source of misperception and a naive belief in the reality of appearances. Sound might be construed as a secondary or corollary sense susceptible to the corruption of racist, nationalist, sexist, and xenophobic assumptions, for beyond sight we tend to create assumptions about identity through the sound of a voice: Does this person sound like a man or a woman? Black or white? Foreign or one of "us"? Touch, beyond being associated with physically reaching out beyond ourselves (either to comfort the other or to do violence to the other), bespeaks not only a novel sense in the realm of the cinematic (a medium dominated by vision and sound) but also a novel sense through which to connect with the other. Laura U. Marks, a film theorist whose work investigates the possibilities of "haptic visuality," aligns the intercultural in cinema with an overcoming of the primacy of the visual. She argues that "intercultural cinema bears witness to the reorganization of the senses that take place, and the new kinds of sense knowledges that become possible, when people move between cultures."[5] In *The Skin of the Film* Marks describes a "turn to the nonvisual senses" as "in part a response to the perceived imperialism of vision."[6] Several chapters in this collection take up this point, investigating contemporary border cinema's invocation of "nonvisual senses."

While the focus of this book is on how recent cinematic aesthetics interact with and intervene in conceptions of global borders and the racial, ethnic, and cultural identities so often defined by them, cinema's apparatus and aesthetics have actually long been interlaced with global borders. It is helpful to consider the relationship between borders and early cinema at a contemporary moment when film theorists have identified a return to the tendencies of cinema's origins in the slew of recent technologies (3-D, 4-D, high definition, and virtual reality) that promise the spectator immersive embodied sensations and experiences very much akin to what attracted the first film spectators in the late nineteenth century, many of whom took the moving image as real (transgressing the borders of the screen) and believing, for instance, that the train in Auguste and Louis Lumière's *Arrival of the Train at La Ciotat* would crash into them. It is thus unsurprising that the filmmaker Alejandro González Iñárritu used virtual reality in his 2017 exhibition *Carne y arena* (Flesh and sand) to break down the borders between "U.S. and Them" by sensorily immersing spectators in the experiences of refugees crossing the U.S.-Mexican border.

The genesis of cinema's apparatus can be understood as one rooted in division, emerging from photographic motion studies that attempted to divide a continuous and indivisible duration into discrete photographed instants, recalling the futile desires driving Zeno's Paradox of Motion and the realization that within the border—the interstice separating two discrete frames—arises the infinite possibility of unpictured, ungrasped frames. It is no wonder, then, that, as Mary Ann Doane argues in *The Emergence of Cinematic Time*, cinema emerged during a nineteenth-century zeitgeist of archive fever, a mania for collection in a period in which technology and industrial progress fueled Europe's colonial expansion (the collecting of territories).[7] All the same, while its mechanism divided and charted an actually continuous duration, cinema's illusion of motion relied equally fittingly upon human vision overlooking and transgressing "borders," perceiving *apparent motion* by overlooking the interstices between frames. Thus, at the heart of the filmic apparatus is the undoing of the borders its mechanism drew in time.

This image of a futile chase to impose divisions, only to find them transgressed by what lies infinitely in between, recalls the paradoxical figure of the U.S.-Mexican border in Anzaldúa's *Borderlands*, in which she presents the figure of the infinitely divisible and evasive razor edge of the barbed wire fence separating the United States from Mexico as her "home" as a Chicana. Her poetic opening to the book figures the fence that cuts the subjects who cross it, spilling their blood, as "*una herida abierta* [an open wound], where the Third World grates against the first and bleeds."[8] She thus disfigures the image of a clean-cut border, just as the geography of the region, the blowing desert sand and the constantly moving ocean, underscore the physical border as a futile fiction.

From the earliest moments of film's cultural history, its makers and consumers have recognized the potential for film to overcome borders (and to traffic cultural and political values across them). An early instance of this potential is Pancho Villa's 1914 contract with the Mutual Film Company to film battles of the Mexican Revolution, a contract that emerged from Villa's recognition of film's propagandistic power to circulate his image as a Mexican Robin Hood both at home and abroad. In the same period, film's potential for geographic transgressions was a point of concern in post-Victorian American society, where Christian leagues called for censoring film as early as 1908 out of concern that prizefighting films shot in the territories of Nevada and New Mexico would import the pugilism of the "less developed U.S. territories" to the civilized East Coast.[9] This concern followed a general anxiety about film's ability to transport the corrupting influence of urban environs to small-town America. Cinema conflated the divide between city and country, the pugilism of the U.S. Western territories with the cradle of its civilization in the East. At the same time, early cinema was key to constructing and reifying borders, in Villa's case through the visualization of a racial line separating Mexico from the United States; cinematic representations of the Mexican Revolution invariably helped Americans visualize the divide between the United States and Mexico as a racial one.

As many of the chapters in this collection contemplate national borders around the globe at a time of heightened political tensions over immigration, it is fitting to recall cinema's use in imagining and reifying divisions based on class, race, gender, culture, and nationality as ubiquitous to early cinema in the United States from the 1910s and 1920s, a period that coincided with a surge of immigration from Asia and eastern and southern Europe. The United States perceived this surge of immigrants from nonwhite, Catholic, and Jewish communities as a threat to its Anglo-Saxon Protestant identity. There were several laws limiting immigration from these regions in the era of early cinema's rise. This series of legislative efforts culminated in the Johnson-Reed Act (also known as the National Origins Act) of 1924, which cemented Asian exclusion by establishing the Asiatic Barred Zone and curbed immigration of "undesirable" Europeans by creating a quota system by nationality for immigrants. Films like *Making an American Citizen* (1912), *Traffic in Souls* (1913), *The Cheat* (1915), and the serial film *Patria* (1917) make explicit cinema's early role in maintaining the borders of America's cultural identity and defining it squarely as white, Protestant, and Western European, an identity these films sought to protect from the encroachments of eastern European Jews, southern European Catholics, Asians, and Mexicans. The latter were represented as aligned with German attempts at attacking the United States following the Zimmerman Telegram, and as nonwhite outlaws, rebels, and peasants through cinematic depictions of the Mexican Revolution.[10]

Indeed, throughout its short history, cinema has proven essential in describing and maintaining the borders that define national and cultural identity through its propagandistic powers. Germany's Third Reich used cinema as a mechanism for educating Germans in how to distinguish Aryan from non-Aryan traits through overtly anti-Semitic films (which were less common in Germany's pre–World War II film production) like Fritz Hippler's *Der erwige Jude* (The eternal Jew, 1940), and through films like *La Habanera* (The

Havanan, 1937), which more subtly depicted the moral and intellectual inferiority of non-Aryan subjects—in this case, Latinos. Cinema's use as a tool for drawing and underscoring national borders through visualizing and constructing racial difference is unsurprising given the emergence of its medium from attempts at the rational separation and ordering of fluid duration, attempts that coincided with the ongoing Western imperial separation and ordering of geographic space during the nineteenth century. As much as cinema has been used in such historical instances as 1910s America and 1930s Germany to delineate national identity on the basis of race, ethnicity, religion, and language, at these same moments it also served as a powerful tool for imagining and forging identities (even as those identities were exclusionary, racist, and xenophobic).

This paradoxical power of cinema to both fix and unfix identity (what Siegfried Kracauer defines as its realist versus formative tendencies), to both reify and reimagine borders between communities and subjects, intensifies in the age of the digital as the ability to artificially create a seamlessly "realistic" world (through CGI) and to record the "real" world (through ubiquitous and affordable means of recording images anywhere and at any time) have both dramatically increased. Considerations of cinema's recent aesthetic contestations to borders manifest themselves in diverse and overlapping ways throughout this volume. For example, Marina Hassapopoulou's "Composite Aesthetics as Cultural Cartographies of Europe in Transition" locates a rupture in the index of national identity represented by and manifested in the "composite" image produced by CGI and the interactive and hypertextual aesthetics of spatial montage in European youth cinema at the turn of the twentieth century. Rebecca Sheehan's "Undocumation: Documentary Animation's Unsettled Borders" locates a similar rupture in the indexes of identity that take place in recent documentary animations about border subjects where documation's avowal of artifice signals the fabricated nature of an image. By underscoring the possibility of intervening in the construction of an image, animation contests the indexical nature of photographic realism and its corresponding indexes of identity, from the visible identity of race to identities defining citizenship.

Both Hassapopoulou's notion of "composite aesthetics" in European cinema after the creation of the European Union (EU) and Sheehan's analysis of the role of animation's artifice in recent border documations resonate with Rosa-Linda Fregoso's argument in "The Art of Witness in Lourdes Portillo's *Señorita extraviada*" that Portillo's use of "poetic" images rather than traditional documentary ones refigure the spectator's relationship to the victims of the feminicides in Ciudad Juárez, Mexico, enabling the film to replace desensitization with activism. These chapters thus register in three distinct ways how the transition from analog to digital filmmaking, a transition hallmarked by the rise of various experimental and interactive aesthetics, reflects the undoing of essentializing and indexical identity claims, constructions of national identity, and the visible and indexes of race, gender, and class. Fregoso demonstraties how Portillo uses "poetic" images in *Señorita extraviada* (Missing young woman, 2001) to intervene in the determinism of documentary images, underscoring the risk that traditional documentary images of victims of Juárez's feminicides will function to desensitize rather than promote activism in the spectator. Fregoso variously identifies in Portillo's film how poetic images replace the visual with the haptic in the film and, unlike expository images more keenly indexed to reality, create an active spectator who learns to empathize with the victims of Juárez's feminicides and who is thereby spurred to activism rather than being distanced from the victims by images spectacularizing the violence.

Portillo's use of a poetic mode to replace a passive spectator with an active one challenges documentary aesthetics to replace the actual with the performative (an extension of the haptic) and the given (about which we can do nothing) with an understanding of a situation in which acting and doing, performance, and self-determination matter. Animation plays a similar role in the documations Sheehan discusses as it imagines granting to children—some of the most powerless border subjects—the power to intervene in the constructed nature of their identities rather than being subject to the essentializing gaze of the camera (and of the state) that the photographic image risks asserting.[11] Hassapopoulou documents the same interventions in the (re)construction of European identity on the part of young audiences, made available through "composite aesthetics" that undo the necessary relationship between national (pre-EU) identity and cultural stereotypes by replacing the linear with the interactive, the visual with the haptic in a number of instances. Thus, Hassapopoulou, Fregoso, and Sheehan argue that the use of postdigital cinematic aesthetics plays a major role in transgressing borders through activating the spectator to *empathize* with cinematic subjects by replacing visual and auditory aesthetics with haptic ones.

Monica Hanna's "The Cinematic Borderlands of Alejandro González Iñárritu's *Babel*" explores haptic aesthetics in mainstream contemporary cinema by illuminating how subtle and complex postproduction editing and sound mixing generate empathic embodied spectatorship through cinema as a universal language imagined as transcending sensory, cultural, and geographic borders. The "haptic" aesthetics that, for Fregoso, replace the dominance of the visual image in Portillo's *Señorita extraviada*, function similarly for Hanna in González Iñárritu's film as culturally and geographically distant characters are brought together with one another and with the audience through match-on-action cuts, sound bridges, and point-of-view uses of sound and image. Hanna argues that *Babel* (2006) uses haptic mechanisms to unite geographically and diegetically distant sound and image in order to elicit sympathy from the audience for characters who represent two groups of people, Mexican migrants and Muslims, both of which are frequently demonized in post-9/11 American politics. Her chapter suggests that the film views affective border crossing as a way to counteract some of the damage of national and political borders.

Contemporary border cinema frequently counters homogeneous conceptions of space, time, and historicity with heterogeneous ones as a means of signaling the replacement of a unifying and hegemonic national identity with heterogeneous cultural identities determined by individuals rather than a state. Reconfiguring time and space to reimagine ways of seeing and knowing the world, many of the films explored in this collection train us to review, reimagine, and reject existing borders. For example, in part following Anzaldúa, Hanna argues that *Babel* creates a "cinematic borderlands" as an antidote to the real and hardening borders of the post-9/11 world, particularly in U.S. interactions with Mexico and Arab countries. Hanna argues that techniques like match cuts and sound bridges aesthetically overcome the violence represented by contemporary bordering practices. The visual and sound editing of the film bring together story lines across national, regional, linguistic, and class differences to create an alternate space through cinematic overlays bridging time and geography and thus highlighting points of connection rather than difference.

Challenging borders by creating empathy through cinematic form is also key to Goran Paskaljevic's *Honeymoons* (Medeni mesec, 2009), according to Anita Pinzi, whose "Challenging European Borders: Goran Paskaljevic's *Honeymoons*" explores how the Serbian filmmaker represents the human toll of the "paradox" that the Schengen Convention of 1990 created: the "removal of internal borders . . . corresponded to a fortification and militarization of Europe's outer border." As Pinzi observes, the formal structure of *Honeymoons* both replicates this border, as the two couples who attempt similar migrations from non-EU countries (one couple from Albania to Hungary and the other from Serbia to Italy) never actually meet in the film, and challenges these borders as the couples' journeys are brought into relation with one another through formal devices such as crosscutting and the frequency of events in the plot. As Pinzi argues, this alignment of journeys through the plot "criticizes intra-Balkan tensions" by "showing how countries that harbor reciprocal hate can tragically undergo a common destiny of intolerance as a consequence of a larger system of exclusion embodied by the border control of the European Union." As with *Babel*, a film whose geographically distant characters have lives that similarly intersect in the ways the couples in *Honeymoons* do, but who never physically meet one another (a testimony to the geopolitical borders separating them), Paskaljevic's film uses cinematic aesthetics to create an empathic connection between characters and between the characters and audience, as do González Iñárritu's match-on-action cuts, sound bridges, and strategic use of point of view. To this end, Pinzi observes that the camera's movements in *Honeymoons* are purposefully aligned with the characters such that the viewer is placed in an empathic position.

Similarly to the contestations of space Hanna notes in *Babel*'s aesthetics, Elena Lahr-Vivaz's "Remapping the Borderlands in *¿Quién diablos es Juliette?*" argues that Carlos Marcovich's 1997 film contests narrow conceptions of Cuban identity by replacing the binary figure of the "border" with an "archipelagic" one. Like Fregoso's work on Portillo's "poetic" documentary, Lahr-Vivaz explores a disruption in the assumed fidelity of the documentary image as the film remixes documentary and mockumentary aesthetics to demonstrate the impossibility of "clear demarcations between people, places, and performances," replacing the *actual* with *actuación* (acting) and essential notions of identity with performative ones. Thus, similarly to Hassapopoulou's, Sheehan's, and Fregoso's underscoring of artifice over essentialism and animation over photography's privileged index in the films they examine, Lahr-Vivaz locates the significance of acting (performativity) replacing the actual (the essential) in Marcovich's unorthodox interventions in the documentary image (a music video, clips from other films, interviews with actors). As the documentary image's presumed hegemony and authority is contested in Marcovich's work, so too, Lahr-Vivaz argues, does Marcovich correspondingly imagine spatial alternatives that challenge the authority of national borders to demarcate identity.

Jennifer Harford Vargas's "Crossing *por el Hueco*: The Visual Politics of Smuggling in Colombian Migration Films" similarly explores challenges to the binary figure of the border by examining the complex figure of *el Hueco* in recent Colombian cinema, demonstrating how this cinematic trope suggests an alternative cartography defined not by stable borders but by the porous, fissured, and marginal ones figured in the bodies of undocumented migrants crossing *por el Hueco*—through a spatial, temporal, and legal gap. This refiguration of border crossing is represented by the nonchronological plot of Simón Brand's *Paraíso Travel* (Paradise Travel, 2008). In counterpoint to the mainly linear and conventional "American dream" plot of Joshua Marston's *Maria Full of Grace* (2004), Harford Vargas locates in *Paraíso Travel* a nonlinear temporality that matches the orientation of its characters' geographic trajectory (which is "[not] strictly south-to-north") across multiple national borders. Thus, Harford Vargas locates challenges to the indexical and binary nature of the border (as a straightforward signifier and a straightforward distinction between "us" and "them," here and there) in the aesthetics of the plot structure of *Paraíso Travel*, which is as unstraightforward as Marcovich's documentary aesthetics are for Lahr-Vivaz. Both authors present important challenges to, and reconfigurations of, borders: the archipelagic border for Lahr-Vivaz, and *el Hueco* for Harford Vargas.

Fissures to temporality and history often structure challenges to identities traditionally defined by national borders in cinema. For example, Alex

Rivera's dystopic *Sleep Dealer* (2009) envisions a future for the U.S.-Mexican borderland that returns its economy to the *milpas* (maize fields) of the past, which defined a simpler and more just relationship between people and natural resources (water and land) unmitigated by the United States' (and NAFTA's) exploitation of both. Frederick Luis Aldama explores this borderland sci-fi film in "Toward a *Transfrontera*-Latinx Aesthetics: An Interview with Filmmaker and Artist Alex Rivera." The beginning of *Sleep Dealer* sees the main character Memo leave his family's impoverished *milpa* for Tijuana, where he joins a "cybracero" factory that expropriates his labor (but not his body) across the border to the United States. This is a futuristic concept Rivera imagines based on the history of the U.S. Bracero Program (1942–1964), with the difference being that the imagined cybracero program (which draws inspiration from current technology like drones and virtual reality) affords Western nations "all the work without the workers." By the end of the film, though, Memo returns to the *milpa* and the mise-en-scène of the final scenes could just as well be from forty years ago as forty years into the future, the period in which the film is set. Similarly, much of *Sleep Dealer*'s mise-en-scène compresses markers from the past, present, and future, dislocating the narrative from a linear temporality. Indeed, in the film, atemporality expressed in elements of mise-en-scène accomplishes what the atemporality of *Paraiso Travel*'s plot structure does for Harford Vargas. According to Aldama, this captures an identity in which "Latinos exist *across* cultural and national spaces."

The heterogeneity of time that Rivera generates in the mise-en-scène through which *Sleep Dealer* represents the U.S.-Mexican borderland is similar to the spaces in which a host of contemporary Israeli films take place. As Anat Zanger and Nurith Gertz's "No-Man's-Land: Shifting Borders and Alternating Identities in Contemporary Israeli Cinema" notes, such films contest a "homogeneous Israeli identity, fortified behind borders that separate it from Palestinian identity." Zanger and Gertz identify the settings of bus stations and neighborhoods divided by checkpoints as spaces where borders are being "drawn, traversed, and violated," spaces that suggest a "world outside the law," thus contesting Israel's hegemonic political and social discourse based on a worldview of national unity. These heterogeneous spaces, which Zanger and Gertz liken to Giorgio Agamben's "camp," Edward Soja's "thirdspace," and Gloria Anzaldúa's "borderland," thus foreground the artificial and performative nature of borders, undermining both their authority and their essential nature, and locating a "postnational society" in a space that imagines "individuals who have not assimilated into the collective," moving "between and within communities."

Heterogeneous spaces granting the individual self-determined identity find a natural correspondence in the kind of technological atemporality demonstrated by *Sleep Dealer*, but they can also contest borders by challenging historical narratives (and temporal trajectories), as well as popular or traditional tropes of a given national cinema responsible for erecting and preserving national borders through securing national and cultural identity. We see such contestations to historical temporality (and narrative) as well as to traditional national cinematic tropes, genres, and plot structures in the Israeli films discussed in Yael Munk's "The Borders We Cross in Search of a Better World: On Border Crossing in Three of Amos Gitai's Feature Films" and in José B. Capino's "Filipinos at the Border: Migrant Workers in Transnational Philippine Cinema," which examines recent Filipino romantic melodramas. Munk argues for a regrouping of Gitai's Israeli film trilogies to understand how the border functions as a thematic trope that links historical moments and traverses chronological time as Gitai's films move from representing the forced expulsion of Holocaust survivors from Europe to Israel in *Kedma* (2002) to representing a much later forced expulsion depicted in *Disengagement* (Itnatkut, 2007), a film that portrays the emotional effects of Israel's disengagement from the Gaza Strip and the internal displacement it impelled. As with the heterogeneous spaces conveyed through *Sleep Dealer*'s simultaneous mise-en-scène references to various temporalities, and such spaces that Zanger and Gertz argue prevail in several recent Israeli films (the bus station, the neighborhood checkpoint), Munk similarly locates mise-en-scènes functioning to reify the "third-space" of the borderlands as two of Gitai's border films, *Promised Land* (Ha'aretz Hamuvtachat, 2004) and *Free Zone* (Ezor Hofshi, 2005), take place on the open road, suggesting the same kind of self-determination that the heterogeneous space and time ironically permits for the individual in Rivera's film and those spaces discussed by Zanger and Gertz.

While heterogeneous space has defined the mise-en-scène of recent Israeli cinema (as well as, temporally speaking, Rivera's science fiction dystopia), and Gitai's films have aligned themes of borders and migrations across historical time and geographic place, Capino points to a similar heterogeneity of form that signals individual self-determination as a challenge to collective conformity and nationalism in much the same way as the heterogeneity of mise-en-scène and historicity has in the Israeli films discussed in this collection. He examines melodramatic film cycles that register and explore the conditions of Filipinos as a growing source of global migrant labor and, in particular, domestic labor. As a variant on the heterogeneity of space and time we've see in other films, Capino registers a heterogeneity of genre in the films comprising the cycles (from the 1970s through 2000) he analyzes, as they assume what he calls a "transgeneric makeup registering historical changes in the situations of migrants." For example, he observes that these films take on at various points more "lachrymose" romantic and domestic tones, betraying the influence of horror in the 1990s and the upbeat tone of the romantic comedy in the new millennium.

Within this variety of melodramatic form, Capino locates a heterogeneous structure that not only challenges genre conventions by hybridizing them but also challenges the conventions of migrant identity by ironically locating in the "tragedies and triumphs" that dominate the endings of melodrama "the melancholy reckoning of opportunities the protagonist may have taken but had instead chosen to forgo," and locating in those "sacrificed possibilities" the "strategies and openings for prolonging one's stay in the host country." Yesterday's wound thus becomes tomorrow's promise as a counternarrative that chips away at the dominant "weepy" trajectory of the typical melodrama. Thus, self-determination for the characters of the Filipino melodramas Capino discusses is found in the formal structure of recent challenges to the conventions of melodramatic genre and plot, which might again be read as analogues for conventions of national and cultural identities. It is within these formal aesthetic fissures that Capino locates a challenge to the borders that define and confine the identity of the Filipino migrant worker. While the genre chosen by Rivera in *Sleep Dealer*—science fiction—has often been used as a contestatory generic mode to question contemporary politics and social structures from the safe distance of the future, we see in Capino's analysis how genres traditionally used to bolster nationalist ideals can hybridize and mutate to function as contestation as well. In the case of the migration films Capino explores, this involves an examination of how contemporary Filipino cinema uses romantic melodrama to question the government's promotion of exported labor by showing the dangers and tolls of working abroad.

A number of chapters in this collection explore how the recent rise of haptic aesthetics in the postdigital era have been employed to challenge borders between subjects, nations, and cultures by generating an empathic relationship between the spectator and the subject on the screen. At the same time, *Border Cinema* considers how cinema can contest the binary configuration of borders with aesthetics that mobilize theories of "thirdness," complicating and muddying the "us" versus "them" divide that so often defines border politics. Almost all of the chapters draw in some way upon Anzaldúa's rich conception of the borderlands as a third space alternative to the United States and Mexico, while Zanger and Gertz deploy Soja's "thirdspace," and many close readings of the politics of cinematic aesthetics are informed by Solanas and Getino's "third cinema." In fact, Harford Vargas's conception of *el Hueco* and Lahr-Vivaz's notion of the archipelagic follow in the footsteps of retheorizations of borders as binary spaces through the contestations of third terms. Thus, this collection's simultaneous focus on cinema's spatial reconfigurations of borders alongside its exploration of border cinema's persistent appeal to the haptic argues for understanding Marks's notion of the haptic in the context of conceptions of "thirdness" used to challenge border binaries. In this sense, the haptic might be considered its own third term in cinema, somewhere between (or beyond) the senses that dominate cinema (sight and sound). Sight and sound are senses that have been traditionally used to reify rather than challenge borders in that they are used to assign, designate, and essentialize markers of identity such as the color of a subject's skin, her accent, or her gender. We see this, for example, in the complex colonial systems of racial classification that continue to resonate today, as this classification system is integral to what decolonial thinker Walter Mignolo, drawing on Aníbal Quijano, describes as the "colonial matrix of power."[12] We also see this in how certain voices and types of sound are raced or gendered. In contrast to sight and sound, the realm of haptic aesthetics has proven generative in challenging borders by replacing the inclination of assigning an onscreen other an identity based on these sensory indexes with an inclination to feel *with* and *for* that other. Thus, with the haptic image, experience and performance are invited to replace stabilizing (and confining) designations of identity. The haptic as a third sense thus performs like Anzaldúa's borderlands in continuously rupturing and undoing the border in its role as a third space.

Together, the chapters that make up *Border Cinema: Reimagining Identity through Aesthetics* focus on how film can reflect the effects of globalization and the proliferation of borders on individuals from various subject positions while producing aesthetic visions that afford a glimpse of possibilities that lie beyond current crises. These films adopt novel genres, styles, media, and technologies meant to move the viewer. We see throughout this volume both convergences and divergences in the means by which the films seek to elicit empathy and challenge audiences to act, through immersion or distancing; hyperrealism, science fiction, and animation; poetic or realist modes; and melodrama or comedy. Some of the techniques these filmmakers employ push in quite different directions aesthetically, such as the exaggerated affect of *Babel* and the romantic melodramas from the Philippines in comparison to the distancing techniques of the metadocumentary *¿Quién diablos es Juliette?* (Who the hell is Juliette?) and the (un)documations. Nonetheless, border cinema tests the plasticity of film's form and aesthetics, as well as the abilities of its moving images to move the viewer—emotionally, intellectually—to some type of action in the world, whether questioning nationalist narratives spurring the current fever of border fortification or pushing for legislative or cultural change. The border is often figured as a liminal space at the margins, and as such it is replete with possibilities for imagining alternative futures. As this collection demonstrates, contemporary cinema offers a set of aesthetic opportunities particularly suited to helping the viewing public imagine those possibilities.

Notes

1 A number of theorists have noted how, in the interest of distributing high-concept (and big-budget) action films to Asian markets, Hollywood studios have increasingly replaced complexities of narrative that necessitate large amounts of dialogue with digitally produced complexities in the visual image and the soundscape of a film that benefit from communicating in a universal language. In some ways, this turn to a universal language of images can be seen as a *return* to the advantages of transnational distribution that cinema enjoyed from its inception through the end of the silent era (1929–1932).

2 Ian Haney López, *Dog Whistle Politics: How Coded Racial Appeals Have Reinvented Racism and Wrecked the Middle Class* (New York: Oxford University Press, 2015).

3 Wendy Brown, *Walled States, Waning Sovereignty* (Brooklyn, N.Y.: Zone, 2010).

4 Ella Shohat and Robert Stam, "Introduction," in *Multiculturalism, Postcoloniality, and Transnational Media*, ed. Ella Shohat and Robert Stam (New Brunswick, N.J.: Rutgers University Press, 2003), 1.

5 Laura U. Marks, *The Skin of the Film: Intercultural Cinema, Embodiment, and the Senses* (Durham, N.C.: Duke University Press, 2000), 195.

6 Ibid, 194–195.

7 Mary Ann Doane, *The Emergence of Cinematic Time: Modernity, Contingency, the Archive* (Cambridge, Mass.: Harvard University Press, 2002), 5–10.

8 Gloria Anzaldúa, *Borderlands/La Frontera: The New Mestiza* (San Francisco: Spinsters/Aunt Lute, 1987), 3.

9 For a detailed history of prizefighting films, see Lee Grieveson, "Fighting Films: Race, Morality, and the Governing of Cinema, 1912–1915," in *The Silent Cinema Reader*, ed. Lee Grieveson and Peter Kramer (New York: Routledge, 2003), 169–186.

10 In 1917, the British decrypted a telegram from German foreign minister Arthur Zimmerman to a German diplomat in Mexico proposing a wartime alliance with the Mexicans in which the latter would regaim Southwest United States territories formerly belonging to Mexico. The Zimmerman telegram helped spur the United States' entry into World War I against Germany.

11 It is also interesting to note the predominant focus on children and youth culture in the border films discussed in many of the chapters in this collection. This coincidence correlates with the alignment of youth and hope with the digital age and globalization, as in Hassapopoulou's chapter on European youth culture on film, as well as a rupture with the past and with historical modes and technologies of cinema. The films discussed in Hanna's and Sheehan's chapters focus on children, while those analyzed by Hassapopoulou (who argues for the importance of a consideration of youth culture and youth films in understanding emergent European sensibilities), Pinzi, Lahr-Vivaz, and Harford Vargas all focus primarily on teenagers and/or young adults.

12 Walter Mignolo, *The Darker Side of Western Modernity: Global Futures, Decolonial Options* (Durham, N.C.: Duke University Press, 2011).

2

Composite Aesthetics as Cultural Cartographies of Europe in Transition

MARINA HASSAPOPOULOU

Amid Britain's controversial vote to exit the European Union (EU), ongoing refugee crises, and the detrimental impact of recent terrorist attacks, Europe finds itself again at a crucial crossroads sure to reshape it topographically, culturally, economically, and politically. Current hegemonic structures such as the EU are being challenged, and immigration laws criticized, while the question still remains of whether shared characteristics of an elusive Europeanness exist and, more important, whether Europeanness can be summoned in times of national crisis to impose a sense of uniformity in decision making and notions of citizenship. Cinema, after the overhyped digital "crisis" that sparked numerous ontological concerns, is about to enter another existentialist phase as a gradual yet steady infiltration of virtual and augmented reality technologies enter mainstream media. These innovations, along with new interactive modes of spectatorship, are bound to bring up familiar (and mostly dead-end) debates regarding cinematic ontology and the supposed death of cinema. Thus, as in the late twentieth century, when cinema's digital turn coincided with the expansion of the EU and the redrawing of the European map, critical moments in European history are again coinciding with new developments in visual and kinesthetic media culture.

This chapter begins by connecting the development of digital cinematic techniques in the 1990s to significant sociopolitical and transnational changes reflected in youth-oriented European films of the late 1990s and early 2000s.[1] During this period, experimentation with new digital aesthetics and their convergence with older filmmaking techniques created a hybrid pastiche of effects. As the European films I will discuss were visually mapping and delimiting the so-called new Europe, they were also attempting to aesthetically map out a new composite cartography of cinema's transition from analog to digital—a transition that should not, however, be treated as unidirectional and deterministic. In these cases, the digital was embedded into questions of cultural specificity and identity rather than a loss of indexicality, as these films attempted to engage with historicity through other avenues besides photorealism, and thus liberated the digital from the realism debates it is still often locked into. In these films, analog and digital techniques were not assimilated into a photorealistic whole but instead drew attention to the process of hypermediation. The resulting hypermediacy "acknowledges multiple acts of representation and makes them visible" through references to other modes of representation and media formats and, I would add, to older and newer ways of mapping sensory experience.[2] I argue that this *composite aesthetic* corresponds to a reflexive process of mapping that evokes yet ultimately transcends topography and photorealism in order to propose a multifaceted philosophical reflection on the cultural and sociopolitical implications of mapmaking. At the same time, the aggregate nature of these aesthetics charts the status of cinema's fluctuating ontology and the epistemological questions that arise from such ontological changes.

The 1990s marked the beginning of a new Europe following the collapse of the Soviet Union, the fall of the Berlin Wall in 1989 and the subsequent reunification of Germany, the dissolution of Yugoslavia, a more centralized bureaucracy of the EU, and the consideration of more countries' accession to the EU (among other changes). But the optimistic contemporary rhetoric surrounding the hope of a reformed Europe failed to fully take into account the nationally specific consequences and difficult transitions of a more geographically connected European continent. The complex relationship between the national and the transnational/international, which includes the dislocating impact of globalization, the challenging process of European integration, postcommunist geopolitical changes, the complicated transition from late communism to late capitalism, and the increase in the mobility of migrant laborers and refugees, is often underestimated in discussions regarding the new Europe.[3] A more complex study of European cinema reveals how it aesthetically mirrored contemporaneous negotiations of Europeanness and challenges to traditional understandings of nationalism as a cultural foundation during this time.

As European borders were being renegotiated in the 1990s, this period also marks a transitional phase for cinema, starting with the mainstreaming of computer-based editing systems. The connection between the so-called crisis in cinematic ontology brought about by the introduction of digital technologies (which severed the photochemical index of analog filmmaking, undoing what many understood to be an ontological premise of the medium) and the simultaneous identity crises occurring in Europe has not yet received enough critical attention. The changes in the nature of cinema—more epistemological than ontological—coincide, as I will argue, with significant transitions in European history in ways that are not mere historical coincidence. In this context the digital, which is frequently perceived as ahistorical, universal, and immaterial, becomes infused with cultural, subjective, and site-specific meaning when used to reflect and visualize European changes.

Connections between the new digital era of filmmaking and the new chapter of European history are visually prefigured in the hybrid analog-digital aesthetics of some turn-of-the-century national and coproduced European youth films, such as Cédric Klapisch's *L'auberge espagnole* (The Spanish apartment, 2002), Tassos's Boulemetis's *A Touch of Spice* (Politiki kouzina, 2003), Tom Tykwer's *Run Lola Run* (Lola rennt, 1998), Jean-Pierre Jeunet's *Amélie* (2001), Tina Ellerkamp and Jörg Heitmann's *Killer.berlin.doc* (1999), and Fatih Akin's *In July* (Im Juli, 2000), as well as international films about the "new Europe" such as Jeff Schaffer, Alec Berg, and David Mandel's *Eurotrip* (2004).[4] By analyzing the hybrid aesthetics in these films, particularly their use of database narratives, interactivity, and spatial montage, I argue that the experimental amalgamation of digital and analog filmmaking techniques translates into a critique of connectivity, globalization, and mobility at a time in which European borders—like cinema's boundaries—were being expanded and renegotiated.[5]

Cinemaps as Alternative Cartography

> The map evinces both a history and a set of formal problems of its own making, outside of the control of the film, that simultaneously summon those of the film itself.
>
> —Tom Conley, *Cartographic Cinema*

Referring mostly to films shot during World War II, Teresa Castro sees the emergence of a "mapping impulse" as a symbolic reminder of the atrocities of the war.[6] This cartographic impulse resurfaces most prominently in the youth-oriented European cinema of the 1990s and late 2000s, suggesting that the mapping impulse in cinema recurs during moments of sociopolitical transition, political unrest, and cultural trauma. A crucial difference between the World War II cinematic maps Castro is referring to and these more recent European "cinemaps" (to borrow a term from Sebastien Caquard) is that, this time, the maps do not aspire to be accurate, comprehensive, or panoramic (as the World War II cinematic maps reflected a posttraumatic impulse to gain control over political geography). Rather than conventionally functioning to advance narrative and provide spatial orientation, the new cinemaps are central to existential, cultural, and geographic journeys, confirming and extending Rosalind Galt's assertion that "in the early 1990s, Europe became, as if it had not been so before, a question of space."[7] Tom Conley argues that cartographic imagery is never fully assimilated into the fiction of cinematic narratives because maps "bring to the image a history that is *not* cinematic; they are written in codes and signs that are not those of the film."[8] In a way, the new cinemaps combine the indexicality and documentary aspects of cartography with cinema's formative aspects to create a complex psychocultural amalgamation of topography, spatiality, and virtuality.

The influence of cartographic techniques on cinematic aesthetics is not unidirectional. Caquard has extensively documented cinema's and cartography's bidirectional impact on each other, with special attention on the influence of computer technology and recent developments in locative mapping. In his work Caquard demonstrates how cinemaps—including atlases, aerial views, and panoramas—actually predate and anticipate contemporary interactive and animated features of digital cartography, such as Google Maps, the geographic information system (GIS), and the Global Positioning System (GPS), which now mark the default ways the connected world navigates physical space. Although Caquard mainly argues for cinemaps predating most of the capabilities of digital maps, the films I will cover not only prefigure future developments in both digital cartography and also cinematic language but also nostalgically incorporate more antiquated navigational methods (like compasses and atlas maps); this nonassimilative amalgamation of the old with the futuristic is reminiscent of the irreconcilable aspects of Europe's past and present. Furthermore, the youthful point of view in each of the films I will discuss serves as a way of reflexively negotiating between past and present, while also—thanks to the youth's generational, cultural, and/or geographic distance from traumatic national histories—attempting to find optimism in the playful restructuring of European identity.

Remapping through Europuddings: Coproduction as Cultural Patchwork

Cédric Klapisch's *L'auberge espagnole* (2002; also known as *The Spanish apartment*, *Europudding*, or *Pot luck*) exemplifies this tendency of negotiating between the past and future of Europe, technology, and (trans)national identity. Mostly conveyed through the perspective of Erasmus University graduate student Xavier, *L'auberge espagnole* centers on French Xavier's study abroad experiences in Barcelona and his interactions with his six roommates from different EU countries. The film interrogates the problematic notion of pan-Europeanism in its own limited way that is reflective of a contemporary Europe that excluded eastern European and European countries not in the EU. At least on the surface, the film's coproduction values, EU financial support, multicultural (though predominantly white and middle-class) cast, multinational locations, mainstream appeal, and youth-oriented perspective seem to optimistically point to new modes of coproduction and inter-European collaboration. The film is a testament to the turn-of-the-century encouragement of European coproductions and the accompanying financial incentives, such as the European Commission's MEDIA Plus Program to advance the European distribution of national and European films and to make these films more marketable.

Nevertheless, the filmic narrative's reluctance to settle on a particular version of Europe and on consistent tropes in European cinema is indicative of its time and of its contemporary anxiety about the future, particularly as related to youth and the impact of globalization on both an individual and cross-cultural level. The film's criticism of the Erasmus study abroad program as essentially a way for students to engage in some European tourism without delving into serious academic study provokes a broader scrutiny of EU bureaucracy and professional nepotism, and examines Europe's inability to rapidly adapt to new processes of globalization, including technological advancement and alternative job markets (such as those thriving on intellectual capital and immaterial labor). The film also perpetuates what Thomas Elsaesser identifies as the European Union's "crisis of representation and legitimacy in the eyes of its citizens."[9]

The film as a cultural commodity paradoxically contradicts the film as cultural dialectic, since its narrative content evokes skepticism regarding the EU, while its mode of production suggests the utility of European funding. For this reason, despite its seemingly paradoxical emphasis on both cultural assimilation (through its melting-pot vision of European youth) and individualism (through Xavier's—and by extension France's and other nation-states'—solipsistic way of envisioning the new Europe in terms of how it relates to his own identity), there is still an obligatory optimism underscoring the film. This optimism extends to the film's status as a multinational coproduction that could potentially pave the way for other inter-European and transnational collaborations.

Despite positive intentions for European collaboration, these multinational coproductions are often met with suspicion and critical scorn, falling under the rather derogatory category of the "Europudding," which is defined by Katrin Sieg as "a blend of cultural ingredients whose sugary superficiality is as pleasing to the cash register as it is aesthetically unhealthy. The very idea of a cultural mixture does not easily rhyme with European traditions of conceptualizing culture as essentially ethnic, homogenous, and distinct, and syncretism as contamination or degeneration."[10] While Europudding coproductions have the potential of destabilizing outdated European traditions and offering alternatives to the homogenizing impulses propagated by the EU, they often fall back on stereotypes and clichéd visual tropes rather than deeply probing the question of cultural diversity and pan-Europeanism. The seemingly conservative aspects of Europudding initiatives and the critical backlash they typically receive resonate with a larger tendency for "inwards turns of politics" in European cinema, which "seem to have revived a longing for traditional structures of kinship and ethnicity."[11]

Nonetheless, in visualizing through various scenarios of cohabitation the issues of a European melting pot forged by EU and other inter-European initiatives, *L'auberge espagnole* examines the local and individual effects of globalization through the more focused lens of Europeanization. The film even seems to suggest that Europeanization's impact is similar to the locally felt effects of globalization that contribute to regional economic, political, and ideological crises. Furthermore, by celebrating cultural amalgamation under the identity of the EU, these Europuddings ask whether revived and nonisolationist aspects of nationalism are inevitably an instinctive cultural response to the locally felt anxieties regarding globalization; this possibility of revived and expanded nationalism should be considered whenever transnationalism and globalism are evoked as neoliberal alternatives to the interpretation of globalization as cultural imperialism.

L'auberge espagnole reflects and speculates—aesthetically, culturally, technologically, and production-wise—on the aftermath of what are regarded as three main catalysts to European globalization: the fall of communism, the fall of the Berlin Wall in 1989 and the subsequent reunification of Germany, and the development of a uniform European market. The film's partially utopian, youth-driven vision of Europe is inevitably counterbalanced with a more critical perspective of a conservative, racially compartmentalized, and technologically backward bureaucratic reality. These two facets of Europe raise questions about the ambivalent role of the EU in either facilitating neoliberal economies or functioning "as a democratic instrument through which the power of capital can be constrained and regulated in the interest of the people."[12]

The multicultural youth perspective offers a chance for Klapisch to experiment with new technologies and novel ways of conveying international mobility through its hybrid aesthetics, which appropriate modes of spectatorship derived from other media, including print culture, television (specifically, reality TV), surveillance footage, GIS and GPS locational systems, and a web interface (see figure 2.1). The tension between capitalism and democracy, internalized through its protagonist Xavier as an ongoing existentialist struggle,

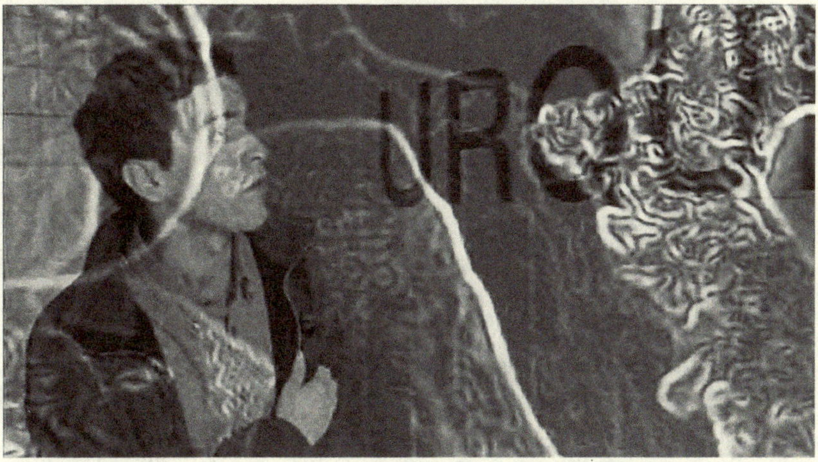

FIG. 2.1 *L'auberge espagnole* (2002): Screenshot from the MRI fantasy sequence, illustrating a convergence of cartographic techniques with the psychic mapping of the mind.

remains unresolved just as the film refuses to settle on a consistent narrative register. As Mireille Rosello argues, Klapisch's narrative techniques contribute to a sense of constant becoming, "Europe is in becoming, unable to totalize, to properly add up what is lost and what is gained"—or, as Xavier puts it, "like Europe, I am all of this, I am a real mess."[13]

Because of its far-reaching allegorical dimensions, *L'auberge espagnole*'s commentary on a variable identity related to emerging developments in global connectivity (on personal, collective, and technical registers) has gone largely unnoticed. My intention here is to bring these questions into focus so as to argue that youth-oriented films do not merely function on an allegorical level, nor should their subject matter be dismissed as lighthearted and frivolous by association. In fact, its youth orientation affords the film a meditation on identity as an ongoing experiential process that adds more depth to insights about Europe at the turn of the century. Rather than arriving at essentialist notions of identity and, at the same time, of cinema in the age of digital and networked communications, the film posits identity as variable.

Variable identity is a term from digital media theory, indicating an elusive, fluid, and nuanced subjectivity that encompasses "the trauma of immigration, the sense of living parallel lives, the feeling of being split between different realities."[14] On technical registers, variable identity is formally constructed through the aforementioned experimentation with the aesthetics of older and newer media and their corresponding modes of navigating the world that converge in the medium of cinema. Identity formation is thus partially influenced by information subjectivity, which is the subjectivity that emerges from the information age—in this film broadly defined to include print culture (through the evocative images of the act of note taking, the typewriter turned computer keyboard, and the dictionary turned digital lexicon, for instance) as well as games, mobile and locative media, networked telecommunications, and the digital interface. This formal convergence points to larger currents of convergence—for instance, between online and traditional distribution and reception, the merging of different national companies, the privatization of industries and processes of deregulation dating back to 1980s Europe, and the public/private overlap precipitated by technologies of surveillance and self-surveillance.

This fusion of older and newer modes of spectatorship and, by extension, identity and citizenship, suggests that, as I have argued in another context, "hybrid identity is not always the result of new or progressive operations of mind and technology, but may also encompass past psychological trauma, especially when that trauma (re)emerges as the result of a life-changing cultural, sociopolitical, and/or technological transition."[15] The inclusion of variable identity into the analysis of European cinema amplifies the argument that "there is no-one in Europe who is not diasporic or displaced . . . and whose identity is not always already split or hyphenated."[16] The films discussed in this chapter, and *L'auberge espagnole* in particular, provide a multilayered visualization of what a European cultural database might look like by including in this vision the technological shifts that cause rifts in the perception of any totalizing version of identity and, by extension, Europeanness.

L'auberge espagnole anticipates the popularity of interactive modes of media consumption through the database narrative, a concept popularized by Marsha Kinder that initially became associated with the first experiments in the recombinatory and computational stories of the University of Southern California's Labyrinth Project in the late 1990s and early 2000s. Through a combination of choice, chance, and design, database narratives are open to revision and resequencing by both producers and consumers—either through production-based editing and remixing or cognitive reconfiguration of different narrative outcomes.[17] Although database narratives have now become incorporated into mainstream production—in cinema, for instance, with Tom Tykwer's *Run Lola Run* (1998), Mike Figgis's *Timecode* (2000), and Christopher Nolan's *Memento* (2000)—Kinder attaches a subversive and empowering potential to the way narratives are nonlinearly and nonteleologically assembled in this mode of active database production, consumption and (now, with transmedia/cross-platform storytelling) distribution.[18] Moreover, nonlinear storytelling and narrative experimentation has been historically symptomatic of cultural and intellectual crises—for instance, Luis Buñuel's surrealist *Un chien Andalou* (An Andalusian dog, 1929) as an intended audiovisual shock and reaction against bourgeois values, Radúz Činčera's pioneering choose-your-own-adventure film

Kinoautomat (1967) as a critique of both communist ideology and democratic utopianism, and Krysztof Kieslowski's multiple-draft/forking-path film *Przypadek* (Blind chance, 1987) as a grim critique of Poland's political and religious status quo in relation to its anti-Semitic past. The cinema that emerges during moments of global crisis and cultural transition inevitably reflects, speculates on, and archives its own version of historicity—a complex mixture of the collective consciousness of its time, contemporary mythmaking, individual subjectivity, aesthetic experimentation, and industry reconfigurations.

From the onset, *L'auberge espagnole* establishes itself as a reflexive database narrative that can be temporally and narratively reconfigured. For example, the "many-windowed" aesthetic of the opening credits of the film is reminiscent of hypertextual ways of navigation.[19] The multiple split-screen framing of the opening credits establishes the film's mosaic- and puzzle-like structure: the split screen remixes excerpts from various scenes of the film and, upon repeated viewing, functions as an anticlimactic preview that gives plot spoilers. The viewer can only retrospectively recall the opening segments in sequential order and mentally assemble them chronologically. This aesthetic encapsulates the intersections between place and subjectively constructed space, and amplifies Walter Benjamin's vision of the city dweller as "a kaleidoscope equipped with consciousness."[20] The ways in which the content of these windows is kaleidoscopically rearranged evokes the ethos of remixing and do-it-yourself practices, as well the process of patching together a Europudding.

The multiwindowed fragmentation of the film's scenes is also reminiscent of the interactive features of selection-driven DVD menus. The formal resemblance of the film to a database also visually alludes to the postproduction editing of digital film. The use of fragmentation as an organizing principle shifts the emphasis from temporal progression and linear storytelling to reflexive and cognitively active ways of making sense of the fragmented information of today's multimediated landscape. The incorporation of multiple windows or other distinct parts into a single frame creates what Lev Manovich calls "spatial montage."[21] Spatial montage conditions viewers to receive bits of information simultaneously and hypertextually as multiple fragments compete for the viewer's split attention. While spatial montage can overstimulate and overwhelm viewers with too many simultaneous streams of information, it can also grant them more agency regarding where to focus their attention within the frame. Additionally, I would argue that films utilizing such techniques typically address and appeal to younger generations; the fact that these techniques became increasingly popular as modes of storytelling in the late 1990s partially attests to an acknowledgment of youth as a main demographic (the MTV generation) and as an influential consumer group within the "new" Europe and beyond.

Unlike the temporally driven montage of narrative cinema, spatial montage involves multiple moving images (and thus multiple temporalities), usually of different sizes, appearing on the screen simultaneously to create a contextual collapse that has been especially linked to digital remixing practices and procedural spectatorship. I have elsewhere defined procedural spectatorship as a type of viewing experience where "the viewer's narrative comprehension essentially converges with the modularity and automation of *Soft Cinema*," a cinema defined by postproduction software-driven processes."[22] Procedural spectatorship is reflective of the process of narration (how the story is conveyed and how it materializes onscreen) over narrative (the content of the story). The topographical and mental maps conveyed in the film thus become a significant narrative component and add a sociocultural layer that corresponds to larger processes of memory functions and informational organization in the digital age.

Spatial montage establishes a type of procedural rhetoric for *L'auberge espagnole* and its relation to Europe. This mosaic collage—which recurs toward the conclusion of the film to provide an existentialist reflection on identity politics—can be related to Elsaesser's observation that the nation-states of Europe are relatively recent, and many of them have resulted from "forcibly tethering together a patchwork quilt of tribes, of clans, of culturally and linguistically distinct groupings."[23] The opening sequence's tentative tethering of a patchwork of disparate narrative fragments reveals its larger creative and distinctly European challenge: that of attempting to weave together different ideologies and institutional agendas into a hodgepodge of a film. Although many critics have seen this rather haphazard cultural (and, arguably, stereotypical) international kaleidoscope as a weakness, I regard it as an appropriate metaphor for the EU's attempts to patch together disparate nations in order to present a holistic, cosmopolitan, and diverse vision of Europe, complete with the film's contemporarily apt omission of profound racial diversity (a common omission in French cinema) and the absence of eastern European representation. Furthermore, if we identify the film as both distinctly French *and* European, its variable nature and hybrid composition reflect the multinational networks of production, distribution, and exhibition that have become essential disseminators of national cinemas and, thus, of prepackaged national identities.

Sieg is perhaps the only scholar who has come close to relating *L'auberge espagnole* to digital modes of production and consumption, likening the film to a "digital diary" and arguing that it is "implicitly framed as a blog—a private expression published, without any industry mediation, on the Web."[24] Taking this comment further in order to highlight the tension between capitalism, neoliberalism, and intellectual utopianism at the core of the film's appropriately heterogenous ideology, it is worth noting that early theories on blogging such as those by Geert Lovink have pointed out the potentially subversive and countercultural potential of blogs while at the same time exposing their nihilistic tendencies. Xavier's ultimate choice to become a writer rather than accepting a more economically stable position at the EU headquarters in Brussels literalizes the act of independent blogging as a subversive vocation, at least at a time where it was not fully incorporated into the business model of today's internet economy. In accordance with Maurizio Lazzarato's argument that immaterial labor alters in potentially productive ways the relationship between producers and consumers, Xavier's decision to forgo a stable career path within an existing European/global market suggests that this type of creative labor departs from earlier factory models of standardized, compartmentalized, quantifiable and mechanized labor (e.g., Fordism and Taylorism). *Les poupées russes* (Russian dolls, 2005), Klapisch's sequel to *L'auberge espagnole*, keeps in check the revolutionary potential of immaterial/intellectual creative labor and alternative modes of cultural production by opening with the portrayal of Xavier as a discouraged, financially struggling writer who has lost his inspiration to write. This revisionist approach to the subversive potential of creative labor comes with the hindsight of a three-year time lapse between the two installments and the subsequent development of corporate structures of monetization for digital labor and virtual content that have obviously not worked in freethinking Xavier's favor.

Cognitive and (G)Astronomical Mapping in Coming-of-Age Films

One of the most overlooked aspects of *L'auberge espagnole* is its meditation on—and mediation of—the increasingly invasive impulse to externalize the mind. Although there is a long history of predigital tools and concepts functioning as mnemonic prosthetics or as externalizations of mental processes (such as Vannevar Bush's memex, René Descartes's sealing wax, Sigmund Freud's mystic writing pad, Hugo Münsterberg's Paramount pictographs, and Plato's cave), digital technologies have accelerated the impulse to visualize memory as a database and project onto digital screens the internal operations of the mind, from magnetic resonance imaging (MRI) scans to Facebook's "What's on your mind?" status update prompt and YouTube's "Broadcast Yourself" tagline. *L'auberge espagnole* exemplifies this tendency through the externalization of Xavier's private thoughts onto the publicly visible digital diary mentioned earlier and, more conventionally, in his voice-over. Xavier's blog is yet another incarnation of other processes in the film (and historically) that externalize and visualize mnemonic operations and cognitive functions, such as the use of MRI scanning to determine the cause of Xavier's mysterious ailment, which gives Klapisch an incentive to amalgamate "objective" scientific ways of mapping the mind with subjective, surrealist, and psychoanalytically inspired representations. By offering us an insight into Xavier's subconscious through the language of processes that both map and abstract the workings of the brain, Klapisch presents mind mapping as a complex multimodal process that formally combines but cannot fully assimilate the technologically rendered visualizations with psychological conditions such as repressed guilt and subliminal fantasies.

Like *L'auberge espagnole*, *A Touch of Spice* (Politiki kouzina, 2003) is a coming-of-age film laden with an air of cosmopolitanism and an existentialist perspective on inter-European and global relations, provoking some similar questions as its predominantly French counterpart. *A Touch of Spice* is famously considered as the first feature-length coproduction between Greece and Turkey.[25] This coproduction marked new territory in inter-European coproductions, and the eventually widespread popularity of the trilingual (English, Greek, and Turkish) film was unexpected due to Greece and Turkey's historically tumultuous political relationship. Through its high production values and elaborate use of computer-generated imagery (CGI), the film also established a higher aesthetic and technological caliber for Greek filmmaking, something that Dimitris Eleftheriotis assigns as part of the reason for its popularity with international audiences.[26] Furthermore, *A Touch of Spice* is exemplary of a perceptual shift in contemporary Greek cinema's focus from esoteric, culturally specific issues to a more exoteric, cross-cultural, and cosmopolitan focus—at least up until the 2008 Greek riots, which once again turned the focus back to the internal problems of the nation (though, this time, acknowledging more openly its multicultural, diasporic, immigrant and exiled populations).[27]

A Touch of Spice is narrated through the perspective of a grown-up Fanis who, through his childhood flashbacks, retells and rewrites his solipsistic version of the events leading up to, and the aftermath of, the mass deportation of Greek/Greek–Turkish nationals from Turkey in the 1960s. Fanis's family history, his traumatic separation from his beloved grandfather, and the forced repatriation of his family, are set against the backdrop of the tumultuous political relationship between Greece and Turkey. The fact that this political history is retold from the perspective of a young boy (and refiltered through his subjective and unreliable recollections as a nostalgic adult) minimizes the collective impact of the trauma of cultural displacement that many Greeks suffered in the 1960s.

As in the other transnational films mentioned in this chapter, the universally relatable lenses of youth, nostalgia, and humor in *A Touch of Spice* create a means of engaging diverse audiences and of "easing" viewers into the historical trauma of national narratives. The burden of representation that most "foreign" films carry for audiences is thus lightened, and the historical aspects of the film can be seen as adhering to a type of subjunctive or revisionist history that resonates affectively rather than factually or ethnographically.[28] The poststructuralist move away from ethnographic and factually oriented versions of onscreen history creates a more complex engagement with the historicity of cinematic images that includes mnemonic processes and displaced trauma as an extended, affectively resonant (rather than strictly factual or ontologically photorealistic) realism.

Although not directly symptomatic of new technologies, these new engagements with history have become more frequent and feasible with the proliferation of interactive media and digital production tools. Eleftheriotis eloquently describes the sequences in *A Touch of Spice* where the use of CGI evokes and ultimately transcends the ethnographic impulse of national cinema to create new hybrid imaginaries, where memories of the past and their traditional modes of representation converge with the technologies and cultural mobility of the present. The use of digital technology thus becomes embedded with cultural and historical specificity, and the dates and location captions that accompany each establishing mise-en-scène render the digital as time- and place-specific despite (or in addition to) its universally resonant aesthetic. To Greek and Turkish audiences, the CGI version of Hagia Sophia and Istanbul has an uncanny effect: it is familiar yet also conspicuously artificial and temporally distant. As Eleftheriotis notes, this CGI re-creation visually compensates for Greek cinema's "historical representational deficit and the national trauma of the loss of the city."[29]

Moreover, the fact that the film's depiction of Istanbul in the late 1950s and early 1960s feels visibly artificial invites reflection on the relationship between digital technologies and collective histories that go beyond mimetic and representational considerations. From our first visual introduction of Fanis as an internationally accomplished astrophysics professor, the relationship between digital reproduction and its indexicality is thrown into question. Fanis is seen closely examining a digitally printed image of a breakthrough astronomical discovery and questioning its claims to truth by humorously wondering whether it deserves a Nobel Prize or whether the unfathomable depiction is the result of a faulty printer, thus further questioning the indexicality of the photochemical properties of digital printing. The empirical skepticism toward the truth claims of digital imaging sets the tone for the entire film's spatiotemporal ambiguity that further complicates the relationship between memory, nostalgia, recollection, and cinematic effects.[30]

Beyond conceptual cartographies, the literal process of mapping in *A Touch of Spice* has escaped critical analysis. The first example of mapping comes halfway through the film in Fanis's flashback of him and his grandfather in the spice shop creating a map of the universe. The grandfather uses spices both topographically and symbolically to teach Fanis about space and the planets, likening the qualities of each spice to a sense-driven description of each planet. This mapping of the universe prefigures Fanis's and the film's cosmopolitan approach to national cinema and shifts the focus from physical place to—literally and figuratively—outer space.[31] *A Touch of Spice* thus presents us with another, sensory-driven version of cartography, one that resonates affectively rather than based on scientific correctness and authenticity. In the final sequence of the film, Fanis, with the help of conspicuous rather than photorealistic CGI, reenacts the process of mapping space using dust and old spices from his grandfather's shop. This final sequence presents a digitally manipulated version of the analog process of mapping space depicted earlier in the film. The fusion of contemporary cinematic technology with childhood memories, individually processed national trauma, and cosmopolitanism—here even more broadly envisioned as a transcendental awareness of the cosmos—"places the hero as the lynchpin of an imaginary (and imaginative) universe before setting it free in its perpetual motion."[32]

Once again, the film creates multiple layers of historicity through the complex interplay of technology, fantasy, memory, and nostalgia to provide an alternative affectively and psychologically motivated historicity. Although cinema cannot technically convey the exact smell and touch of spice (à la Sensorama), the haptic and olfactory associations that are evoked and amplified through CGI imagery expand the capacities of digital cinema to effects beyond its representational, indexical, and archival capacities. The mapping of physical place (the Turkish spice shop) onto a fantasy (outer) space thus becomes infused with mnemonic, emotional, and technological associations. The hybrid composite aesthetic of the "bleeding through" of physical location onto digital fantasy space created by the fusion of CGI with the photographic properties of the medium reminds us that our sense of place is technologically assisted (particularly with our increasing reliance on locative GPS technology and augmented reality), hypermediated, mnemonic, and always subjectively experiential.[33]

Bleeding through Past and Present, Digital and Analog

Tom Tykwer's *Run Lola Run* (Lola rennt, 1998) also exemplifies this "bleeding through" effect in relation to the digital-analog-locative fantasy. Since much has been written about *Run Lola Run*, and for the sake of prioritizing my examples, I would like to instead focus on a lesser-known yet aptly fitting German film, *Killer.berlin.doc* (1999) that also makes the case for youth films as particularly primed for contestations to entrenched and essentializing identities. Like *Run Lola Run*, *Killer* imagines Berlin after the fall of the Berlin Wall as a playground and, as *A Touch of Spice* is for Greece, it is a testament to a more exoteric turn in German filmmaking. Part documentary, part reality show, and part fiction, the hybrid experimental film *Killer* captures a multicultural group of real artists who sign up to play an improvisational adaptation of the German children's game Killer, in which each participant is assigned another player to "kill" using makeshift symbolic weapons such as letter bombs. The artists come from different places, including Berlin, England, Japan, and the United States. Imagining Berlin as an improvised playground is a suitable metaphor for a city in transition, an emerging city in scaffolds yet to be fully unveiled. Fittingly, the impressions of Berlin are mediated through multiple and often irreconcilable perspectives, creating a kaleidoscope of visions that is filtered through a third-person surveillance point of view, as well as each player's confessionals, video diaries, Polaroids, Super 8 films, journals, and other media. At a time in which Germany was being reconfigured culturally, economically, politically, and architecturally, "the film superimposes on this public remapping a more subjective and marginal cartography."[34]

Psychogeographic play in this case additionally serves to highlight the increasingly networked counterculture in Germany (with Berlin quickly becoming its cosmopolitan center)—a counterculture of diverse artists and intellectuals that, in the film, is uncharacteristically given agency in remapping the creative terrain of the "new" Berlin by allowing both cultural insiders and outsiders to have a stake in the multiple redrawings of the map. While some of the game participants in the film see the new urban model of fragmentation and dislocation as "a liberating rather than paralyzing force," others see a city that increasingly looks like an artificial "computer graphic" with the intention of "democratic transparency" being just a facade for building "little control palaces" (quotes from *Killer.berlin.doc*). Both of these perspectives respond positively to a Debordian and Oulipo-inspired rule-based game that uses the idea of the *dérive*—of urban drifting and a "will to playful creation"—to create unpredictable phenomenological cartographies of Germany-in-transition.[35]

Besides the superimposition of the private and subjective onto the public, there is another process of superimposition that once again brings about the convergence of technology and history. The resulting composite aesthetic of the film corresponds not only to the negotiation between actual, subjective, and multiculturally negotiated space but also to the film's unique technological history. *Killer* was originally shot in digital video, but was printed to thirty-five-millimeter film, resulting in a cinematography that lies in between digital and analog. This "undigitization" was made in order for the film to be submitted to the Berlin International Film Festival, the Berlinale, which at the time did not accept digital formats. The film's title thus became rather ironic after its acceptance into Berlinale, since the title alludes to the film's "computerized" name (as a .doc file). As the film became "undigitized" for festival screenings, it was also adapted into a cutting-edge online interactive version.

The online interactive version of *Killer* turns the viewer into an active user by offering multiple ways of navigating the Killer game (see figure 2.2), including tracking each player's daily activity on a map, and exploring each player's journals in a nonsequential order. Like *Run Lola Run*, the film capitalizes on the 1990s hype surrounding emerging interactive media technologies while also

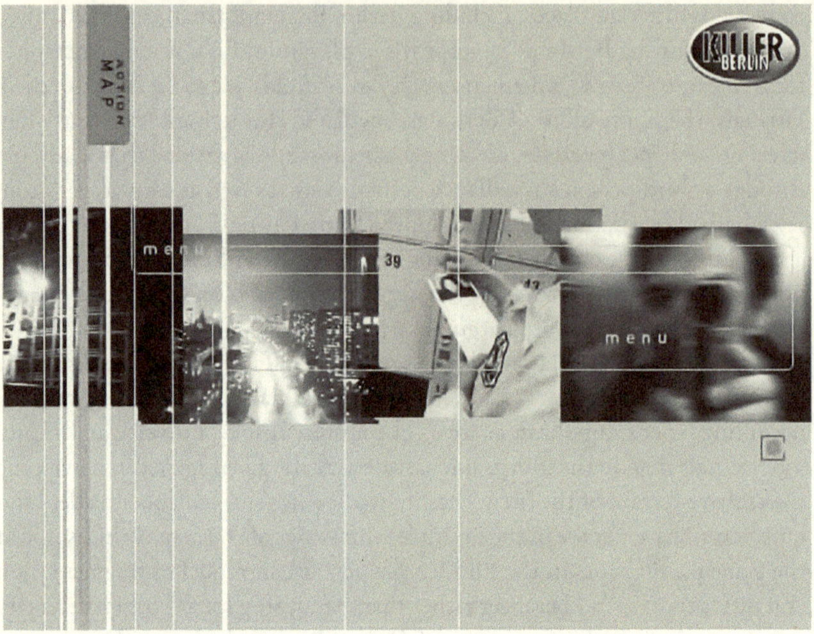

FIG. 2.2 *Killer.berlin.doc* (1999): The technically innovative main menu of the interactive version of the film (a prototype of early CD/DVD-ROM menus).

maintaining ties with the past. For instance, the web version of *Killer* is both innovative in its interactivity and nostalgic in its cartography, presenting a new navigational format against an older map of Berlin that is still divided into east and west. The Berlin-Mitte on the interactive map refers to the center of East Berlin, prior to the 2001 reform that turned the area into a larger borough now known as the city center. Notably, in all its iterations, *Killer* technically marks the time at which cinema's new digital ontology was entering a transitional and contested phase, just as it thematically charts the renegotiation of national identity at a time of historical transition.

Europe? Which/Whose Europe? Cartography as Contested Territory

In European films that resonate with international audiences, the idea of Europe emerges not only from a partial transcendence of national specificity "but also from a new understanding of Europeanness in relation to global actors" and from cross-cultural modes of spectatorship.[36] The consideration of the cult U.S. youth-oriented travel film *Eurotrip* expands the discourse on Europeanness to outsider views of Europe to reveal certain European notions that travel across media industries and audiences. *Eurotrip* centers on a group of U.S.

teenage high school graduates who decide to travel to Europe for various reasons, including tourism, new experiences, and connecting with a long-distance German pen pal. The European backpacking trip inevitably evokes several stereotypical impressions of Europe and its residents in an even more controversial way than does *L'auberge espagnole*. Due to its predominantly American point of view, the film has received harsher criticism from European audiences, who assess this fictional film based on criteria of cultural authenticity, realistic representation, and indexicality. Instead of rehashing debates on media representation and stereotyping, I will instead focus on more critically productive aspects that tend to get marginalized in such debates.

What has escaped most critics is the fact that *Eurotrip* is actually a cross-cultural production mostly filmed in the Czech Republic (now a popular lower-cost filming location), with additional filming in Germany, Paris, Vatican City, the United Kingdom and the United States. The scenes filmed in Germany, Paris, Vatican City, and the United Kingdom correspond to the places traveled in the film, thus adding a sense of "real" place to the narrative locations. Besides its multiple production sites, *Eurotrip* is aesthetically and structurally influenced by European cinema. The iconic Paris train station in the film, for instance, brings to mind other contemporary depictions of Paris in European cinema, such as Tom Tykwer's short *Faubourg Saint-Denis* in the *Paris Je T'aime* anthology (2006), in which a vividly visual and visceral stop-motion sequence represents a mental montage of Paris filtered through the subjectivity of its blind protagonist. In *Eurotrip* a similar collage aesthetic is evoked in a visually fragmented, kaleidoscopic view of Paris that provides a *sense* of place rather than a topographically bound representation of it. *Eurotrip* also features translated versions of popular, youth-oriented English-language songs, such as the French version of the Who's 1965 hit "My Generation" in the opening credits sequence, perhaps hinting that youth culture more easily traverses cultural borders.

Eurotrip additionally references monumental historical events through pop culture. For instance, a fantasy sequence featuring David Hasselhoff singing in German hints at his inexplicable pop icon status in Germany (starting in East Germany), and at his even more unlikely connection to the Berlin Wall (Hasselhoff famously performed at a celebration in Berlin after the fall of the wall in November 1989 with his song "Looking for Freedom," which had become a local anthem in the months leading up to the fall and the final years of the Cold War). And yet, the cross-pollination of aesthetic, cultural, and historical influences in the film has largely gone unnoticed because critics instead focus on more conspicuous representational aspects. The online scrutiny of even the accuracy of the European map shown in the credits sequence reminds us of the tendency to read cinematic maps with real-life geographic considerations in mind. A testament to this are the various fan-made and tourist attraction maps that reimagine city cartographies alongside movie locations.

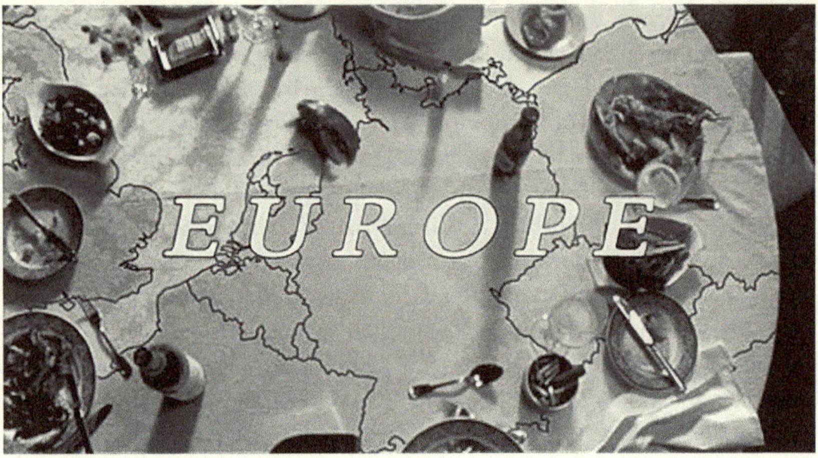

FIG. 2.3 *Eurotrip* (2004): The improvised table map that becomes the main navigational compass for the rest of the film, with captions digitally superimposed over each object to indicate the country it represents.

The maps depicted in *Eurotrip* shift from the conventional atlas and spherical globe to more subjective, process-oriented and improvisational ones once the protagonists arrive in Europe. When all of the protagonists reunite in Paris, they turn their restaurant dinner table into a collaborative do-it-yourself map to chart their upcoming trajectory across western Europe. The teenagers' map uses objects from the table as props: a wine bottle for Paris, Brussels sprouts for Brussels and Germany's Black Forest, and a Heinz ketchup bottle for their final destination of Berlin (see figure 2.3). The film returns to this map several times to revise it and add new destinations, taking into consideration unpredictable detours—including ones in Bratislava and Rome—that occur along the way to Germany. This hybrid cartographic aesthetic becomes the loosely used compass through which the protagonists and audience track the inter-European journey. Its use in the DVD menu for the film makes it an even larger organizational motif.

The fact that the film's humor is largely derived from the cultural disconnect between the American tourists and the local European cultures they experience has been interpreted by audiences as a sign of U.S. cultural imperialism. In particular, the film's desolate depictions of Bratislava—as a reductive symbol for all of eastern Europe—have offended eastern European viewers in particular. The accusations of maps operating as a form of cultural imperialism is reminiscent of earlier criticism regarding the propagandist and imperialist aspects of maps, such as Hans Speier's important 1941 article "Magic Geography," which focuses on World War II–era cartography.[37] The fact that Bratislava and, by extension, eastern Europe do not fit into touristy and unified impressions of Europe is indicative of inter-European divisions and the issues of reincorporating postcommunist nations into a uniform European market after the Cold War. And yet, through the reductive inclusion of Bratislava in *Eurotrip*, the film superficially expands the notion of Europe beyond its (then) typical tourist destinations. By depicting a derelict Bratislava (represented on the map as a dirty ashtray annotated with question marks), the film could be hinting at—albeit through the problematic lens of cine-tourism—the transitional challenges that former communist countries were facing despite the optimistic rhetoric surrounding the idea of a new Europe.

Borders, Reconfigured

Although the films discussed in this chapter were made prior to the 2004 incorporation of new countries into the EU, the concerns regarding inter-European divisions, territorialization, and cultural segregation are still very much present; in fact, these issues have arguably always been at the core of notions of European nationhood. Beneath the "new Europe" positivist rhetoric of opening up new capitalist markets and sanctioning a greater sociopolitical equilibrium between east and west lay new sets of concerns that are now more conspicuous than ever. While the time after the "new Europe" is no longer defined by long-lasting divisive clashes (e.g. between east and west, Orthodox and Catholic or Protestant, communism and capitalism), are the new divisions that have emerged (north and south, capitalism versus late capitalism, free trade versus protectionism, open versus closed borders, conservativism versus liberalism, liberalism versus neoliberalism, EU/eurozone versus actions such as Brexit, and so on) reconfigurations of Europe's enduring walls and boundaries? Can we even envision European identity without its internal clashes and divisions?

Cinema's composite aesthetics during the 1990s and early 2000s gesture toward ideological conflicts that have only recently become clearly articulated and confronted within political and public discourses. As in the case of other transnationalisms, a more transnational Europe—and similarly, a more diverse film industry—carries with it both positive and negative consequences. The emancipatory potential of the proliferation and different variations of Hamid Naficy's notion of "accented cinema," as well as the aforementioned exoteric turn in previously insular national cinemas, is often counterbalanced by new inequalities and uneven structures of civic participation. Beyond a technovisual phenomenon, composite aesthetics can be considered as a metaphor for the paradoxes of collapsing borders: as some walls break down (digital versus analog, national versus transnational), other boundaries take their place (Global North versus Global South, globalization versus Americanization, etc.) that, in their seeming polarity, often mask further divisions within the schisms. Composite aesthetics serve as a reminder of the transitional liminal stage between border collapse and boundary rebuilding that is often masked under the rhetoric of progress and connectivity.

Notes

The author would like to thank the generous support of New York University's Tisch School of the Arts and the Department of Cinema Studies for the grant for the archival research for this project. Special thanks to Jörg Heitmann and the Arsenal archive for publication permission for the image from *Killer.berlin.doc*.

1 For historical accuracy, it should be noted here that analog computers were used in the creation of moving images by pioneers such as John Whitney Sr. as far back as 1957, and digital computers began to be used to create moving images as far back as the 1960s (with media historians going even farther back in time to trace this trajectory). However, even though digital cinema has a much longer prehistory, it was not until the late 1990s that the notion of digital cinema as a powerful influence in contemporary visual culture became a topic of interest in the industry, popular media, and academia.

2 Jay Bolter, and Richard Grusin. *Remediation: Understanding New Media* (Cambridge, Mass.: MIT Press, 1999), 33–34.

3 Daniella Berghahn, and Claudia Sternberg, eds. *European Cinema in Motion: Migrant and Diasporic Film in Contemporary Europe* (New York: Palgrave Macmillan, 2010), 18.

4 Although most of the films I focus on in this essay are predominantly western (and western southern) European, I am hoping that my critical framework can be extended and modified to analyze other instances of border cinemas; for instance, there are strong connections between this theory on composite aesthetics and the *rasquache*-like aesthetics and techniques in turn-of-the-century South American media. In a forthcoming article, I extend the framework of composite aesthetics to virtual reality coproductions that deal with other historically transitional moments in eastern Europe and in the post-9/11 United States.

5 For an animated "map" of this chapter, see Marina Hassapopoulou, "Cine-Mapping Europe," November 20, 2017, https://prezi.com/nndpg-rb3j_7/cine-mapping-europe/.

6 Teresa Castro, "Cinema's Mapping Impulse: Questioning Visual Culture," *Cartographic Journal* 46, no. 1 (2009): 9.

7 Rosalind Galt, *The New European Cinema: Redrawing the Map* (New York: Columbia University Press, 2006), 1.

8 Ibid, 4.

9 Thomas Elsaesser, "Real Location, Fantasy Space, Performative Place: Double Occupancy and Mutual Interference in European Cinema," in *European Film Theory*, ed. Temenuga Trifona (New York: Routledge, 2009), 253.

10 Katrin Sieg, *Choreographing the Global in European Cinema and Theater* (New York: Palgrave Macmillan, 2008), 63.

11 Elsaesser, "Real Location, Fantasy Space, Performative Place: Double Occupancy and Mutual Interference in European Cinema," 58.

12 Sieg, *Choreographing the Global in European Cinema and Theater*, 64.

13 Mireille Rosello, "Imagining European Subjects as Chaotic Borders: Cédric

Klapisch's *Pot Luck* and *The Russian Dolls*," in *Zoom In, Zoom Out: Crossing Borders in Contemporary European Cinema*, ed. Sandra Barriales-Bouche and Marjorie Attignol Salvodon (Newcastle, England: Cambridge Scholars, 2007), 18.

14 Lev Manovich and Andreas Kratky, *Soft Cinema: Navigating the Database* (Cambridge, Mass.: MIT Press, 2005), 17.

15 Marina Hassapopoulou, "Reconfiguring Film Studies through Software Cinema and Procedural Spectatorship," *NECSUS: European Journal of Media Studies* 3, no. 2 (2014), http://www.necsus-ejms.org/reconfiguring-film-studies-software-cinema-procedural-spectatorship/.

16 Elsaesser, "Real Location, Fantasy Space, Performative Place: Double Occupancy and Mutual Interference in European Cinema," 48.

17 This anticipation of technological interactivity has a much longer tradition of other forms of predigital social and cognitive interaction, including the supposed "democratization" of the post-Cartesian spectator's gaze through public art such as the panorama, and mobile protocinematic contraptions such as the phenakistoscope and the zoetrope. In the history of cinema, Kinder and Manovich have cited Luis Buñuel, Peter Greenaway, Dziga Vertov, and others as predigital database filmmakers.

18 Marsha Kinder, "Narrative Equivocations between Movies and Games" in *The New Media Book*, ed. Dan Harries (London: British Film Institute, 2002), 58–60.

19 Jim Bizzocchi, "The Fragmented Frame: The Poetics of the Split-Screen" (2009), http://web.mit.edu/comm-forum/legacy/mit6/papers/Bizzocchi.pdf (accessed October 3, 2018), 1.

20 Walter Benjamin, *Illuminations*. Translated by Harry Zohn (London: Fontana, 1973), 177.

21 Lev Manovich, *The Language of New Media* (Cambridge, Mass.: MIT Press, 2001), 322.

22 Marina Hassapopoulou, "Reconfiguring Film Studies through Software Cinema and Procedural Spectatorship," unpaginated.

23 Elsaesser, "Real Location, Fantasy Space, Performative Place: Double Occupancy and Mutual Interference in European Cinema," 48.

24 Sieg, *Choreographing the Global in European Cinema and Theater*, 71.

25 Theo Angelopoulos's *To Vlemma tou Odyssea* (Ulysses' gaze, 1992) is an earlier example of cross-cultural collaboration between France, Greece, and Italy but, like *A Touch of Spice*, is still regarded as predominantly Greek. Greek cinema presents a notable exception to Galt's generalization that the frequent European coproductions after World War II render any idea of "pure" national film cultures a myth (paraphrasing Galt, 2).

26 Dimitris Eleftheriotis, "*A Touch of Spice*: Mobility and Popularity," in *Greek Cinema: Texts, Histories, Identities*, ed. Lydia Papadimitriou and Yiannis Tzioumakis, 18–36 (Bristol, England: Intellect, 2011).

27 This critical shift from the *chora/esoteriko* to *exoteriko* in Greek cinema is historically outlined by Eleftheriotis.

28 For more on subjunctive history, see Hillman (2006).

29 Eleftheriotis, 25.

30 Although Eleftheriotis uses the term "spatio-temporally ambiguous" for a specific sequence in the film taking place in the Istanbul hospital (25), I argue that spatiotemporal ambiguity characterizes the composition of the entire film.

31 The fascination with space is a common yet rarely analyzed trope in other

European youth-oriented films, including Wolfgang Becker's *Good Bye Lenin!* (2003) and Penny Panayiotopoulou's *Dyskoloi apohairetismoi: O babas mou* (Hard goodbyes: My father, 2002) where young boys' interest in astronauts and the galaxy are nostalgically transposed into adulthood.

32 Eleftheriotis, "*A Touch of Spice:* Mobility and Popularity," 33.

33 Kinder's collaborative interactive works from the Labyrinth Project conceptualize the "bleeding through" effect as a result of a layered memory that enables one to navigate both past and present simultaneously—as evidenced, for instance, in the simultaneous layering of archival, private, and Hollywood images in Norman M. Klein, Rosemary Comella, Andreas Kratky, and Marsha Kinder, *Bleeding Through: Layers of Los Angeles, 1920–1986,* DVD-ROM and book (Los Angeles: Anenberg Center for Communication, University of Southern California, 2003).

34 Galt, 95.

35 Guy Debord, *Brief Moment in Time: The Situationist International 1957–1972*, ed. Elisabeth Sussman, 135–139 (Cambridge, Mass.: MIT Press, 1989).

36 Mariana Liz, "From Europe with Love: Urban Space and Cinematic Postcards," *Studies in European Cinema* 11, no. 1 (2014): 11.

37 Hans Speier, "Magic Geography," *Social Research* 8, no. 3 (1941): 310–330.

3

Undocumation

Documentary Animation's Unsettled Borders

REBECCA A. SHEEHAN

Over the past twenty years, a spate of films has emerged that uses documation, a hybrid form of documentary and animation, to address border crises. This chapter focuses on a handful of these works that use actual sound from interviews with subjects whose lives have been affected by national borders, placing that sound over animated, and sometimes rotoscoped, images.[1] The rise of these films in the digital era is unsurprising for a number of reasons linking technological forms and structures to political and economic forms and structures. In this chapter, I consider these films in the context of a postdigital age as they emerge from and reflect the relationship between the globalizing impact of technology and its destruction of national borders and the transglobal movement of capital and of humans that has resulted from globalization and digitalization. The evident rise in commerce and trade spurred by the digital age has produced a series of dislocations stemming from the demand for the cross-border transport and movement of labor and capital, dislocations from which causes national borders and nation-states writ large to find the stability of their identities naturally under threat. This threat of dislocated goods and people compares metaphorically and literally to the dislocations that the digital image presents to analog film and photography and the impact of this dislocation on how we understand the cinematic image's relationship to the real.

At its inception, digital filmmaking was understood by film theorists to have severed the cinematic image's indexical relationship to the world. Whereas the analog image was thought to be the by-product of an ontologically privileged photochemical reaction, film theorists saw digital images as breaking that index and replacing it not only with code but—more often than not—the human hand, which could suddenly, as Lev Manovich has put it, "paint with pixels."[2] Manovich also makes the striking and insightful claim, however, that the digital returns film to its origins of artifice and animation, means of production that never went away with photography but were only increasingly well disguised from the spectator through it. For Manovich the digital makes the cinematic image more honest about the tenuousness with which it can claim a necessary or natural relation to the world. In a similar way, the postdigital age's dislocation of bodies, capital, and labor only makes tangible the arbitrariness of the relations that subtend national identity and national borders. In both cases the digital age has starkly illuminated something the nation-state and the moving image (especially when it has been used at the behest of ideology) have had us conveniently forget: that the relationships between signifiers and referents are arbitrary (as Ferdinand de Saussure might argue) rather than necessary or fixed. That is, the identifiers of nation and citizenship, just like the cinematic image, are never the complete and natural transfiguration of an absolute reality for which they are so often mistaken; rather, they are intricately constructed, painted, and figured just as the digital image in the postproduction editing room.

The digital's unfixing of the bond between signifier and referent (image and reality, nationality and individual) and the mobility this unfixing invites, has been met with anxious attempts to refix and reorder referents into stable signifiers and identities. In cinema, we saw this exemplified by the sudden vogue of movements like Dogme 95 in Europe, which premised itself upon fidelity to an unadulterated realism in the 1990s when computer-generated imagery (CGI) was infiltrating cinema. This period when CGI was transforming cinema's relationship to the "real" also witnessed the rapid rise of reality television, another conceptual backlash against threats to the index, though one that at the same time thoroughly ironized a concern with the real by transforming reality into performance. In the context of global politics (which is now, at least in the United States, inextricable from reality TV), we also see this backlash against the unfixing of indexes in what Wendy Brown has brilliantly theorized as a paradox of national borders in which as the sovereignty of a state wanes the visibility of its borders waxes; whenever a nation's identity and stability is under threat, the more money it will put into militarizing its border. Thus, as the sovereignty of a state is actually threatened, the visibility of the borders that index its power, its sovereignty, and its national independence increases. This paradox of visibility is central to Brown's argument and is deeply connected with the digital age's movement, which has been able (through invisible or virtual forces) to challenge and unfix the control of nation-states. The attempts of nations to build up and make more visible their literal borders (e.g., the $27 billion wall President Donald Trump wishes to construct between the United States and Mexico) as an attempt to re-establish the index of nationality, a *visible* sign with an unquestioned and unquestionable relation to reality, in an age of global trade and commerce. It is thus unsurprising that the same political supporters urging the expensive construction of a visual index defining the United States' physical borders would include a subsection of nationalists unsubtly attempting to revive another visual index of American nationality: whiteness. But just as the digital image has put cinema's indexicality into question as always having been a matter of artifice (according to Manovich), so too has the movement of the digital age thrown the necessity of walls between nations (and racialized definitions of nationality) into question as themselves constructs serving arbitrary (politically and ideologically constructed) interests rather than essential purposes. In other words, the postdigital age's mobility returns us to realities we have forgotten or overlooked about both the nature of cinematic representation and the representations of the nation-state's boundaries and citizens: that both are signifiers with relationships to their referents that, rather than being essential, are intricately constructed and mediated by culture and politics.

Gloria Anzaldúa's conception of the "borderlands" in her seminal text *Borderlands/La Frontera: The New Mestiza* is premised in large part upon the "unnatural" quality of the boundary separating the United States from Mexico. The contrast between the barbed wire that Yémaya, the Yoruba goddess of the seas, blows down in the poem that begins Anzaldúa's text, the "fence rods" staked in the sea that "cannot be fenced," underscores the constructed rather than essential nature of the border, whose physical and ideological artificiality are constantly undermined by the ocean and the desert sands that resist such defining and confining.[3] The artificiality of the border as literally "drawn" by national, political, and economic interests has become a theme uniting cinematic representations of the U.S.-Mexican border. For example, Shaul Schwarz's *Narco Cultura* and Vicki Funari and Sergio de la Torre's *Maquilapolis* (both documentaries) and the TV series *The Bridge* utilize what has become an imagistic trope in cinematic depictions of the U.S.-Mexican border where a line is literally drawn, *animated*, over an aerial photograph picturing the border as a swath of desert: El Paso's glimmering buildings against Juárez's dilapidated shacks; the vacant desert of the U.S. side of the border contrasted with the *maquiladoras* (foreign-owned factories) that run up against the Mexican side; the consequences of the North American Free Trade Agreement. The line artificially traced over a photographic reality suggests a mechanism for interrupting and interfering in the omniscience and power of the state (implied by the aerial perspective). The drawn-in or drawn-over line communicates to the audience how artificial means reify a view of the border that is totalizing in its "truth-telling" abilities; aerial images connote the power of surveillance via the state-owned satellite or drone. These are images that are also generally used to reveal a previously undisclosed reality; thus the trope ironically uses the authority of the aerial image to reveal the artificiality of the border. As an *artificial* visual construction of the border (traced over the photographic image), these animations also locate and recall a history of photography's and cinema's authoritative participation in the construction of this border, often taken to be natural, always already there. This dynamic finds its origins in an earlier circulation of border images: the early twentieth century postcards Claire Fox analyzes in which photographers and correspondents often felt compelled to draw in a border where none was otherwise visible.[4] The contemporary aerial views that feature in so many U.S.-Mexican border films also feel this compulsion, and their performance of drawing that line documents both the reflex and the work that goes into making visible an unnatural boundary. The fact that this drawn line has become a visual trope in representing the border registers the extent to which the border's efficacy has depended upon and exploited a collective investment in and visualization of a line separating "us" from "them."

While animation plays a rather incidental role in the feature-length documentaries I have mentioned, even as it provides a trope that frames the forced visualization and manufacture of the U.S.-Mexican border, it plays a more central role in the largely experimental shorts I will examine here. (Even television series produced for mainstream audiences such as *Seeking Refuge* or Agniezka Piotrowska's *Running for Freedom* are quite experimental.) In these works animation not only underscores the artifice and considerable arbitrariness involved in signifiers such as the border wall, nationality, or immigration status, which are so often taken unquestionably as natural or essential signifiers, "signs taken for wonders"; it also represents the subjectivities that can intervene in and participate in the construction of the image, recovering the agency of the subject and the filmmaker in constructing reality through (re)imagining it.[5] This is the case in Jacqueline Goss's *Stranger Comes to Town*, which interviews non-U.S. citizens about their encounters with the Transportation Security Administration (TSA), matching actual sound from interviews with animated characters from the multiplayer video game *World of Warcraft*. In key moments, these characters (and the audio from the interviews) are superimposed onto rotoscoped versions of animations the TSA itself uses in instructing passengers about procedures they will encounter upon deplaning in the United States. In a couple of instances the characters are at the computer, where they type in their personal information but instead what appears on the screen in the

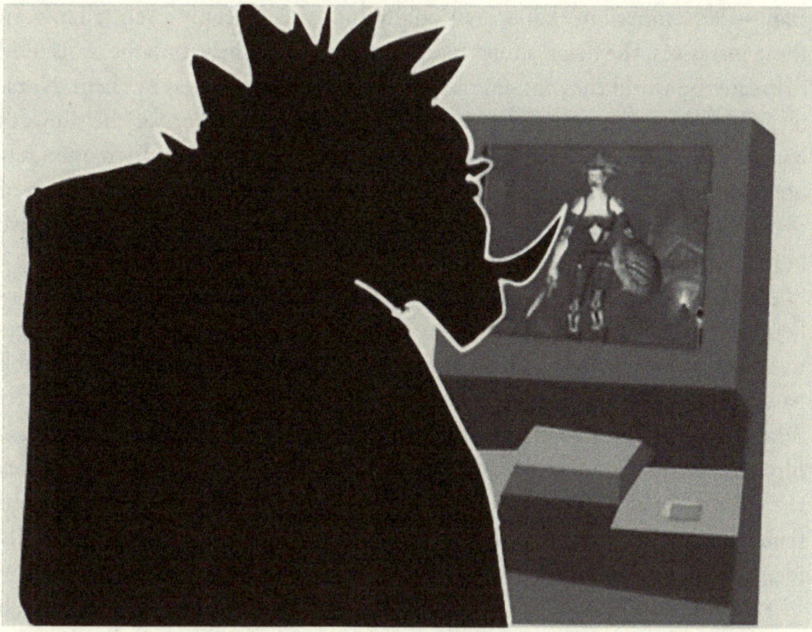

FIG. 3.1 *Stranger Comes to Town* (2007): Here, Goss has superimposed characters from *World of Warcraft* onto a TSA instructional animation. The "monstrous" foreign figure is thus permitted to choose his or her own body as a reflection of the cyberavatar permitted *World of Warcraft*'s players.

film is the *World of Warcraft* menu offering them several avatar options (see figure 3.1).

Goss's use of animation thus imagines the ironic agency of the subject placed under the demands of a state to "identify" him- or herself. Similarly, an episode of the BBC documation series *Seeking Refuge*, "Ali's Story: A Journey from Afghanistan," which briefly depicts the self-narrated story of a boy separated from his parents at an airport en route to London, concludes with an animation of the boy sitting in front of cutouts of drawings, pasting cut-outs of himself, his mother, and his father on the same sheet of paper as his voice tells us, "My first wish would be my mum and dad coming to this country." In both Goss's more experimental *Stranger Comes to Town* and "Ali's Story," the experience of the subject "choosing" his own identity through animation is featured in a way that permits the form of documation to resonate with the stories the films tell. In both cases, animation's use within the film's diegesis echoes its use as a formal choice for the entire work, making it into a metaphor for the subject's agency within the story world to move against the formal dictates and constraints of that same world (its animated rather than live-action pictures), which might be seen as metaphoric of the determinations of the state—determinations that are nationally and, often, racially essentializing. In these instances, the films' subjects are empowered by the very same tools used to create the world they inhabit rather than being subjugated by them. Notably, animation's loosening of the index becomes a metaphor for the subject's contestations and interventions in the state's determinations, which often rely upon indexing the body of the immigrant. Especially relevant to the notion of the index are *Stranger Comes to Town*'s representations of the TSA's extensive biometric data gathering (finger printing, retinal scans) and the ironic absence of different skin colors in the TSA's instructional video on which Goss bases her film. The absence of diverse skin colors in the instructional video attempts to deracialize the subjects, either subliminally instructing TSA agents to look past race as perhaps the most prominent biometric in a post-9/11 world or overtly disavowing the TSA's own culpability in using race as a prejudicial index. Goss's film reveals the irony of these videos by depicting the TSA's use of race (an index the instructional video makes invisible), playing over these images the sound from interviews with Middle Eastern subjects who recall feeling visually identified as suspicious by the TSA *because* of their race and ethnicity.

In these ways *Stranger Comes to Town* documents some of the backlash against postdigital mobility found at the U.S. border. As an entirely animated documentary, the film makes the spectator aware of the distance and artifice between visual signifier and the embodied referents of the subjects Goss interviews. The subjects relate stories of the TSA's attempts to use biometrics to identify them and at times ironize the separation of this indexical data from their minds, desires, and personal histories (all of which should be of actual concern to the TSA, but through this process of tracing, physical indexes go undocumented and undetected). One subject specifically talks about his "desires that don't translate into a document." Goss's use of *World of Warcraft* characters as the "identities" of these subjects both gives them the freedom of disguise and points to the *digital* world as one in which the disembodied subject can move freely, albeit virtually. Like the TSA's actual world, *World of Warcraft* is a game in which players must negotiate travel through spaces regulated by borders (walls, city gates, etc.). Players inhabit bodies of their choosing, but their movement depends on the outcome of processes that Tess Takahashi calls "discursive": "[examining] the category of citizenship . . . as a juridical construct that evokes both legal public protection, and its flip side: constraint and restriction of freedom."[6] In a number of instances, an interviewed subject acknowledges difficulties complying with a dominant culture's presumed image of him or her, as when an Egyptian man speaks about the assumption that he is Muslim even though he does not believe in God: "Regardless of whether I care about Islam or not, I am Muslim, because I am considered by other people to be so. That's part of describing who I am; you're describing what it means to them, not necessarily what it means to you." The first time we see a *World of Warcraft* character in the film, she is quite unexpected, as she suddenly appears while the first subject being interviewed is speaking over Goss's rotoscoped version of a TSA animation. In this moment, the subject speaking is construed as a monster, which is at this point both humorous and appropriate, as the subjects' stories are identified with these figures of the inhuman, the monstrous, suggestions of how they are being seen by the border agents for whom they are simply suspicious bodies trying to get from one point to another. Thus Goss suggests the monstrous as a political and cultural construction that affords both subjugation *and* the freedom of deconstruction (being artificial). Just as the migrant or the other can be arbitrarily labeled a monster (as in Trump's assertion that Mexican immigrants are rapists), the digital world envisions how the subject might derive power from taking advantage of the arbitrary nature of the (racist, nationalist, sexist) sign to imaginatively determine his or her own identity through the choice of an avatar that does not align with the subject's "real-world" racialization (in *World of Warcraft*, the player can choose to be a pink- or a blue-skinned monster, for example). While the gaming world suggests the virtual transgressions of movement afforded the subject who can recover self-determination even within the "constraints" of the "category of citizenship," it also pictures citizenship and the borders that protect it as constructions (of the coders who produced the game, of the cultures and interests that produced the nation-state).[7]

Just as the digital's departure from the indexical also puts into question the faith placed in the correspondence between the analog image and reality, so too does the image that *shows us* its means of production rather than hiding those means suggest the means of ideological and economic production behind categories of citizenship taken as inherent and natural. One of the ways in which Goss makes the means of production visible in her film is through her apparent rotoscoping over the animated films the TSA uses to explain its procedures. Takahashi describes these images as "purposefully crude," and I would argue that they make what we can imagine to be the originals even more abstract, the lines defining objects and persons more squiggly, less exact.[8] Goss's interruption of the TSA's representation of its own border security processes with her own animation draws our attention to the constructed and arbitrary nature of not only the TSA's representation of itself but also the very border processes and procedures represented in these films. Much as the first subject interviewed by Goss wonders whether her fingerprint will be the same if her hands are sweaty, Goss's abstracted rendering of the TSA's more refined drawings points to the tricky business of indexing humans whose movements (both physical and mental) inherently contest fixedness through change.

Karen Beckman has argued that in the wake of a nostalgia and concern for the lost analogic index in cinema, animation becomes a crucial counterpoint to the notion of the indexical.[9] This seems particularly important in the context of Goss's film and other documations concerned with borders. Beckman theorizes that while the index symbolizes fixity, animation as a process that subtends all cinematic production undoes film's indexical identity (its photographic basis) with one that instead symbolizes movement and change. Just as all cinema consists of animation, all identity consists of movement and change. This is an important relationship between documentary and the issues of subjectivity at issue in documation; just as cinematic images have enjoyed the assumption of containing a privileged indexical or *real* relationship to the world, so too have identities (on the basis of race, sexuality, gender, nationality, and religion, for example) enjoyed (or suffered) the assumption of offering a privileged index of the real, effectively defining the person they describe. Animation's subversion of documentary's privileged relationship to the real through documation is thus philosophically compelling for challenging this privilege (and the essentializing fixity it assumes) with animation's qualities of movement and change, a compelling analogue for documations that use their form to undo fixed and essentializing understandings of identity, replacing them with animation's qualities of movement and change that acknowledge identity as a product of subjective agency. In Goss's film, animation acts as a formal counterpoint to indexicality (as the indexical voices of the subjects are laid over animated images) and as a conceptual counterpoint in the way Beckman imagines. That is, while the TSA agents attempt to fix the identity of subjects moving across the border (through biometrics and physical data), their movement voids the correlation between data and body, signifier and referent. The business of refixing an unfixed world is positioned as an unending chase, similar to Zeno's Paradox of Motion (and cinema's very attempt at capturing duration in successive still images) and the way that Anzaldúa has theorized the infinitely fine, infinitely divisible, tip of the razor wire that in some places constitutes the border between the United States and Mexico, a metaphor for the unending work of division that borders invite as well as their arbitrariness set against the wilderness of geographic space. Goss's film uses images from *World of Warcraft* to visualize an unnecessarily and arbitrarily divided landscape (as it is in the game) whose borders are crossed and contested through negotiations between avatars that are really people sitting in front of computers in different countries, often on opposing sides of real-life borders. The encounter between humans mediated by the virtual world of the game thus appears somewhat more realistic in the postdigital age than the encounters mediated by and at the U.S. border. In the gaming world, individuals untethered from their nationalities can move and act with a freedom afforded by the internet's contestations to global borders.

Like Goss, Ari Folman uses a process akin to rotoscoping in his 2008 film *Waltz with Bashir* (Walz im Bashir). Unlike traditional rotoscoping, though, instead of tracing *over* live-action images, Folman had his animators draw *from* such images, putting them at another remove indexically from the "reality" they represent. Folman's film is an autobiographical quest to understand his role as a young Israeli soldier in the 1982 massacre at the Sabra and Shatila refugee camps in West Beirut and consists of interviews with his fellow soldiers who recount how they willfully ignored information and signs that the Phalangists, Israeli allies, were committing genocide at the camps. The film's use of documation points to larger questions about the extent to which reality is mediated by subjective and ideological desires and beliefs, and the extent to which we see what we want to see, what we *believe*, what our mind constructs for us given our political priorities and biases. As Israeli soldiers, Folman and his friends did not want to see the overwhelming evidence of what was occurring: a systematic ethnic genocide of Shiites by right-wing Christians. Folman's use of documation as a self-reflexive form that asks the viewer to constantly question the image's means of production (and therefore, much like events of the past that surface through the memory and testimony of those Folman interviews, human subjectivity's mediation of the world) can help us to understand the use of documation in Goss's film and others. The reality of the massacre to which Folman and his fellow soldiers had repeatedly turned a blind eye is represented at the end of the film by the only live-action images of the entire work. Thus Folman associates the live action with the real, but by doing so hauntingly poses the question of what happens to "real" historical events that occur when no cameras are watching.

The rotoscoped image in *Waltz with Bashir* and other films intervenes and interrupts with the human hand an automatic process that, as André Bazin has theorized, has a privileged ability to present and embalm the events of the past. What does this intervention mean? On the one hand, as I have argued, there is the symbolic nature of this intervention illuminating the ways in which real-life images are always perceived by way of a mediating subjectivity and are thus not the purely indexical representation of the world; their presentation of the world does nothing to bring us objectively closer to it, as our very seeing is a matter that defies objectivity, our mind sketching over the visible world. On the other hand, this intervention of the human hand is also an act of human agency over the automatisms of a world of mechanically produced images. As I have suggested, the digital image's unfixing of the index has returned film studies to questions about cinema's basis in reality, challenging Bazin's conception of the photographic image preserving the world and cinema's orientation being toward a total representation of reality. However, as Beckman notes, "Among the problems that have arisen from the over-emphasis on the 'indexical' may be that André Bazin and the conversations about realism that grow out of his work have become too exclusively aligned with an oversimplified sense of the indexical, photo-based image."[10] Beckman goes on to quote Thomas Elsaesser, who notes that "Bazin's realism was taken as naively pertaining to truth-claims, announcing a correspondence between what was on screen and what was in the world, clearly a fallacious or 'ideological' position. . . . Bazin had always maintained a more nuanced, aesthetic view, arguing that *realism is a function of artifice, and that realism comes by way of belief.*"[11] I would like to focus on Elsaesser's claim about the centrality of artifice and belief to the ontological theories of Bazin, because it makes a philosophical claim that subtends not only the question of cinema's fixity to reality but also other signs taken for wonders—in particular, the fixity of national identity and borders. Belief is certainly at the heart of Folman's experiments with animation and his frustrations with recovering truth from the memories and beliefs that mediate the past. A central question arises from Folman's meditations on the power of belief and from photography's power to evoke belief: If realism comes by way of belief, what is the effect of documation images that invite disbelief through their reflexivity—showing their seams, as it were? If a subject's belief is realism's means, might this suggest that disbelief is a potent means for challenging an image's (or a signifier's—i.e., an identity's, a nationality's) basis in reality? While recognizing that our subjectivity is itself inescapable, interrupting the mechanical processes of live-action image making is a gesture that underscores the subject's power to move and animate in opposition to the fixity and determination of the indexical image or the nationally drawn border or ideologically defined other. This unfixing of reality through acknowledging the power of our own beliefs in determining that reality is essential to documation.

Returning to Goss's use of *World of Warcraft* avatars, it is clear that this choice serves another important function: it uses animation to *disguise* the identity of the subjects she interviews. Hanna Heilborn and David Aronowitsch have similarly used animation as a means of disguise, as they document legally undocumented subjects and those who wish to remain invisible to the state. From 2000 to 2012, they made three short films, all focused on children placed in extremely difficult and dangerous situations because of geopolitical borders. The first film, *Hidden* (Gömd, 2002), documents an interview with Giancarlo, an undocumented Peruvian migrant to Sweden; the second, *Slaves* (2008), interviews a South Sudanese child who was enslaved by a government-sponsored militia; and the third, *Sharaf* (2012), interviews a child about his dangerous migration by boat from the coast of Morocco to Spain's Canary Islands. Although all three films are animated, the strongest case for animation as a means of disguise is made in the first film, *Hidden*, and one wonders if they used the same form for the following two films more as a visual language that communicates in the images we associate with children—images that enunciate a child's simplistic worldview or perhaps invites the possibility of play and role-playing as yet another challenge to the fixity of signifiers to referents (bodies with nationalities, images with realities). As with *Stranger Comes to Town*, *Hidden* uses actual interviews with its subjects and pairs

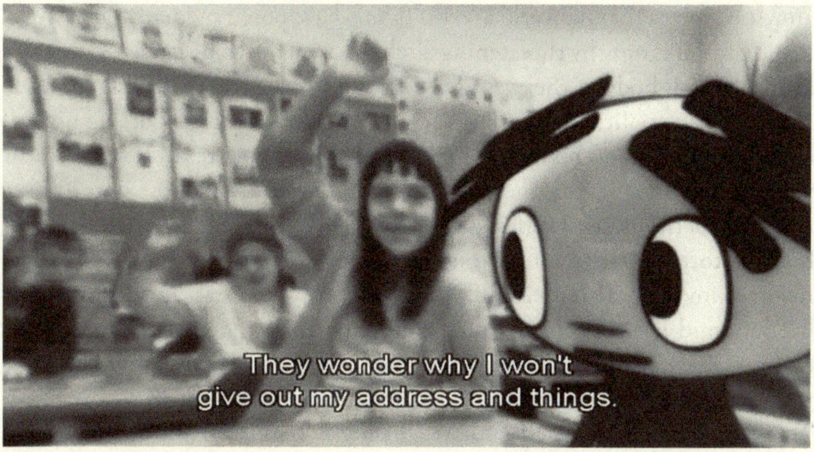

FIG. 3.2 *Hidden* (2002): The filmmakers use animation to comment on the dehumanizing effect of Giancarlo's undocumented status, which forces him to become invisible to his peers as he must hide details about his home life and his background at school.

sound from those interviews with animated images. What is striking about the use of animation in the film is that it simultaneously represents the invisibility of the subject, Giancarlo, to the state who will not recognize him as a citizen, and the invisibility of his life and struggles to those children he interacts with on a daily basis but from whom he must keep his life a secret (see figure 3.2). It also represents Giancarlo's own desire to hide from what he perceives to be the state's all-powerful, all-seeing eyes, his experiences as the subject of immigration raids and police chases.

Within this matrix of motives for the animated image, there is the fact that the visually impoverished nature of the information about Giancarlo's and his family's ethnic identities within the animation shifts our attention to the *sound* of the interview. While Giancarlo can communicate with the interviewers in Swedish and the translator in Spanish, his parents, not knowing Swedish, must communicate via the translator. Giancarlo's language and his two years in Swedish schools have thus moved him across the linguistic and cultural borders that still exist for his parents during the interview. If we were to just *listen* to Giancarlo's voice, if not his words (as the animation encourages us to do by offering us very little to visually identify Giancarlo), we would think he was Swedish. Despite Giancarlo's movement beyond linguistic and cultural barriers, however, his identity remains generically fixed for the state as an undocumented migrant living illegally in Sweden. Near its end, the short film shocks the audience with a simple intertitle informing us, "That winter Giancarlo attempts suicide. This time the authorities take him seriously and the family is allowed to stay." The question of the body and its visibility to the state that the animated images of Giancarlo and his family have posed suddenly takes a dramatic turn. It is only by threatening to eliminate his own body that Giancarlo legitimates his body in the eyes of the state. At the threat of erasing his body from the body politic (which has been the state's desire in deporting him all along), the state grants his family a stay, reasserting its power only at the moment when self-erasure, suicide, the ultimate threat to the power of the state, evokes the power of the most powerless individual (a child, an immigrant) over his own body, in total opposition to the state's authority over a person it has mostly rendered invisible. This invisibility, underscored by Giancarlo's cartoonish figure set amid live-action images of children at his school, suggests that he, unlike them, does not enjoy the legitimacy of being real or even human. Here the state acts to fix the unfixed movement of the body that will erase itself. To fix Giancarlo, whose actions have threatened removal of his own body and its dislocation from the legal purview of the state, the state must contradict itself. Assigning Giancarlo citizenship and thus locating and indexing him is a response to his ultimate threat of moving past the state's power over his body, delegitimizing its control. Suicide reminds the state of the radical limits of its ability to determine and to police the destiny of the human subject, the slippery business of assigning a signifier to a referent when the referent can take its disappearance into his own hands. The agency articulated by the animated image is conflicted in *Hidden*: it represents both Giancarlo's ability to hide himself from the state and the fact that he is forced into hiding by the state while remaining paradoxically visible (as his family hides from the state) and invisible to the law, which views him only generically as another undocumented alien.

It's Like That (2005) by the Southern Ladies Animation Group, independent animators based in Melbourne, Australia, uses stop-motion and traditional animation techniques to disguise the identities of its subjects, much like *Hidden* and *Stranger Comes to Town*. But, like *Hidden* and Heilborn and Aronowitsch's other films, it also uses animation to evoke a child's worldview, suggesting that the limitations to a child's understanding of the legal circumstances of borders and migration can defamiliarize those circumstances for the audience. This is another way of making us question the necessity of these borders, and ultimately undoing our beliefs that construct and support them. Notably, the film does not give us any explanation of who the children speaking are, where they are, or the actual circumstances of the detention they describe until five minutes into the seven-minute film. In this way, the children's voices (interviews conducted with them by an ABC correspondent in 2002, after they had been detained for a total of twelve months) animate in our minds—with the help of their bird puppet live-action surrogates (animated through stop-motion)—the conditions of their lives confined behind bars, remembering a place to which their parents cannot return for fear of their lives. The effect of these interviews and the unlocalizable nature of the animated images is to universalize the experience of these children. Their detainment could be anywhere: they could be the voices of Central American children detained at the U.S. southern border or migrants detained on the shores of southern Europe. It is only after the interviews, when the screen goes black, that we learn we have been listening to children being held in one of six offshore detention centers in Australia built to accommodate the 1993 passage of an act mandating detention for individuals unauthorized to enter the country. The children have arrived in boats seeking political asylum from countries that are not specified. The universal nature of the children's stories in the film is echoed in the non–site specific nature of the animations. In fact, it is in the film's dislocations that the filmmakers are most sharply able to suggest the global nature of contemporary migrant crises. As borders have tried to contain the movement and dislocations of bodies in a postdigital age of globalized capital that has veritably fueled this movement, they have only dislocated and replicated their own conflicts. In the words of Anzaldúa, borders are sites where "the third world grates against the first and bleeds," and in the age of global capitalism, facilitated by a rapid movement of bodies and goods across borders with the help of the internet, the binaries that constitute the singular border have become binaries that constitute every border, that spread and move like a contagion to borders throughout the world.[12]

I have examined animation functioning in these border documations as at once a reminder of the artificiality and arbitrariness of border walls and citizenship, signs often "taken for wonders," mistaken as essential, and as metaphors that locate the agency of the subject or the filmmaker in contrast to the power of a nation-state's laws. Turning to the ethical implications of using animation to portray child subjects, I would like to examine this choice beyond its obvious value of protecting children from punitive consequences and to protect their stories from being exploited for the purposes of spectacle, no doubt some of the reasons a filmmaker would turn to the time-consuming and demanding labors of animation to tell their stories. That is, there may also be an empathic value to the distance created between the spectator and the subject when the photographic, live-action representation of a subject or of his or her past is rejected in favor of an animated image. Here a similar situation presents itself as the one Rosa-Linda Fregoso observes is the case with Lourdes Portillo's *Señorita extraviada*, a film about the feminicides that plagued Ciudad Juárez, Mexico, in the 1990s through the early 2000s, which chooses to avoid using the same "lurid pictures of the girls' dismembered bodies" that were published in newspapers, which "added to the brutality of their murders."[13] Fregoso borrows from Susan Sontag in describing Portillo's attempts to avoid the paradoxical potential for traumatic photographic images to both anesthetize and traumatize the viewer (in addition to retraumatizing the subjects whose oral testimonies in the film bear witness to the disappearances and deaths of their daughters, sisters, and friends). Fregoso also points out a concern that has been registered by other documentary filmmakers when it comes to the representation of sensationalized violence or victims: Portillo hoped to avoid exploitative representations or spectacularizing depictions of the feminicides, which the use of images of tortured bodies of the deceased, already widely circulated by newspapers, would threaten to do. As Fregoso explains, instead of using these more graphic images, Portillo "opened up . . . an alternative to image-based proof, an aesthetics grounded in embodied sensory knowledge about the impact of dehumanizing violence."[14] Fregoso describes Portillo's "haptic visuality" (using the term coined by Laura U. Marks): the aesthetic means for accomplishing such a shared sensory knowledge: empathic communication between the spectator and the witnessing subjects in the film as they recall the disappearances of the women. Fregoso's reading of what Bill Nichols might call the "poetic mode" of Portillo's film suggests that by refusing to provide for us documentary's typical photographic image, Portillo allows her spectator to be moved and to relate to the murders and their toll on the community through processes of "feeling" rather than "intellectualizing." For Fregoso, by replacing the optical with the haptic, Portillo's aesthetics activate a process of empathy and emotional movement (which Fregoso argues is better capable of activating the spectator to take action), which threatens to be short-circuited by the stark immediacy and brutal nature of a photographic representation.

Similarly, many of the documations that represent border subjects (many of whom are children) tend to provoke in the cinematic spectator feelings of helplessness akin to that which the audience experiences with the victims of Juárez's feminicides in *Señorita extraviada*—especially the powerlessness of the families in the face of the state's impunity, which compares to the powerlessness of the children in these documations in the face of the state's legal procedures. These documations are able to provoke feelings of empathic helplessness with an eye toward transforming active empathy into activism by using animation in a similar way to how Portillo uses "documentary poetics." At one point, Folman's *Waltz with Bashir* explicitly comments on the function of photographic images in relation to empathy. In a key interview in the film, a psychoanalyst tries to explain the phenomenon of disembodied witnessing (or remembering a traumatic event as an "out-of-body" experience) as a symptom of post-traumatic stress disorder. The psychoanalyst gives as an example an ex-soldier, whom she describes as a "photographer," who witnessed the events of the 1982 Lebanese war "as if he was looking through a camera." The moments that "really emotionally affected him in the moment" were those he witnessed when he "put the camera down," when he beheld dead and dying Arabian horses, thinking, "What had they done to deserve this?" The horses themselves are a mediation of violence in this instance; they are standing in for the dead and dying people of the town. The mediation or transference of violence resonates with the story that begins Folman's quest for his memory of participating in the Sabra and Shatila massacres, when a fellow ex-soldier comes to him and relates to him his recurring nightmare of twenty-six dogs who pursue him. As the friend relates to Folman (and to the viewer), these were the dogs his battalion made him shoot as they entered a Lebanese village so that they would not bark and alert the town to their presence. The soldier tells Folman he was incapable of shooting a human, so his fellow soldiers made him compensate for that by shooting these dogs. The impact of the Arabian horses on the "photographer" buffers and mediates his no doubt more gruesome encounters with the dead and dying bodies of innocent humans. The bodies of animals thus function in a similar way as the animation of Folman's film, permitting the only access to memory and perception that the mind can bear without itself experiencing the perpetrated trauma.

The so-called photographer's mediation of the events through a real or fictive camera lens would of course be ineffective in the context of a film where the photographic image is a given, and so, in a way, the choice to animate *Waltz with Bashir* reflects Folman's out-of-body memory of the events, his mind buffering itself from trauma and thus also buffering viewers from it. Much like the ways in which *Señorita extraviada* forces us to sympathize with the helplessness felt by the families of the victims of Juárez's feminicides through the work of feeling provoked by a poetic mode of documentary rather than seeing or intellectualizing through more graphic, direct images of the atrocities that might have been offered by an expository mode, Folman also uses animation to provoke feelings of frustration and helplessness in sympathy with his own attempts at recovering a repressed past and in sympathy with the ex-soldiers interviewed in the film who remain helpless in preventing the massacre they now know they were also helplessly enabling as adolescent soldiers.

Borrowing in this way from Fregoso's descriptions of the effects Portillo's formal "poetic" choices have for the subjects of her film as well as for her audience, I would like to examine whether animation functions in a similar way for other documation subjects discussed in this paper. Is animation also able to create a relationship between the spectator and its subject on the level of *feeling* rather than *seeing* that accomplishes something the photographic image cannot? Sontag begins her essay *Regarding the Pain of Others* by interrogating Virginia Woolf's reflections on responses to gruesome photographs of the Spanish Civil War circulated in 1936–1937. As Sontag observes, "Invoking this hypothetical shared experience ('we are seeing with you the same dead bodies, the same ruined houses'), Woolf professes to believe that the shock of such pictures cannot fail to unite people of good will. Does it?" Of the photographs of mangled bodies of women and children and bombed out houses, Sontag argues, "Not to be pained by these pictures, not to recoil from them, not to strive to abolish what causes this havoc, this carnage—these, for Woolf, would be the reactions of a moral monster. And, she is saying, we are not monsters, we are members of the educated class. Our failure is one of imagination, of empathy: we have failed to hold this reality in mind."[15]

Sontag's observation about the relationship between imagination and photography in Woolf's thoughts about war photography is a startling one for our contemporary world and its positive inundation with images of war and its victims, many of them children. I would like to argue not only that such an inundation results in the kind of anesthetization that Sontag later discusses and Fregoso points out as a reason behind Portillo's use of poetic aesthetics rather than graphic photographs but also that our relationship to such live-action footage is one that allows our imagination to fail by asking us only to passively see rather than to *create* and thus to engage with the world in our minds that these subjects must inhabit far away from our everyday visual witness. That is, I would like to argue that animation, much like Portillo's use of poetics to evince embodied empathy, requires real imaginative work on the part of the spectator that risks easy elimination at the sight of a live-action photograph, a real-life image. The inherent role of animation as a mediation, an enunciation of the artifice subtending the representation of reality and even the ideological, social, and political constructions of that reality that I have examined earlier in this chapter thus here takes on yet another dimension. Animation not only stands for this work of artifice and creation but compels its viewer to work from and through traces of the story related through images that might be regarded as impoverished or diminished from their live-action counterparts.

Should we regard animation as prompting the work of imagination, we might also regard animation as a fertile formal choice in these instances for provoking an empathic relationship between the spectator and the subject that might be short-circuited by the self-evident and "totalizing" tendencies of the photographic image—totalizing not just in the representational privileges assumed by documentary filmmaking, as Trinh Minh-ha has observed, but also in a way that closes off the world of the subject, making its effect on the spectator negligible in comparison to the reality with which it concerns itself. In fact, the totalizing nature of the photographic image in this sense can also relate to its tendency to refer to or index something that *has happened* rather than something in the present tense, compromising the status of an ongoing crisis and thus its ability to motivate of our activism.

Should animation carry a privileged ability to activate (or *animate*) the imaginative participation of the viewer, it is no wonder that documation has assumed a preferred status in the genre of television programming and web series devoted to raising awareness about issues ranging from political and economic refugee crises to homelessness in America (as with the web series produced by Seattle University, *American Refugees*). This reading of animation's abilities to activate empathy and action on the part of the spectator depend in large part upon a reading of animation as (perhaps controversially) an ironically *impoverished* representation, one that tends to comprise the only incomplete representations we have of events to which no camera was able or present to bear witness. It is worth reading animation's ironic value as an impoverished or lacking representation in this way, particularly as it accompanies the real voices and testimonies of border subjects. Photography's ontology has conditioned us to privilege as evidentiary the photographic or filmic image and to question or suspect claims for which there is no such "hard" evidence (despite all of the recognition in film and documentary studies of the myriad ways in which *what* the photographer chooses to show and *how* he or she chooses to frame the information given in a photograph can radically change or shift its content). By positioning us *before* we can invest belief in an image (and thus endow it with realism), as if giving us a choice to condition what we see as fiction or fact, animation puts pressure on realism's means, so often taken for granted with photography's automatisms and its photochemical index. It reminds us that, as Elsaesser points out regarding Bazin's ontological theories, realism comes by way of belief. Could it be that the belief activated by animated images requires a mobilization of the very imagination, the activity of empathy rather than the passivity of pity, which may fail us when it comes to photographic images—according to Sontag, images of a reality we may "fail to hold in mind"?[16] The animated documentary thus asks us to be copresent in a way that the live-action image does not; there is a sense in which the latter will exist without us, when no one is watching, but that the other *needs* us.

By contrast to animation's status as an impoverished image, it is worth assessing from the perspective of experimental filmmaking practices what claims to realism (and thus "complete" rather than "incomplete" representations) animation makes. Arguments that early avant-garde filmmakers and abstract painters before them made suggest the relationship between abstraction and psychological and subjective experiences and perceptions that transgressed photographic realism. For instance, the German expressionist painter Franz Marc wrote to his wife, Maria, from the Western Front of World War I that the psychological reality of his experiences in the trenches and his subjugation to the first forms of chemical warfare were unsuitable to realist representation.[17] Marc signaled the psychological realism of images that were not realist in the traditional *visual* sense but were clear representations of the reality of psychologically and physically traumatic experiences and their memories. In his theoretical writings, the French impressionist filmmaker Jean Epstein charts the capacities of cinema as a medium of representation that could exceed the "reality of the eye" to express "the heightened awareness of poetry," noting that "the fifteen hundred million who inhabit [the world] can see through eyes equally intoxicated by alcohol, love, joy and woe, through lenses of all tempers, hate and tenderness . . . we can see the clear thread of thoughts and dreams, what might or should have been, what was, what never was but could have been, feelings in their secret guise, the startling face of love and beauty, in a word, the soul."[18] If we view animation as a *more* complete rendering of the kind of psychological realities expressed by Marc and Epstein, rather than an impoverished rendering of the real (though I see no reason why it cannot function *at once* as teeming and impoverished), there emerges a host of representational possibilities animation makes available to the filmmaker and to his or her subject.

Agniezka Piotrowska gives us some perspective on the at once teeming and impoverished nature of animation in her essay "Animating the Real: A Case Study." In discussing the documentary series she produced for television, *Running for Freedom*, she points out that she was obligated to use animation as a mediating device for distancing the subjects who would break down so much over their own stories that they became inviable television subjects. Here we might see animation as impoverishing, but in this very gesture we see that it becomes laden with meaning (the unfit-for-television nature of the performance of memory in the case of these subjects and thereby of memories that exceed their subject's capacity to endure them). Animation's impoverished nature represents the "unsymbolizable nature of trauma," what goes beyond comprehension, beyond the socially acceptable. As Piotrowska puts it, "in attempting to get at a trauma, words fail."[19] Animation's impoverished rendering of a live-action image (existent as a fiction of the past or a real-life image that the animator has chosen not to use or has chosen to trace through rotoscoping) thus symbolizes what exceeds the "symbolic," that for which we otherwise have no means of common expression. Piotrowska notes that her creation of images to depict the experiences of Teresa, a Colombian refugee, mirrored the fact that the subject herself was "writing an account in her mind, which had elements of complete factual truth in it and maybe a little bit of fiction"—namely, that the romantic relationship she idealized with her disappeared husband was more a fantasy than the reality in which her husband's desires were mercurial and personally damaging.[20] The role of animation as standing in for how the subject's desires and fantasies can cloud her memory, determining and intervening in a representation of the "truth," is resonant with Folman's use of animation in *Waltz with Bashir*. Piotrowska refers to the work of Jacques Lacan to contextualize her experience, "transcribing" Teresa's memories of her traumatic escape from Colombia, as she notes that "in the *Running for Freedom* project, I must say that I was indeed the person who somehow was supposed to know how to translate their silent pain into a symbolizable story . . . Lacan defines transference as 'the enactment of the reality of the unconscious' . . . and has been known to often repeat that analysands' fictions can be just as truthful as any correct factual accounts."[21] Earlier in her essay, Piotrowska refers to the work of surrealists in discussing her animation choices: "[Julie Innes,

Piotrowska's codirector] and I decided on a visual language, which was in some way reminiscent of the work of surrealists such as [André] Breton and [Joan] Miró. We were very wary of attempting any 'realistic' representation, which would be too figurative because we did not want to pretend that somehow we were able to capture the tragedy of the pain of our contributors."[22] Thus the elements of "fantasy" that could be seen as animation's impoverishment (for its lack of indexical privilege in relation to the world) is here noted as a gain, offering a more complete representation of the truthfulness of the fictional (a subject's fantasies as they color the past) and of the *true* nature of a trauma so painful and beyond belief as to be "beyond words"—that is, beyond the capacities of the symbolic. It is clear from Piotrowska's words that animation symbolizes a recognition on the part of the filmmaker that she cannot fully capture the trauma and tragedy experienced by her subject and that eliciting empathy from the spectator can never be the same as having full access to the experience. Here animation in the service of empathy respects the uniqueness and profoundness of the experience without reducing it to what Trinh T. Minh-ha might call a "totalizing" vision.

While audiences have come to expect live-action images from documentary (part and parcel to our naive expectations of documentary's and photography's ability to reveal the "truth"), animation's use in documentaries about borders and their subjects reveals the intrinsic artifice behind *all* representations, and particularly those that suspiciously disavow their own artifice. Documation thus imaginatively exploits the digital's severing of cinema's indexical claims to locate within the very mistaken assumptions about cinema's ontology revealed by the digital the mistaken nature of ontological assumption about other indexes: nationality, race, and immigration status, which are so often taken to be (similarly to the photograph) unmediated and unconstructed documents of the truth. The distance between animation and the world to which an animated image points in these films thus underscores the extent to which our understanding of borders is mediated and constructed by culture, ideology, and politics but, most of all, our *belief* in these things. Correspondingly, the drawn border becomes a site where subjects can take the artifice that constructs a border to locate the power to intervene in and deconstruct borders. As the latter part of this chapter has argued, the distance between the animated image and the worlds described by the subjects of these films also prompts the spectator to work at constructing the world of the film in ways the live-action image's apparent clarity and transparency can allow him or her to avoid doing. Documation does this through prompting the spectator to actively imagine the world sketched by animation and thus to actively engage with the suffering of subjects rather than passively observing live-action images that "document" it. Animation's rootedness in movement and the coconstruction of the world it evinces from the audience place it in the present tense in a way that contrasts with the historicity and pastness of the live-action documentary image. There is an agency for both subject and audience implied by animation's emphasis on the present, the evolving and mutable rather than the always already. Thus, the animated image not only becomes a resource for respecting the privacy of victims (especially children) and their families (while not exploiting tragedy for spectacle) but also an aesthetic means for cultivating activism through creating an *active* spectator. Finally, alongside the imagination of the spectator prompted by the distance between the animated image and the various worlds it indexes (including the interior worlds of subjects), animation's anonymizing function is able to disguise, and thereby question, the primary visual index of otherness: race. Removing the index of race (as we see in films like *Hidden* and *Stranger Comes to Town*), animation underscores the relationship that subtends the plights of diverse border subjects and the economic and social inequality that threads together and spreads across border crises in an age of globalized capitalism.

Notes

1 Rotoscoping is a process whereby an animator either digitally or manually traces over live-action images. Depending upon the degree of fidelity between the traced image and the photographic image, the resulting images bear what has been described as an "uncanny" resemblance to the real.

2 Lev Manovich uses this expression when he argues that in the postdigital age, "cinema can no longer be clearly distinguished from animation. It is no longer an indexical media technology but, rather, a subgenre of painting." Lev Manovich, *The Language of New Media* (Cambridge, Mass.: MIT Press, 2001), 295.

3 Gloria Anzaldúa, *Borderlands/La Frontera: The New Mestiza* (San Francisco: Spinsters/Aunt Lute, 1987), 2–3.

4 Claire Fox, *The Fence and the River: Culture and Politics at the U.S.-Mexican Border* (Minneapolis: University of Minnesota Press, 1999), 78.

5 I borrow this phrase from Homi K. Bhaba, "Signs Taken for Wonders: Questions of Ambivalence and Authority under a Tree outside Delphi, May 1817," *Critical Inquiry* 12, no. 1 (1985): 144–165. Bhaba uses the expression to refer emblematically to the "discovery" of the English book in cultural writings of English colonialism in the "wild and wordless wastes of colonial India, Africa, the Caribbean," where the book functions as "an insignia of colonial authority and a signifier of colonial desire and discipline" (144).

6 Tess Takahashi, "Experiments in Documentary Animation: Anxious Borders, Speculative Media," *Animation: An Interdisciplinary Journal* 6, no. 3 (2011): 238.

7 Ibid.

8 Ibid.

9 Karen Beckman, "Animation on Trial," *Animation: An Interdisciplinary Journal* 6, no. 3 (2011): 259–275.

10 Ibid., 260.

11 Ibid.; emphasis added.

12 Anzaldúa, *Borderlands*, 3.

13 Lourdes Portillo, "Filming *Señorita Extraviada*," *Aztlán* 28, no. 2 (2003): 229.

See also Rosa-Linda Fregoso, "The Art of Witness in Lourdes Portillo's *Señorita Extraviada* (2001)," chapter 4 in this collection.

14 Fregoso, "The Art of Witness."

15 Susan Sontag, *Regarding the Pain of Others* (New York: Farrar, Straus and Giroux, 2003), 6, 8.

16 Ibid., 10–11.

17 In the letter, Marc writes about this sense that "the war is not turning me into a realist—on the contrary: I feel so strongly the meaning which hovers behind the battles, behind every bullet, so that the realism, the materialism, disappears completely." Franz Marc to his wife, Maria, September 12, 1914, in *Letters from the War*, ed. Klaus Lanheit and Uwe Steffen, trans. Liselotte Dieckmann (New York: Lang, 1992), 4; the letter also appears, slightly modified, as Franz Marc, "Im Fegefever des Krieges" [In the purgatory of war], *Vossische Zeitung*, December 15, 1914.

18 Jean Epstein, "On Certain Characteristics of Photogénie," in Richard Abel, ed., *French Film Theory and Criticism: A History/Anthology*, vol. 1: *1907–1929* (Princeton, N.J.: Princeton University Press, 1988), 314.

19 Agnieszka Piotrowska, "Animating the Real: A Case Study," *Animation: An Interdisciplinary Journal* 6, no. 3 (2011): 340.

20 Ibid., 342.

21 Ibid., 342.

22 Ibid., 340.

4

The Art of Witness in Lourdes Portillo's *Señorita extraviada*

ROSA-LINDA FREGOSO

"The art of film can be used in the service of the unprotected," Lourdes Portillo once wrote in an article on her highly acclaimed documentary *Señorita extraviada* (Missing young woman, 2001), adding, "And documentary can take a stance and inform, activate, promote understanding and compassion."[1] *Señorita extraviada* is compelled by a poetic politics and ethics aimed at transforming the terror inflicted upon communities on the border.

Portillo's film is one of the first documentaries to investigate what was once considered Mexico's number one human rights issue: the murder and disappearance of hundreds of women and girls in the violence-torn border city of Ciudad Juárez. Instead of employing an expository mode centered on informing the audience of the details, scale, and ramifications of this issue, Portillo's film employs what might be described as a poetic mode. The documentary's poetics encourages an understanding and compassion for the victims and survivors of human rights violations that can potentially generate relations of solidarity and political action. "Our task is to communicate heart to heart, to join our forces that will put an end to violence and brutality perpetuated on those without voice," she stresses.[2] While an expository approach might communicate to the *minds* of Portillo's audience, her poetic approach communicates to *hearts*, building sentiments of solidarity that are likely to be more effective at inciting political action.

Although its true effects may be difficult to gauge, *Señorita extraviada* is above all driven by a desire to change the hearts and minds of its viewers, and primarily those with limited awareness of state-sanctioned violence against Mexican women. In the years following its release, Portillo became a crusader for women's human rights, screening the film before international audiences and raising awareness about the persistence of feminicidal violence in Mexico.[3] As Portillo explains in the essay she published shortly after the release of the documentary, "I traveled endlessly, to Italy, Greece, Norway, Canada, Spain and other countries to get the word out, and to gather signatures and letters to both President [Vicente] Fox and President [George W.] Bush. I have spoken to influential journalists in many countries, who have taken it upon themselves to carry the banner for justice in Juárez. No foundations were willing to support this human rights crusade, so I refinanced my house in order to take a year off to do this work."[4]

Señorita extraviada has screened before members of state and intergovernmental bodies like the European Parliament, the U.S. Congress, and the International Criminal Court, and at human rights conferences and forums like the Ninth World Summit of Nobel Peace Laureates in Paris. At major international/national film festivals the documentary has garnered over twenty awards, including a Special Jury Prize at the Sundance Film Festival; Amnesty International's first ever Award for an Artist; the Nestor Almendros Award from Human Rights Watch; First Prize "Grand Coral" for Best Documentary at the Havana Film Festival; and the FIPRESCI Award at the Thessaloniki Documentary Film Festival. Portillo has toured with *Señorita extraviada* beyond the festival circuit, screening the film before organizing and activist groups in Europe, Latin America, and the United States. This public visibility and recognition has given her a platform for bearing witness to human rights injustices on the border and denouncing the Mexican government for its complicity in terrorizing women. *Señorita extraviada* informs its viewers about the issue of feminicidal violence in Ciudad Juárez, but it goes beyond the informative level; it incites the imagination and inspires creative participation in social action.

Early on Portillo chose to frame the documentary's narrative in ways that explicitly echoed the organizing strategies of the mothers and other women's rights activists whose social justice campaign intensified around the time of *Señorita extraviada*'s release, which coincided with the assassination of human rights lawyer Digna Ochoa in 2001 and the unearthing of the tortured bodies of eight women in *el campo algodonero* (the cotton field) adjacent to the headquarters of the Asociación de Maquiladoras in Ciudad Juárez. The documentary makes no pretense to "objectivity" but instead explicitly assumes the perspective of the mothers/activists in their demands for justice. In an early interview, Portillo discusses the social impact and role of the documentary in activist politics:

> So that was really the whole intention of the film . . . to create a kind of consciousness, to incite people to act, and it did that. I think every time that the film showed someplace people were outraged, which they should be. Everywhere I went people wanted to know "What can I do?" So it was at that moment that I said "yes, I need to figure out what they can do." And I need to have addresses and I need to have people for them to connect with and things to do. Everywhere I went it was always the same, you know? People wanted to do something, everywhere. There was never a screening where people didn't stand up and say I'm going to write a letter to the Mexican consulate. It was amazing. I remember in Quito, Ecuador, I showed the film and an old man who's about eighty stood up and he said, "Well I'm outraged and I think this is a *vergüenza*, this is shameful for the Mexican government and today I'm going to write a letter when I get home to the Mexican ambassador. And who in this audience," he asked about two hundred people, "is going to write a letter like mine?" And they all raised their hands. It was so touching, so beautiful that people felt that kind of compassion for the girls and were willing to do something.[5]

This astounding effect of moving an audience to action is the highest mark of achievement for a political documentarian like Portillo—or, for that matter, any political arts movement like Latin America's *tercer cine* (third cinema).[6] Portillo has consistently embraced an aesthetics of social justice, one that is illustrated in such films and documentaries as Glauber Rocha's *Deus e o diabo na terra do sol* (Black god, white devil, 1964), Fernando Solanas and Octavio Getino's *La hora de los hornos* (The hour of the furnaces, 1968), and Patricio Guzman's three-part *The Battle of Chile* (1975, 1976, and 1979); it is an aesthetics whose "common denominator," one of its exponents, Argentinean filmmaker Fernando Birri explains, is a "poetics of transformation . . . a creative energy which through cinema aims to modify the reality upon which it is projected."[7]

This chapter highlights the power of *Señorita extraviada* to incite the imagination and inspire creative participation in social action. In a series of conversations that span a decade, Portillo and I have discussed the making of the documentary and the role of the artist in the politics of social justice and human rights. We have explored the discursive and aesthetic strategies behind a poetics of transformation, the responsibility of the artist and the intellectual in bearing witness to state terrorism and on behalf of people suffering persecution and human rights violations. Our conversations began when she first decided to make a documentary about the murders and disappearances of women in 1998, which was the year we both began our research into the subject of feminicide on the border; in my case, this culminated in two coedited collections and numerous essays on feminicide.[8]

In presenting this reading of the film, and discussion with Portillo, I make no pretense to "objectivity" nor do I assume the stance of the disinterested/distanced spectator. It would be not only disingenuous for me to occupy or claim this position but also an impossibility: I know things about the process, history, and making of this documentary due in large measure to my close friendship with its director.[9] My intimacy, ongoing conversations, and interviews with Portillo for over ten years have given me a unique perspective on the film, but so too has my own ongoing research on the subject, close contact with mother-activists in Mexico, and my political commitment to and solidarity with the movement to end feminicide. I occupy the position of an interested *and* intimate spectator, and this vantage point colors—and, I daresay, improves—my reading of *Señorita extraviada*. Yet divulging my position as an interested/intimate spectator is not meant to invalidate other possible readings of the film, for mine is simply one specific and historically situated reading of many possible analyses.

Possessed by the Subject Matter

Portillo first heard about the murders of women and girls in Ciudad Juárez from our mutual friend, filmmaker Renee Tajima-Peña, who referred to an article written by Debbie Nathan for the *Nation*.[10] As Portillo recalls, "Renee said 'Look at this, I can't believe what's happening in Mexico.' I couldn't believe that all these murders went unnoticed; almost a hundred girls had been killed at that point. And Renee said to me 'Don't do this project. I know that it's very tempting for you to do, but you shouldn't do it. It's pretty scary.' So when Renee said that it was kind of scary, I thought to myself, 'Oh this is something that I'd like to do.'"[11]

Portillo's family is from the border state of Chihuahua and the "harrowing panorama of what might be taking place"[12] in the border region is something that captivated and ensnarled her. The notion of "being possessed by an idea" is one that Portillo has used in another context to describe how a story takes hold of her imagination: "My world was shaken to its core, and the fear experienced by the people of Juárez became part of my own daily life for the next three years."[13]

By the time Portillo first started filming, women's rights groups had documented the cases of 162 murdered women between 1993 and 1999, and hundreds more disappearances. Until then Ciudad Juárez had Mexico's highest rate of sexually violent crimes. Apart from media sensationalism about serial killers/sexual predators exterminating young women, speculation about the motives behind the killings were just as macabre: some alleged that women were murdered and disappeared by sex traffickers, while others suggested an underground economy of pornography and snuff films; a satanic cult; criminal gangs, for their bonding rituals; or even unemployed men envious of women maquiladora workers. But no one knows for sure.

In her funding proposal to the Soros Documentary Fund, Portillo mentions the "ghoulish theories that the women were victims of a crime ring that smuggles human organs into the United States for transplant surgery."[14] Behind all this loud sensationalism, Portillo discovered "a deafening wall of silence: most people were too terrorized to speak out. The authorities, when questioned, gave only cavalier and confused responses."[15] It was "the silences, the elusiveness, the lies, the misrepresentation, the misinformation,"[16] the lack of an evidentiary basis for a conclusive story that gave Portillo the impetus for making a different type of film.

The Art of Witness

Portillo opens the documentary by declaring, "I came to Juárez to track down ghosts and to listen to the mysteries that surround them." What she discovered in the border city were the unseen presences, the unspoken violence, the unrepresentability of terror. She was so haunted by what she witnessed in the course of tracking down ghosts, so horrified by the sexualized nature of the violence and the enormity of the disappearances, by the indifference, subterfuge, and impunity surrounding gender crimes, by so much grief, fear and despair, that she invested *Señorita extraviada* with her outrage.

"After realizing that I couldn't get to the bottom of it, it became a different thing. It became a human rights cause," she confided to María-Christina Villaseñor.[17] "Now I'm not investigating. I am witnessing and denouncing something that is unacceptable to human beings."[18] In referring to this dual purpose, witnessing and denouncing, Portillo signals the complex discursive construction of the documentary. She could not get to the bottom of things, could not produce conclusive evidence about the gender crimes, nor of the identity of the perpetrators and their motives for murdering and disappearing so many women and girls. The film's ending is inconclusive and open-ended not just by the force of Portillo's own volition but because feminicide was then (and continues to be) an ongoing phenomenon, its perpetrators and motivations difficult to pin down with categorical certainty:

> It's a never-ending story that you could go on and on with. . . . So you have to finish when you know you have no money. Then the question becomes, how do

> you make it important, and how do you make a film that doesn't neatly tie up into an ending. I mean that was the real challenge. And I think a lot of people that are not used to this kind of storytelling, are a little bit up off by the story. You know, "You didn't solve it." . . . This is a documentary in which you cannot tie the end into a neat bow.[19]

Unable to tie the end into a neat bow freed Portillo from the documentary burden of veracity. Questions of truth and referentiality became less central to *Señorita extraviada*'s discursive construction than, say, questions of "documentary poetics."[20] "Witnessing" and "denouncing," as Portillo suggests, are key components of its poetics, but the witnessing dynamics inscribed in *Señorita extraviada* are less about supplying evidentiary proof of the event or the legal act of proving than they are about the art of witnessing.

Portillo's coupling of "witnessing" with "denouncing" reminds me of Shoshana Felman and Dori Laub's observations about Claude Lanzmann's 1982 film *Shoah* regarding film's "capacity for witnessing."[21] The capacity of art and film to witness involves more than just the documentation of an event; it refers to the act of testifying and to art's "responsibility for truth." As Felman and Laub explain, "To testify is thus not merely to narrate but to commit oneself, and to commit the narrative to others: to take responsibility—in speech—for history or for the truth of an occurrence, for something which by definition, goes beyond the personal in having general (non personal) validity and consequences."[22]

In *Señorita extraviada*, testifying to the truth of an occurrence involves the recognition of *both* the literal plight of border women who have been murdered or disappeared *and* the general (symbolic) consequence of feminicide for the social world in which we live. To explain the documentary's allegorical figuration, Portillo has cited the observations of colleagues like performance artist Guillermo Gómez-Peña, who once said, "*Señorita extraviada* is a metaphor for what is happening in the world today," and those of Mexican filmmaker María Novaro, who upon seeing the documentary at its premier in San Antonio, Texas, recognized its literal and symbolic truth: "Esta película es una bomba" (This movie is a bomb), she said, then insisted that it be screened in Mexico because *Señorita extraviada* spoke to the truth of the government's complicity: its failure to intervene and act on behalf of its citizens. In this sense, the documentary bears witness to a truth beyond the occurrence of feminicide—"something which, by definition goes beyond the personal, in having general (non personal) validity and consequences."[23]

As many of us who study feminicide in Latin America maintain, the state's failure to exercise due diligence—to investigate, prosecute, and ultimately stop the killings—in effect perpetuates the historic structure of impunity, a hallmark of authoritarian regimes throughout the region. *Señorita extraviada* does not "bring proof," as Jacques Derrida writes about the act of testifying, but rather "promises to say or to manifest something to another . . . a truth, a sense which has been or is in some way present to [her] as a unique and irreplaceable witness."[24] What is this truth or sense that has been present to her?

In the first place, there is the truth of suffering, fear, and horror that exceeds the limits of didactic documentaries, as I will discuss shortly.[25] Then there is the truth of what impunity represents. As manifested in *Señorita extraviada*, the truth or sense that has been revealed to and by Portillo are cases of Giorgio Agamben's *homo sacer*: "the bare life" of those who can be killed with impunity since in the eyes of the Mexican state, their lives no longer count. As Portillo notes, "A poor brown woman in Mexico doesn't have a lot of value. They are worthless. They are sex objects. When you kill one woman, then there are twenty to replace her."[26] The sense of Derrida's notion of *sacramentum*, or oath, gestures to the truth that conjoins the witness and the addressee. "The same oath links the witness and his addressee," he writes, "but this is only an example—in the sense of justice: 'I swear to speak the truth, the whole truth, and nothing but the truth.' This oath (*sacramentum*) is sacred: it marks acceptance of the sacred, acquiescence to entering into a holy or sacred space of the relationship to the other."[27]

Portillo testifies to this reality. In accepting this oath, she commits herself and the narrative to others, and in so doing forges "intersubjective relations that ground the act of bearing witness"[28] in human connections: between survivor/witness (addresser) and filmmaker (witness/addressee); between filmmaker (addresser) and audience (secondary witness/addressee), between survivor and audience. This form of witnessing differs from and even goes against the grain from the "disengaged, guilt-ridden viewing of atrocity-as-spectacle that many forms of spectatorship take."[29] In contextualizing the historic structure of impunity, violence, and trauma, *Señorita extraviada* makes a call to us in the present, to be present in the space of the "figurative witness," as witness to the witness of the atrocity of feminicide. Portillo's form of bearing witness "opens to another poetic and semantic space."[30]

This alternative poetic and semantic space involves a third way of testifying, "not in the sense of 'in favor' or 'in the place of,'" as Derrida explains, "but 'for' someone in the sense of 'before' someone. One would then testify for someone who becomes the addressee of the testimony, someone to whose ears or eyes one is testifying."[31] Kelly Oliver calls this third way of testifying "an ethical-political sense of witnessing." As she explains, "This sense of witnessing not only involves testifying to the events, observed historical facts, but also to the meaning of those events, which goes beyond what the eyes can see."[32]

Portillo is keenly aware of the film's power to act and interpret a reality "which goes beyond what the eyes can see" as well as what the ears can hear.[33]

And she recognizes the ethical and political responsibility entailed in testifying before someone about the meaning of those events. As she expresses it, "I think the truth for me is in the experience, in the purity of the experience. That's where it resides. If we're to understand each other as human beings you know we have to look at each other in the most truthful kind of way and that has to do with our happiness and with our suffering, and with our feelings, *todo lo afectivo*."[34] Bearing witness in film is an image-based process, but here Portillo's form of witnessing "opens to another poetic and semantic space": *lo afectivo*, the affective, the unseen presence, that which is beyond what the eyes can see.

From the beginning of the film Portillo insists on this other form of bearing witness ("I came to Juárez to track down ghosts"), a witnessing that demands our engagement and communion with the truth she re-presents for us. The willful infliction of harm and injury devastated an entire community, as she so compassionately explains, referring to "the amount of suffering that people have gone through" and adding, "Because the suffering that the mothers suffered or the husbands or Maria for example who was kidnapped when she came back to Juárez, yes, I'd like to go back to document the suffering of the children, the girls, the families, and how it's destroyed family after family. The destruction. It's not just five hundred girls that have been murdered. It's thousands of people whose soul has been wounded."[35]

Touching Visuality

Señorita extraviada makes a radical intervention into documentary rhetoric. In her long and accomplished career, Portillo has demonstrated a mastery over documentary form by both embracing and rejecting the conventions of documentary realism and utilizing its realist aesthetics in provocative and playfully self-conscious ways. Even as she deploys well-established techniques for communicating documentary truth (i.e., in interviews, actuality footage, and voice-over narration), she often interrogates the criteria for truth and accuracy in documentary, its reliance on visual evidence, and directs our vision to the plurality of truths and the constructedness of the image. In her earliest documentaries, the use of voice-over leaned toward the poetic and speculative, often relying on a wide array of multisensory images to conjure an experience beyond the visual and informative realms. Portillo's style is innovative in its embrace of "irreverence" as a technique for transcending the literal, explanatory mode for apprehending and interpreting reality. Some of her signature techniques involve playing with the narrative's linear forward-moving temporality as well as the summoning of "disqualified" sources of knowledge passed on in the form of legends, gossip, *canciones rancheras*, corridos, myth, and proverbial wisdom.[36]

Señorita extraviada continues and expands Portillo's distinctive documentary praxis. This time, however, Portillo eschews irreverence and playfulness for a more solemn tone, basing the factual (explanatory) parts of the narrative on journalistic sources (newspaper reports and television news), yet moving beyond the numbers and statistics. Portillo explains this desire for a "new kind of experimental approach," noting "I realized early on that there was no way that the footage that had been shot by other people could be used in this new approach. In discussing all this with Vivian, my editor, we realized that this film was just not lending itself to that kind of playfulness because it was so serious and so tragic. . . . You couldn't go back and forth and play with time when things were accumulating, deaths were accumulating; the numbers were increasing."[37] The film demonstrates a unique stance toward evidence, one that sits less in the realm of factual or empirical truth and more in the domain of the truth of emotions. Here Portillo infuses explanatory documentary discourse with a poetic layer, an alternative and evocative mode of framing truth, that has even sparked criticism about *Señorita extraviada*'s "truth discourse." When the documentary was first shown in Ciudad Juárez, local authorities publicly denounced the testimony of Maria, one of Portillo's main witnesses, as a fabrication. Then, a congresswoman in Chihuahua's Chamber of Deputies accused Portillo of "amarillismo" (yellow journalism) for allegedly perpetuating "urban legends" that attributed the murders and disappearances to the collusion of the government and the narcotrafficking industry.

In the design of *Señorita extraviada* Portillo envisioned a "documentary approach with visual metaphors, impressionistic B-roll footage, and exegetic sound-track to enhance the film's coherence and force."[38] She gleaned a number of visual techniques from previous documentaries. Her 1985 *Las Madres: The Mothers of the Plaza de Mayo* integrated black-and-white footage excerpted from an experimental film to provide a stylized representation of torture. Similar techniques are utilized for visualizing the corporal consequences of trauma, such as the use of canted framing and elliptical editing to render a stylized representation in the scene of Maria's testimonial, as survivor-witness account of the torture of women. As she did in *Las Madres*, Portillo draws on photographs of the murdered and disappeared children; from *The Devil Never Sleeps* (1995), she appropriates the inconclusive ending of a murder mystery; from *Corpus: A Home Movie about Selena* (1995), *Las Madres*, and *The Devil*, she takes the requiem style of storytelling—that is, a composition for the dead.

Making a film about an unfolding traumatic event raises the concern about the ethics of trauma imagery both from the perspective of viewing subjects and that of the subjects portrayed. The experience of personal loss for family members had been (and continues to be) such a life-altering trauma that Portillo considered a more reverential approach to the subject matter, as a way of dealing with the ethics of the image; as she explains, "Lurid pictures of the girls' dismembered bodies were published and added to the brutality of their murders. Their deaths remained no more than statistics for the press for many years. But the increasing number of murders without recourse to justice was devastating to the communities."[39]

This preoccupation with the ethics of visualizing the corporal effects of atrocity is not Portillo's alone. There is a long-standing skepticism toward visual representations of human suffering—torture, rape, dismembered and mutilated bodies, the monstrosities of war, and so forth—in documentary photography and film, partly because, as Frances Guerin and Roger Hallas remind us, "no representation can begin to convey the truth of the traumatic experience."[40] Apart from this skepticism, Portillo faced the paradox of trauma imagery that Susan Sontag wrote about in the 1970s. Images may indeed figure as one of the major forms through which artists bear witness, yet, as Sontag suggests, trauma photography (and by extension trauma documentary) generates a secondary, albeit unintended, effect. Writing about photographs of atrocity she encountered at the age of twelve, Sontag tells us, "What good was served by seeing them? They were only photographs—of an event I had scarcely heard of and could do nothing to affect, of suffering I could hardly imagine and could do nothing to relieve. When I look at those photographs something broke. Some limit had been reached, and not only that of horror; I felt irrevocably grieved, wounded but part of my feelings started to tighten; something went dead; something is still crying."[41]

Sontag hints at the fine line between trauma photography and traumatic photography, the latter being photography that traumatizes its spectator. Photographed images of atrocity, horror, and abjection demand an ethically responsible viewing, at the same time as the viewing process itself—through repetition, familiarity, and ubiquity of the images—can inure us, produce numbness in the viewer ("something went dead"), as much as they can traumatize us ("something is still crying"). Documentary photography (and film) of atrocities inadvertently spawns indirect/ancillary (secondary) trauma on viewing subjects (from the shock at witnessing the suffering of others) and tertiary trauma (from our inability to intervene).

In the course of making *Señorita extraviada*, Portillo and I talked at length about this dreadful paradox of trauma photography and film. We revisited time and time again our skepticism about images that simultaneously demand an ethically responsible viewing and corrupt the viewing process through repetition and familiarity, as Sontag indicates in the following passage: "To suffer is one thing: another thing is living with the photographed images of suffering, which does not necessarily strengthen conscience and the ability to be compassionate. It can also corrupt them. Once one has seen such images, one has started down the road of seeing more and more. Images transfix and images anaesthetize. An event becomes more real than it would have been if one had never seen a photograph. But after repeated exposure to images it also becomes less real."[42]

In our image-saturated world of YouTube and social media, the abundance (and circulation) of images of violence—what Sontag calls "image-glut"—may portend an era of social insouciance. For others, visual portrayals of human suffering are vital to the forging of a politics of solidarity and intervening into the wider political and cultural arena. "The tortured bodies of the victims were necessary," Diana Taylor writes about images of atrocity in Argentina. "They made a difference in that they made difference visible."[43] Images, in this sense, participate in the transformation of the social world.

Yet Sontag's reflection on the paradox of photographs that can both traumatize and anesthetize the viewer raises another concern regarding trauma photography: the exploitation of subjects. In an earlier critique of the work of journalist Charles Bowden, I voiced my skepticism about Bowden's decision to publish an enormously disturbing photograph of the tortured body of a young girl that even newspapers in Mexico (notorious for publishing virtually pornographic images of sexualized violence) refused to publish because the image was so terrifying. Bowden notes "the lips of the girl pull back, revealing her white teeth. Sounds pour forth from her mouth. She is screaming and screaming and screaming."[44] From my perspective, whatever Bowden's intentions were, his decision to publish the image did nothing other than double the abjection and victimization of this murdered young woman. Visualizing the violent procedures of torture and human suffering in cases like Bowden's is a form of trauma pornography that compounds the exploitation and victimization of the victims of feminicide in the borderlands.

Making visible the violent procedures of disappearance and torture that authoritarian states refuse to recognize may indeed "make a difference" insofar as it serves to rally the international human rights community, but imaging tortured bodies also undermines the full humanity of the deceased and the survivors of atrocities. The ancillary trauma affecting viewers of atrocity is even more severe and tangible for the relatives and friends of the deceased and disappeared who must live daily with their personal loss and the repeated experience of compounded trauma from each new announcement, media report, or image of a murdered or disappeared woman.

In the editing phases of the documentary, Portillo grappled with precisely such questions: How could she convey a human story about atrocities without further dehumanizing the victims? How could she denounce the abjection and desecration of female bodies without compounding the trauma of survivors? How could she portray the dead without further desacralizing their semblance? How could she do so in a manner that was respectful of their relatives' grief and honors the memories of the deceased women's existence?

Portillo abstained from visualizing images of mutilated female bodies that had been lasciviously photographed and published because she did not want to exploit the suffering of the relatives, add to their trauma, nor double the victimization of the murdered and disappeared women.[45] This refusal to show the tortured bodies of the deceased opened up a space for an alternative to image-based proof, an aesthetics grounded in embodied sensory knowledge about the impact of dehumanizing violence that did not sacrifice the veracity of the experience. "We aimed for feeling, for something evocative, something that touches you," Portillo explains. "People wanted to feel the presence of the girls and not just hear numbers and see bodies."[46] This evocation, as opposed to imaging, of the presence of the victims led to the design of a distinctive aesthetics, what I term "touching visuality."[47]

The quest for an alternative to the vision-centered sensory experience of film has been an enduring consideration for feminist film and video makers. In the early 1970s feminist avant-garde filmmakers Barbara Hammer and Carolee Schneemann first explored the sense of touch in the visual field. Hammer's film *Dyketactics* (1974) probes the erotics of the female body by appealing to a more tactile kind of vision, a style she called "experiential cinema." This emphasis on film as an embodied practice of "touching" over the modernist "privileging of sight" is crucial to a feminist aesthetics for, as Hammer posits (riffing on John Berger's "The child looks and recognizes before it can speak"), "children know the world through touching before they can ever see." As an embodied practice, experiential films aim to move beyond the modernist segmentation of the senses and appeal to a full range of sensory experiences that capture what Laura U. Marks calls "the unrepresentable senses such as touch, smell and taste."[48]

Like Hammer, Marks theorizes film as an embodied, experiential practice in her illuminating study of "haptic visuality" in the intercultural cinema of diasporic and exilic filmmakers like Trinh T. Minh-ha (*Reassemblage*, 1982), Mona Hatoum (*Measures of Distance*, 1988), Rea Tajiri (*History of Memory*, 1991), and Julie Dash (*Daughters of the Dust*, 1992), among others. For Marks, haptic visuality refers to films and videos that conjure a fuller range of sensory impressions, beyond optical viewing alone. Intercultural cinema qualifies as haptic because it "calls upon the memories of the senses in order to represent the experiences of people living in the diaspora."[49]

Films and videos that deploy haptic visuality encourage a "more embodied and multisensory relationship to the image" through representations that evoke memories and engage the sensual in vision."[50] The emphasis on the tactile is a sensual one—as Marks explains, "as though one were touching a film with one's eyes."[51] Its sensual effects result from the fusion of images with sound, editing and camera movement. By gleaning from other modes of sensory experience, haptic visuality encourages corporal closeness between the viewer and the image, one that surpasses optical viewing on its own. Whereas viewing through the eyes privileges the modernist separation between viewing subject and viewed object, haptic visuality, Marks observes, "invite[s] the viewer to respond to the images in an intimate, embodied way, and this facilitates the experience of other sensory impressions as well."[52]

Portillo's touching visuality involves the careful design of multisensory mixes in the form of touching imagery that enhances the viewer's contemplation, vulnerability, and bodily relationship to the image. In developing this touching visuality, Portillo aims to represent the unrepresentable experiences of deep sorrow and grief in ways that invite the viewer to feel vulnerable, intimately connected to and present in the corporal experience of a mother's (and one father's) mourning and feelings of loss: "That was my intention for the film: for the viewer to feel rather than to intellectualize and try to figure out what's happening. We wanted it to be an experiential film. I wanted viewers to feel what it's like to be in Juárez; to feel what it's like to lose a beautiful young girl."[53]

The film mourns the loss of countless young women and girls and conveys the experience of grief through the mothers' testimonials. The viewer's sensory impressions are further enhanced by a series of lyrical images accompanied by a soundtrack of solemn Gregorian chants. First is the recurring close-up image of a flowing dress shot in slow motion as a pair of mature female hands arranges it carefully on a bed. The scene is shot in slow motion, with low-key lighting and warm tones serving to conjure the erotics of a mother's love. Throughout the film, a repetitive stream of photographs of young women and girls—with the dates of their disappearance/murder listed underneath—reappears. The movement of the camera across each photo, accompanied by reverential music, makes it seem as though our eyes are touching the film. The composition, repetition, and sensory enhancement of these two different types of scenes, followed by a dissolve to a black screen, invite viewers to contemplate the images onscreen. They evoke deep feelings of sorrow and appeal to our sentiments and vulnerability (more about these photographs later).

This, after all, is Portillo's intention, "for the viewer to feel rather than to intellectualize": to make ourselves vulnerable to the image; to abandon our ocular mastery for another bodily relationship between ourselves (the viewers) and the image.[54] Portillo developed this touching visuality by working closely with her production team, planning the narrative structure and techniques that would stimulate other sensory impressions. During a retrospective of her work in Madrid in 1999, Portillo and I visited the Museo del Prado's exhibition of Goya's dark paintings, which later inspired the documentary's somber tone. As Portillo explains, "I thought these paintings are just astounding. And I showed Kyle [the cinematographer] the book of Goya paintings I had purchased and said 'Look, these are the paintings. I want them to inspire us.' One of the things about those Goya paintings is the sky, that sense of doom, the sense of gloom, darkness and mystery, it's what we used for the skies in the film. You see the sky go from light to dark and these clouds passing, well they are inspired by those Goya paintings."[55]

As Portillo notes in another context, "What the documentary does is to give you a sense of fear and claustrophobia. It starts closing in on you."[56] If Portillo had retained this ominous tone as the film's sole register, to convey the darkness of the "vortex of Juárez," as she calls it, then viewers would have more likely felt shattered and disheartened, "irrevocably grieved and wounded," as Sontag felt on seeing her first photographs of atrocity. To mitigate these feelings of distress and offset the sense of fear and claustrophobia inspired by Goya's dark paintings, Portillo resorts to counterpoint, incorporating into the film's narrative structure, aesthetic techniques drawn from what I have elsewhere called "the discourse of religiosity."[57]

Portillo employs religious symbolism and iconography subversively. The strategic placement of images of crosses, montages of crucifixion and home altars, the crescendo in the Gregorian chants, including the solemn chant for the dead ("kyrie eleison"), together establish a meditative, hieratic rhythm in the film. Lourdes describes *Señorita extraviada* as a "requiem." She has in effect resignified the requiem as an artistic composition for the dead, and transformed the solemnity of the chant for the dead into a form of healing, as a salving effect for the soul. Viewers may be subjected to the dark emotions of fear, despair, gloom, and grief, but at the same time, the film refuses to leave us with an unbearable heartache, with feelings of helplessness and distress.

A central component of Portillo's touching visuality is the emotional charge that aesthetic religiosity conjures, stemming from her own deep feelings for the subjects in her film. She explains,

> It is a very intense emotional connection between the subject and myself, one that goes beyond words. I really have no words for it. You can call it "compassion," you can call it "connection," you can call it "understanding." There are many words that you can use, it's not even about thinking. Suddenly that moment of intense emotional connection is just happening. . . . Time just stands still and sometimes things are just very intense and very deep, and it's an emotional connection, an understanding that happens between two people. Like the vortex that you mentioned, time does stand still.[58]

Portillo translated the energy, emotional intensity and connection, the time standing still, into narrative form to arrest the film's forward-moving temporality and communicate her emotional investment with its human subjects.

One further example of this translation is found in the placement of photographs of deceased and disappeared young women and girls.[59] The insertion of the photographs between interviews, narration, and news stories is a deliberate and calculated use of them to arrest the narrative's forward momentum and mark the rhythmic pace of the documentary. As noted above, the combination of photo stills with hieratic music, camera movement, and montage makes it seem as though we are touching the images. The photographs in this sense are not just about evidence or bringing proof, as in the expository documentary. They are elements in a subjective documentary, marking Portillo's compassion, deep connection, and emotional closeness to the women and girls. In this sense, the photographs are hagiological because they honor the women's existence and in the process serve to quell viewers who may potentially feel traumatized by the horrific drama unfolding.[60]

In mobilizing this hagiographic effect, the photographs embody the dialectics of still life, a visual rendering of the death (absence) and life (presence) of Portillo's subjects. The dialectical tension between negation of life in the present tense of feminicidal violence (violation inscribed on the female body) and the affirmation of life in the past tense (repetitive images of radiant women and girls) punctuates the entire documentary. For Portillo there is more to this violence and suffering. There is also the future tense of redemption. Although the photographs appear to conjure victimhood (deceased and disappeared women), they simultaneously reclaim subjecthood (the vitality and sensuality of female existence). The photographs capture moments of happiness in the women's lives and, as such, the dialectical tension between the imaging of victimhood and subjecthood reaffirms female subjectivity more so than victimization/abjection. Were it not for the opening and closing scenes, it might have been the other way around.

As Sergio de la Mora writes about the opening and closing sequences, the ephemeral superimposed shots of young women in the act of witnessing the events unfolding convey women as social actors, "looking at the world as subjects rather than as objects of the gaze."[61] In opening and closing the film with these poetic, ethereal images of women's agency and subjectivity, Portillo redeems and rescues life from death's nullifying force.

The Ethics of Documentary Poetics

In our conversations about the effects of her touching visuality, this penetrating movement into the affective realm of truth, Portillo confides, "We're channeling people's feelings and we're capturing them in this great machinery. . . . We are invoking their suffering and we're portraying it and disseminating in in the art we create. I'm being honest with you. It's our way of disseminating the truth of suffering in a way that will activate people after they see the film. That they will feel a sense of goodness from doing something."[62]

In many ways, this ethical insistence for us to stand as witnesses to the dead and survivors seems very akin to the Latin American tradition of *testimonios*;

it aims to compel the viewer to action. As Anne Cubilié, in a discussion of Alicia Partnoy's testimonial novel *The Little School*, explains, "Distanced spectatorship is not allowed to remain the 'unmarked' default position, but is marked as the position that refuses the full humanity of the dead and the survivors of atrocity."[63]

Even as trauma and violence in Portillo's film exist outside the frame, *Señorita extraviada* troubles the space of distanced spectatorship. Portillo's demand is similar to Judith Butler's call for "modes of public seeing and hearing that might well respond to the cry of the human within the sphere of appearance."[64] The film insists on our hearing and recognizing the "cry of the human," on our recognizing the humanity of "women who are being sacrificed" because as, Portillo laments, "they are viewed as worthless women. They're poor, they're brown; everything that is worthless in Mexico, they personify."[65] In recognizing the humanity in the "cry of the human," Portillo reappears the disappeared and murdered women from the profoundly hidden space generated by the state's denial and erasure of feminicide. *Señorita extraviada* recognizes violence as both a witness against life itself and against a particular kind of identity: poor, racialized women.

Channeling the spectator's feelings and disseminating the truth of suffering in a way that will activate an audience after they see the film reflects the long-standing aspirations of the new Latin American cinema, a poetics of transformation that "generates a creative energy which through cinema aims to modify the reality upon which it is projected."[66] This poetics of transformation calls for the overthrow of systems of domination rooted in and permissive of violence, slavery, conquest, genocide, and feminicide. Portillo shares this understanding that images participate in the transformation of the social world: "If you are going to talk about human rights, you can't be didactic, you have to be compassionate, you have to be humane and you have to be emotional. You have to be all the things that make a person act on behalf of another person. How can you protect a child or denounce violence against women? With your heart. You may be saying 'here are the human rights violations' yet it's all words. But if you show it and you see it and you feel it, then you become a part of it and it becomes a part of you." Yes, we become part of it, and it becomes part of us. We enter into "the sacred space of the relationship to the other."[67]

Notes

A different (and abridged) version of this article was published as "Transforming Terror: Lourdes Portillo's *Señorita extraviada* (2001)," in *A Companion to Contemporary Documentary Film*, edited by Alisa Lebow and Alexandra Juhasz (Hoboken, N.J.: Wiley-Blackwell, 2015).

1 Lourdes Portillo, "Filming *Señorita extraviada*," *Aztlán* 28, no. 2 (2003): 234.

2 Portillo, "Filming *Señorita extraviada*," 234.

3 Following the work of Latin American researchers, I prefer the terms *feminicide* and *feminicidal* over *femicide* and *femicidal*, particularly since in English, the latter can indicate "the killing of a woman or girl by a man on account of her gender." In contrast, I define *feminicide* as the murder of women and girls rooted in a gender power structure and encompassing systematic, widespread, and everyday interpersonal violence. There is also the level of impunity involved, since feminicide involves state-sanctioned violence committed by state or institutional actors (directly or indirectly) and nonstate or individual actors, and is systemic violence, rooted in social, political, economic, and cultural inequalities. See Fregoso and Bejarano (2010); and Fregoso (2011).

4 Portillo, "Filming *Señorita extraviada*," 234.

5 Interview with Lourdes Portillo, 2003 (unpublished).

6 *Tercer cine* is also known as the New Latin American Cinema.

7 Fernando Birri, "For Nationalist, Realist, Critical, and Popular Cinema," in *New Latin American Cinema*, vol. 1, *Theories, Practices, and Transcontinental Articulations*, ed. Michael T. Martin (Detroit: Wayne State University Press, 1997), 96.

8 See Fregoso (2000, 2006); Fregoso (*meXicana Encounters*, 2003); and Fregoso and Bejarano (2010).

9 For further discussion of the limits of "objectivity," see Fregoso (2001). See also Minh-ha (1991).

10 The documentary's original working title, "Death Comes to the *Maquilas*," was taken from the title of Nathan's article in the *Nation*, January 13–20, 1997.

11 Maria-Christina Villaseñor, "Lourdes Portillo Interview," *Felix: A Journal of Media Arts and Communication* 2, no. 3: *Risk/Riesgo* (2003): 170.

12 Interview with Lourdes Portillo, 2011 (unpublished).

13 Portillo, "Filming *Señorita extraviada*," 233.

14 Lourdes Portillo, "Death Comes to the *Maquilas*: A Border Story," proposal to the Soros Documentary Fund for a preproduction grant of $25,000, on file with the author.

15 Portillo, "Filming *Señorita extraviada*," 229.

16 Interview with Lourdes Portillo, 2003 (unpublished).

17 Villaseñor, "Lourdes Portillo Interview," 174.

18 Interview with Lourdes Portillo, 2002 (unpublished).

19 Ibid.

20 See Renov (1993).

21 Shoshana Felman and Dori Laub, *Testimony: Crises of Witnessing in Literature, Psychoanalysis, and History* (New York: Routledge, 1991), 5.

22 Ibid., 204.

23 Interview with Lourdes Portillo, 2003 (unpublished). On July 19, 2002, the documentary was screened in a public plaza, el Jardín Hidalgo in Coyoacán, Mexico City, followed by a panel with notable Mexican intellectuals including the late Carlos Monsiváis, María Novaro, and Elena Poniatowska.

24 Jacques Derrida, "A Self-Unsealing Poetic Text: Poetics and the Politics of Witnessing," in *Revenge of the Aesthetic: The Place of Literature in Theory Today*, ed. Michael P. Clark (Berkeley: University of California Press, 2000), 194.

25 For further discussion of these techniques as they apply to *The Devil Never Sleeps*, see Fregoso (1998).

26 Interview with Lourdes Portillo, 2004 (unpublished).

27 Derrida, "A Self-Unsealing Poetic Text: Poetics and the Politics of Witnessing," 194.
28 Frances Guerin and Roger Hallas, "Introduction," in *The Image and the Witness: Trauma, Memory, and Visual Culture*, ed. Frances Guerin and Roger Hallas (London: Wallflower, 2007), 12.
29 Anne Cubilié, *Women Witnessing Terror: Testimony and Cultural Politics of Human Rights* (New York: Fordham University Press, 2005), 11.
30 Derrida, "A Self-Unsealing Poetic Text: Poetics and the Politics of Witnessing, 188.
31 Ibid., 199.
32 Kelly Oliver, *Women as Weapons of War* (New York: Columbia University Press, 2007), 161.
33 Interview with Lourdes Portillo, 2004 (unpublished).
34 Ibid.
35 Ibid.
36 Ibid.
37 Interview with Lourdes Portillo, 2003 (unpublished).
38 Portillo, "Death Comes to the *Maquilas*."
39 Interview with Lourdes Portillo, 2003 (unpublished).
40 Guerin and Hallas, 2
41 Susan Sontag, *On Photography* (London: Penguin, 1977), 19–20.
42 Ibid., 20.
43 Diana Taylor, *Disappearing Acts: Spectacles of Gender and Nationalism in Argentina's Dirty War* (Durham, N.C.: Duke University Press, 2003), 157.
44 Charles Bowden, *Juarez: The Laboratory of Our Future* (New York: Aperture, 1998), 103. For a complete analysis of Bowden's abjection of the murdered women of Juárez, see Fregoso (*meXicana Encounters*, 2003), chap. 1.
45 See Portillo (2003).
46 Interview with Lourdes Portillo, 2007 (unpublished).
47 Writing in another context about the production of presence, I consider the language of the ephemeral as a way to animate the unseen but felt presences, the memories of *las desaparecidas* (the disappeared). *Señorita extraviada* is part of a new politics of the body taking shape around poetic, ethereal representations that animate an alternative sense of presence or what Kevin Hetherington calls a *praesentia*, the manifestation of "an absence" within the "material presence of social life." Originally concerned with the manifestation of the holy dead (saintly relics) in "insignificant fragment of ordinary material" or saintly relics, *praesentia* is "concerned with performance and presence . . . with the experience of mingling: distance and proximity; presence and absence; secular and divine; human and non-human; subject and object; time and space; vision and touch." In "making those discursive categories appear uncertain and blurred," it brings to the surface the unseen but felt presence, the memories of the subject no longer living, the socially haunting forces; see Hetherington (2003, 1937). *Praesentia* points to the centrality of alternative cosmologies for understanding and imagining subjectivity, and in particular the subject of human rights; see Fregoso (2006). For a compelling analysis of the allegorical elements in *Señorita extraviada*, see Carroll (2006).
48 Laura U. Marks, *The Skin of the Film: Intercultural Cinema, Embodiment, and the Senses* (Durham, N.C.: Duke University Press, 2000), xvi.
49 Ibid., 168.
50 Ibid., xi.

51 Ibid., 172.

52 Ibid., 2.

53 Interview with Lourdes Portillo, 2007 (unpublished).

54 Here Portillo is paraphrasing Marks (2000, 164).

55 Interview with Lourdes Portillo, 2002 (unpublished).

56 Villaseñor, "Lourdes Portillo Interview," 171.

57 See Fregoso (*meXicana Encounters*, 2003), chap. 1.

58 Interview with Lourdes Portillo, 2003 (unpublished).

59 Writing in another context elsewhere, I note that *Señorita extraviada* is an example of the inscription of normative gender identities. The exclusive focus on the murder and disappearance of "young women" has had a similar effect of normalizing traditional gender identities—in this case, by coding the murdered women as "virgins." As I have argued, the film's emphasis on the purity and innocence of the victims is strategic, designed to counter the state and the media's campaign of "blaming of the victim" by attributing female nonnormative sexuality as the cause for their murders and disappearances. Yet the film's title including *Señorita* is problematic from a feminist perspective for its failure to unsettle traditional meanings about women's sexuality, especially the assumptions regarding the patriarchal regulation of women's sexual behavior implicit in that word. The term *señorita* refers to several things: it translates into "young woman" (the film's titles translates as "missing young woman"); "unmarried woman" (in contrast to *señora*, "married woman"); and, most tellingly, it refers to a woman's virginity (*es señorita*), derived from Catholic prohibitions on premarital sex and patriarchal valorization of the "purity" (read: virginity) of a woman. The documentary privileges the young and innocent victims at the expense of the other, older (less pure) victims of feminicide (i.e., single, divorced mothers; sex workers; etc.), and this can in turn leave viewers with the impression that violence against women is somehow more egregious if the victim is young and innocent. See Fregoso (2006).

60 Theresa Delgadillo characterizes the film as a form of "spiritual mestizaje," and Portillo's identification as "mother" as solidarity with the mothers of the murdered and disappeared women; *Spiritual Mestizaje: Religion, Gender, Race, and Nation in Contemporary Chicana Narrative* (Durham, N.C.: Duke University Press, 2011), 128–136.

61 Interview with Lourdes Portillo, 2003 (unpublished).

62 Ibid.

63 Cubilié, *Women Witnessing Terror*, 187.

64 Judith Butler, *Precarious Life: The Power of Mourning and Violence* (New York: Verso, 2006), 44–45.

65 Interview with Lourdes Portillo, 2003 (unpublished).

66 Birri, "For Nationalist, Realist, Critical, and Popular Cinema," 96.

67 Interview with Lourdes Portillo, 2002 (unpublished).

5

The Cinematic Borderlands of Alejandro González Iñárritu's *Babel*

MONICA HANNA

Alejandro González Iñárritu's feature film *Babel* (2006) opens in a desolate stretch of desert landscape in rural Morocco. Near the end of this short but central first scene, two young brothers, Ahmed and Yussef, tend their family's herd of goats. Appearing bored, the two decide to test the rifle their father has just purchased from a neighbor to defend the herd from jackals. Ahmed, the older brother, is skeptical of claims of the rifle's precision, so he aims the rifle at a moving car on the road in the distance, below their position on the mountainside. He misses. Yussef then takes a turn, aiming the rifle at a passenger bus on the same stretch of road. A few seconds after Yussef takes his shot, the bus stops. The long shot capturing the desert scene from Yussef's point of view through the viewfinder of the rifle cuts to a close-up of the two Berber boys as they realize they have made contact. They run. As this first scene ends, a match-on-action cut links this rural scene in Morocco to a domestic scene in San Diego, California, the setting of the next sequence. The action of Ahmed and Yussef running from the left to right of the frame, the camera following them from behind, is continued after the cut with a shot of the back of Mike Jones, a freckled blond boy, running as the camera pans (again from left to right and then around a corner) to reveal his little sister Debbie already in her hiding spot as the two white American children play a game of hide-and-seek with their Mexican nanny, Amelia.

This match-on-action cut that transitions the first scene to the second offers insight into the central motifs and techniques of González Iñárritu's transnational vision in *Babel*. The two scenes are divided by time, as the second scene takes place at a remove in the film's chronology (the audience later learns that these scenes take place out of chronological order), while the two pairs of siblings are visibly separated by nation, class, and race, marked by the sequences' contrasting mise-en-scènes. At the same time, the two pairs of children are connected by two kinds of shots: by the match-on-action cut joining the shots displaying the movements of their bodies, but also by the rifle shot, as the audience later learns that the two Moroccan boys unintentionally have shot the American children's mother, a tourist in Morocco on that bus. The children are also linked in *Babel*'s story as they all experience familial tragedy and loss, though the audience will learn later in the film that the causes of those losses are pointedly different; the American family's loss of a child is caused by an unpreventable health condition, while the Moroccan family's loss of a child is motivated by post-9/11 politics. The split-second act that opens the film is misinterpreted by governmental and media sources who immediately label the shooting a terrorist act, and sets in motion the plot of the film, which takes place in various geographic locations and involves characters who occupy vastly different social positions.

This transnational frame allows *Babel* to meditate on the functions of borders and the disparate experiences of border crossers in a post-9/11 world in which those borders are hardening. Specifically, the film takes aim at post-9/11 U.S. concerns with migration and terrorism, anxiety regarding national security, and the reassertion of sovereignty. The 2002 Homeland Security Act placed immigration enforcement under the auspices of the newly formed Department of Homeland Security. This legislation enacted into law the conflation of immigration and terrorism, and the film depicts the ways in which brown bodies are made suspect to U.S. notions of sovereignty even in cases when those bodies are essential to the functioning of the U.S. economy. The film portrays vividly the ways in which some experience border crossing as effortless, as is the case for the First World characters and goods (the rifle) traveling with ease, while the Third World characters suffer through the resurgence of national border protections as their bodies are policed and threatened. The film's choice of Third World locations in Mexico and Morocco precisely points to the shifts in U.S. politics after the attacks of September 11, 2001, which saw further militarization of the U.S.-Mexican border under the new justification of keeping out Muslim terrorists. Morocco was not a site of the post-9/11 wars (which took place in Afghanistan and Iraq), and is considered a strong political ally of the United States (as one of the countries believed to have hosted CIA "black site" prisons, in which terror suspects were interrogated and tortured, during the post-9/11 period). Nonetheless, it is a majority-Muslim country and thus the film shows panic regarding the possibility of terrorism fomenting there.[1]

The cinematic and narrative techniques employed by celebrated Mexican director González Iñárritu, cinematographer Rodrigo Prieto, and screenwriter Guillermo Arriaga provide a key to *Babel*'s transnational critique of borders as constructed emanations of power bolstered by racism, hatred, and fear, that are damaging to all, though most concretely to those excluded by such borders and left without protection.[2] The film creates cinematic and narrative borders, primarily through the use of striking visual cuts, nonlinear chronology, and disparate languages, echoing the various national borders presented onscreen. At the same time, González Iñárritu upends this logic by presenting an aesthetic that gives equal time and attention to the characters across U.S.-defined borders, humanizing rather than othering. This offers a kind of corrective to media representations of Latina/o/xs and Muslims, particularly in U.S. news media and in Hollywood. The visual and sound editing, alongside the narrative linking of stories across geography and language, elucidate this film's reading of borders as lines that paradoxically divide and connect simultaneously.

Gloria Anzaldúa, the foundational Chicana queer feminist scholar, explains that borders attempt to divide and distinguish. While they do indeed accomplish this goal in some (often violent) ways, Anzaldúa argues that these borders also simultaneously function as points of contact. Rejecting geopolitical and identitarian borders, she theorizes the concept of a "borderlands," a space where "two or more cultures edge each other." She envisions the borderlands as a place where "a third country—a border culture" forms through the "merging" of "the lifeblood of two worlds." It is "a vague and undetermined place created by the emotional residue of an unnatural boundary."[3] Anzaldúa's work is instructive here because it is possible to read González Iñárritu's film as an experiment in creating a cinematic borderlands, a space in which disparate cultures meet despite the vast differences in power between the characters and nations represented, rejecting boundaries that separate the characters geopolitically and interpersonally as unnatural because those characters ultimately share an essential humanity. This humanist argument showcases the bonds common between parents and children in the face of tragedy and loss. While national borders work through distinction and differentiation, striving to atomize and desensitize, the film's borderlands offer a space promoting empathy as an affective bridge across borders, allowing people to see others and feel what those others feel. The film's aesthetic choices help create this empathic bridge for the audience through use of close-ups and point-of-view shots that facilitate the audience's focus on the characters' bodies and subjectivities, and visual and sound editing that creates cinematic borderlands improbably joining distant cultures.

Framing Borders

Structurally, much like the first two films in González Iñárritu's "Death Trilogy"—*Amores perros* (*Love's a bitch*, 2000) and *21 Grams* (2003)—*Babel*, the third installment, focuses on the unexpected intersections between the seemingly divergent story lines, which revolve around four sets of characters. Richard and Susan Jones (played by Brad Pitt and Cate Blanchett) are a white American married couple on a guided tour in Morocco. They take the trip in an attempt to reconnect after their infant youngest son's death. After a few tense interactions between the couple, the two board a tour bus on which Susan is shot. This incident leads to a manhunt by local police for the "terrorist" suspects, and the story is picked up by news networks around the world. Amelia (played by Adriana Barraza), meanwhile, is a Mexican woman working as an undocumented nanny in San Diego for the Joneses. She takes their children Mike and Debbie with her to her hometown across the border in Mexico so that she can attend her son's wedding when no other caregiver is available after Richard and Susan become stuck in Morocco. Amelia's attempt to return across the border to San Diego leads to her being stranded in the desert with her charges; Border Patrol eventually detains and deports her. Chieko Wataya (played by Rinko Kikuchi), a Japanese teenager who is deaf and mute, struggles after her mother's suicide; she does not feel that she belongs, and acts out her frustrations sexually, making advances on various boys and men throughout the course of the day in an attempt to lose her virginity. Her story seems the most removed and tangential to the others, though the audience eventually learns that the connection lies in her father, Yasujiro, who gave his rifle as a gift to Hassan, his hunting guide in Morocco, where he took a big-game hunting trip some time before. This is the rifle that the guide sells to Abdullah Adboum to protect his herd, and which Abdullah's sons use to shoot Susan.

The complex story lines of *Babel* are divided through the diversity of languages and actors, multiple geographic locations, heavy use of jump cuts, temporal disjunction, and varying film techniques. The borders that emerge in *Babel* are national, economic, linguistic, and affective. As Anzaldúa describes them in her own theoretical work, "Borders are set up to define the places that are safe and unsafe, to distinguish us from them. A border is a dividing line, a narrow strip along a steep edge."[4] This description suggests several key features of borders, including that they are meant to mark difference, and that they are narrow, imposed divisions. This framing of borders and their functions is applicable to *Babel*'s aesthetic depiction of borders, as González Iñárritu generates narrative, thematic, and formal borders (through editing and mise-en-scène) as markers of differences that the film presents as cleaving humans. While *Babel* focuses on affective divisions in the form of families whose members are unable to communicate and demonstrate care for each other, the film links these divisions to larger political and economic systems that produce affective failures, with subjects unable to recognize the humanity in one another. As in Anzaldúa's theorizations, *Babel* investigates borders that are both geopolitical and emotional. By focusing on these borders and the difficulties of crossing them, the film highlights the fissures and paradoxes of globalization. One of these stems from the fact that the system facilitates the movement of capital, information, and privileged First World inhabitants across national borders, while Third World residents' bodies are policed and regulated through border apparatuses, their ability to cross borders and attain recognition (and empathy) denied. This leads to a paradox in which borders are simultaneously easier and harder to cross than ever before; borders are permeable and even invisible for some, while they are sites of policing and danger for others.

There are certainly limitations to the reflections on the larger sociopolitical questions in González Iñárritu's film and the success of some of its aesthetic choices.[5] Nonetheless, what is most innovative about *Babel* is its experimentation with a cinematic language to access the experiences of global borders and their crossers, along with attempts to sensitize its First World audience to the humanity of those lives framed as less worthy by First World media and political rhetoric. Here I use the term *frame* consciously for its double meaning, referencing both the visual and rhetorical realms.

Babel seeks to frame and thus *make visible* the ways in which borders assert their power through selectively regulating bodies in a supposedly globalizing world marking their demise. At the same time, the film also frames and thus makes visible the lives of the characters whose bodies are rendered invisible through political frames that perceive them as inconsequential; through such a reframing, *Babel* combats popular media representations that depict some lives as being more meaningful than others. Reductive and false media representations are present in the film, but they are backgrounded and contradicted. In one of the Japanese scenes, a television news program playing in the background misrepresents the shooting of Susan Jones as a terrorist act. The film's action, though, foregrounds a more complex story about the accidental shooting and provides multiple perspectives rather than relying on clichéd tropes. The film, then, implicitly responds to media misrepresentations with alternative framings that picture the shared humanity of the characters across representational boundaries established by the media's framing of the Third World.

This reorientation occurs through the aesthetic choices of González Iñárritu, Guillermo Arriaga, and Gustavo Santaolalla (the composer). One of the most striking of these is the film's use of abrupt cuts that jump from one scene to the next, which can at times disorient the viewer by interrupting the action and shifting to a totally different time and space. One example of such a jarring cut occurs less than twenty minutes into the film, just after a scene depicting the shooting from the point of view of the tour bus (the counterpoint to the opening scene, which depicts the same incident from the perspective of the brothers). This scene displays the dysfunction of the Jones couple's relationship as the two travel through Morocco; their resentment toward each other becomes evident in arguments alluding to past wrongs, and their distance is visually rendered in scenes at a café and on the bus when the two do not look each other in the face. The scene culminates with the bullet entering Susan's shoulder through the window and her husband calling for the driver to stop the bus, before a sudden cut that shifts the scene to a volleyball court in Japan. This scene introduces Chieko, an angst-filled teenager dealing with her difference as a deaf young woman navigating a world in which she feels invisible (especially to potential male sexual partners) and misunderstood (by her father). She vents her frustration at her father in the car, signing, "You never paid attention to me. . . . Mother paid attention to me," her use of the past tense indicating her mother's death. These two scenes are different geographically, linguistically, aesthetically (a handheld camera was used in the Moroccan scene, but not the Japanese one), and narratively. The only connection one might draw between the two is a thematic one: these are two families with emotional distances that have led to miscommunication and misunderstanding. By the end of the film, the audience also learns that both of these families are dealing with recent deaths (the Joneses have lost a child/brother to sudden infant death syndrome, while the Watayas have lost a mother/wife to suicide, both deaths having happened before the action of the film). While the characters deal with emotional and geographic distances, the film space joins them in proximity.

This scene is indicative of the ways in which the film represents borders both metaphoric (sociopolitical and affective divisions) and physical (the U.S.-Mexican border is the one national border that is presented twice). The editing, camerawork, and narrative strategies suggest a world that is sharply divided with institutions and individuals complicit in enforcing borders as a way to maintain existing power structures. To highlight the differences between developed and developing nations in *Babel*, the film uses visual tropes of the desert and city. The developing world is dusty and arid in the scenes depicting Amelia's hometown in Baja California, Mexico, and the Moroccan village of Tazarine in the mountains inhabited by the Adboum family. Indeed, the two landscapes are represented as similarly dry and brown-hued, and they are both visually and thematically linked throughout the film. Some scholars have critiqued the reduction of the Third World to dusty desert spaces, and while this critique is valid, this representational flattening can also be read as strategically marking the similar effects of globalization and the post-9/11 political world order on nations like Mexico and Morocco.

These scenes depicting landscapes of the developing world are visually opposite to those of the one major developed world metropolis depicted: Tokyo. The short San Diego scenes present primarily a single domestic space, and no cityscapes; as a result, Tokyo comes to stand in for the developed world. These scenes focus primarily on signs of modernization: skyscrapers, elevated trains, and neon lights. This imagery suggests a world divorced from the realities encountered in the Mexican and Moroccan scenes. The hypermodernity of urban Japan in relation to the desert locations also marks the difference of the experiences of the characters and visually reinforces geographic differences between the First and Third World locations. Film scholar Dolores Tierney has argued convincingly that film technique, and specifically the use of different film stocks, visually highlights differences across borders, especially between Third World and First World settings in the film.[6] Like the copious jarring cuts, these differences in stocks and techniques are another example of an aesthetic border meant to echo the functions of geopolitical borders in the lives of the characters.

At least on their visual surfaces, then, the various locations and characters in the film are framed as separate, distinct, and incomprehensible to each other. This presents a veritable babel, in which communication has broken down on many levels as a result of this enforced separation. Language becomes a central metaphor through which the film explores miscommunication and divisions. Its title references the biblical story of the Tower of Babel, which explains the origin of linguistic difference as a separation imposed as punishment for human hubris (Genesis 11:1–9). In the film, language is a key border between characters, which accentuates the miscommunications and misunderstandings that saturate the film. Characters in the film speak Arabic, Berber, English, Japanese, Japanese Sign Language, and Spanish, and there is some background dialogue in French and Russian. Many characters have to speak across languages in order to communicate. This is the case with Chieko (who communicates in Japanese Sign Language and through writing; she faces challenges in communicating with her father, whose sign language is rudimentary, and the hearing people she encounters throughout the film), Amelia and the Jones children (while they seem to understand each other, Amelia usually speaks to them in Spanish while the children usually reply in English), and the Joneses in Morocco (the tour guide, Anwar, can translate, but the Joneses do not share a language with some of the locals or the law enforcement official in the village of Tazarine, where the couple wait out the arrival of aid, producing frustration for all involved). While technologies of mass communication (cell phones, television, radio) are evident in various scenes, these technologies are unable to breach the divides between the characters. Instead they aid in miscommunication, particularly in the scene that includes a Japanese television news story that labels the shooting incident a terrorist event, with mug shots of Abdullah and Yussef visually and rhetorically framing them as terrorists. The cinematic space of the film is what allows for the challenging of these rhetorical frames through aesthetic ones that reframe the Moroccan family in an alternative context.

Unsurprisingly given the legislative conflation of anti-immigration and antiterrorism efforts in the United States, the characters in *Babel* whose bodies are policed and made vulnerable are those from Mexico and Morocco. In the film, law enforcement officials regard them with suspicion as menaces in need of disciplining. Amelia is cast by Border Patrol agents as a criminal for her work caring for the Jones children in the United States without proper legal authorization, while the Moroccan boys in the secluded mountains are branded terrorists by the media and U.S. diplomats. Most of the action of the film takes place outside the United States. Despite the characters' connections through their disconnectedness, *Babel* bears witness to the vastly unequal ways in which people are affected by borders depending on national and class affiliations. Political scientist Wendy Brown describes this as one of the paradoxes besetting the recent fervor for fence and wall building at national borders, especially in Western countries: the fact that these border fences and walls also afford "passageways" that "segregat[e]" based on class and national origin.[7] In *Babel* this differentiation between characters at the border is evident in the representations of travel. The physical border crossings of First World travelers are elided in the film, so that there is no visual representation of Yasujiro Wataya or the Joneses entering Morocco. Why bother representing a quick stamp on a passport at an international airport? In contrast, the audience views two crossings of an international border that U.S. audiences are familiar with simply as "*the* border" (the U.S.-Mexican border). The first crossing is from the United States to Mexico, a scene that is atypically exuberant in an otherwise somber film, with a fast-paced *cumbia* by Celso Piña playing as brightly colored and movement-rich scenes of the border and border communities of Tijuana flash onscreen, including border patrol trucks and crosses that dot the border fence to commemorate dead migrants, but also vendors, shops, roadwork, pedestrians, families, prostitutes, and a donkey painted to resemble a zebra. This crossing is depicted as easy, with no stop at the checkpoint entering Mexico, just a clear highway. Santiago, Amelia's nephew (played by Gael García Bernal) who is driving the car, tells the children, "You see how easy it is to get into paradise?" If that crossing is one that leads to paradise, the reverse crossing is one that is the opposite for Amelia.

The second crossing is very different—the crossing into Mexico was set in the daytime, loud, populated, and unobstructed, while the crossing to the United States is set at night, quiet and lonely, with almost no ambient sound, heightening the focus on the tension between law enforcement and the two Mexican characters. In this crossing Amelia faces danger, humiliation, dehumanization, and ultimately effective deportation. After a tense interrogation in which an inebriated Santiago lies and states that Amelia is an aunt to the Jones children, he is directed to a secondary investigation area by a Border Patrol official whose badge ironically gives his name as "Freeman." Santiago drives the car forward, as if to comply, but then drives off recklessly into the night in an attempt to escape. He then leaves his aunt and the children in the desert in order to continue the escape in his car. In the daytime, lost, dehydrated, her red dress torn, her face dusty and tear-stained, sweating and with matted hair, Amelia seeks help for the overheated and dehydrated children she leaves under a tree. When she approaches a Chicano Border Patrol officer (played by Michael Peña), he handcuffs her before listening to her pleas to search for the children. She is met equally unsympathetically by the official who speaks with her in detention. When she asks about the children, she is told, "That's none of your business." When she replies that she raised them, he replies coldly, "They are not your children, ma'am. Plus, you've been working in this country illegally." When he convinces her to accept voluntary departure, she begins to cry. Her sobs do not move the officer, who does not look her in the face and repeats typical anti-immigrant rhetoric that emphasizes criminality despite the United States' reliance on those same immigrants for its labor. The U.S.-Mexican border here is represented as physical and powerful insofar as it is enforced by the might of the security apparatuses of the United States, trained not to see the humanity of the border crossers whose work it exploits. The positioning of the camera places the viewer in the role of the border agent, but gives a close-up of Amelia's face, making the audience see Amelia, humanizing her, rather than adopting the agent's attitude.

While the Moroccan characters do not cross national borders, we see them similarly made subject to U.S. state apparatuses legitimized by President George W. Bush's Middle East policies. *Babel* links the injustices perpetrated at the U.S.-Mexican border to those effected in the name of the "global war on terror." The film represents this conflation and ensuing civilizational divisions by depicting the experiences of the Mexican and Moroccan characters as more closely aligned, while those of the Japanese and U.S. characters resemble each other, as those experiences are shaped in part by the First World/Third World divide. The audience sees Amelia become vulnerable to state power at the border, losing her job, her belongings, and access to a life she had made over almost two decades. We also see the suffering of the Moroccan family at the hands of law enforcement officials. Unlike in the case of Amelia, though, the Moroccans are made vulnerable by an officer who looks and speaks like the shooter he hunts, though the film does not make clear whether the official is a member of a local police or national military force. *Babel* ties these actions to pressures from the U.S. government, as the audience hears bits of the dealings of U.S. legislators and diplomats through media sources and negotiators. Because it is immediately presumed a terrorist incident (by both media and officials), the unintentional shooting becomes an international incident, putting pressure on the Moroccan government to solve the case. That resolution comes at the cost of infringed rights, beatings, coercion, the death of one brother, and the presumed arrest (and uncertain future) of the surviving brother and his father. Several scenes attest to the ways in which the Moroccan characters are subject to the long reach of American power, ironically at the hands of their own officials, such as when the elderly Hassan and his wife are beaten by the investigator who has traced the rifle to the hunting guide. One of the most affecting scenes, however, is after a gunfight that pits young Yussef against the police force, leaving Ahmed shot and dead, their father in tears and grieving, and followed by the youngest son's surrender. Calling for the police to stop shooting and help his brother, the boy breaks and tosses the rifle aside then walks forward with his hands up, pleading with the officers in a child's voice. The lead investigator tells the boy to get on his knees. The camera then sinks low, to Yussef's kneeling height, filming the back of the boy's head and angled upward to frame the impassive investigator's previously sunglass-covered face (he now has removed his sunglasses to better examine the "terrorist" he has captured). The audience may see a parallel here to the border patrol agent; both look at the people over whom they have power with impassivity, not registering the affective mourning in the faces of their victims, though representing this lack of affective recognition serves to inspire empathy in the viewer.

While the losses suffered by the First World characters are personal (due to suicide and illness), the losses suffered by the Third World characters in the film are determined by their nationalities and ethnicities: death and deportation at the hands of officials attempting to "protect" the United States from "criminals" and "terrorists." In *Babel* U.S. fears of terrorism are primarily damaging to those viewed as outsiders and thus threats to the nation—in this case, immigrants or terrorists. The film also shows that the ensuing paranoia is damaging to U.S. citizens. Political wrangling between Morocco and the United States leads to a delay in medical aid reaching Susan, as the countries negotiate who can help in an environment of heightened tension. Richard becomes frustrated with both Moroccan and U.S. officials as he waits in limbo in Tazarine, in fear that his wife will die as they await help. This is the irony of the obsession with sealing off America and (white) Americans (citizens). As Wendy Brown argues, walling may be meant to wall others out, but it also walls in, imprisoning. Carla Marcantonio notes that in *Babel,* the Jones couple is portrayed almost exclusively in enclosed spaces (a bus, a room in Tazarine, a helicopter), this "structure of confinement" highlighting the notion of American exceptionalism and the enforcement of national sovereignty even abroad.[8] This confinement is double-edged, replicating Brown's border paradox: the very structures of confinement, safety, and exceptionalism are the same that jeopardize the lives of the Americans abroad by isolating them from help. The film represents and critiques these tendencies, showing that Susan's survival is placed at risk by the rush to label; she suffers for a prolonged period after American diplomats will not accept local aid because Moroccan officials refuse to label the shooting a terrorist act.

The differences in the treatment of the white American body of Susan and the brown bodies of Amelia and Ahmed recall Judith Butler's arguments in *Frames of War* regarding the effects of the United States' post-9/11 wars on perceptions of subjectivity:

> The notion of the subject produced by the recent wars conducted by the US, including its torture operations, is one in which the US subject seeks to produce itself as impermeable, to define itself as protected permanently against incursion and as radically invulnerable to attack. Nationalism works in part by producing and sustaining a certain version of the subject . . . and . . . what gives power to their version of the subject is precisely the way in which they are able to render the subject's own destructiveness *righteous* and its own destructibility *unthinkable*.[9]

We see these concepts at work in the film when the violence against the American subject, Susan, sparks outrage and mobilization on an international level. The violence against migrants and perceived terrorists, meanwhile, is invisible, quotidian, or, in the case of the Adboum family, justified in the media. The affective economy that the film critiques is one in which the perceived threat of migrants and Muslims forecloses the possibility of empathy toward them. Butler's points here are consonant with Marcantonio's about the visual enclosure of the Joneses' bodies within the film as a reflection of American exceptionalism. At the same time, *Babel* strips away the view of American destructiveness as "righteous" by focusing on experiences of the victims of that destruction. Despite the fact that Susan suffers the loss of a child and is wounded, the film focuses its empathy more on Amelia and Yussef, as the two latter characters' suffering is not just unjust but also preventable. The camera lingers on their stories and bodies longer than on Susan's, reorienting the audience's affective response.

Cinematic and Narrative Bridges

In *Borderlands/La Frontera: The New Mestiza*, Anzaldúa uses spatial metaphors to consider ways of rejecting the violence of national and identitarian borders. Two of those metaphorical counterpoints to the border are the borderlands (discussed earlier in this essay) and the bridge. The bridge metaphor can be applied to the techniques *Babel* uses to imagine connections across geographic divisions, cultures, and people. The film does not present an imaginary that upends the United States' vast political reach and ability to harm others who are perceived as threats. It does, however, suggest that affect has the potential to sensitize viewers to others and otherness, offering a reframing of U.S. power for its own citizens. In a global system that prizes capital over humans, personal relationships suffer, even among family members; yet the film's aesthetics suggest an alternate path that focuses on shared humanity across borders. Emotional borders within families are healed in *Babel* through communication and care afforded by moments that exact vulnerability. The film models the potential for empathy across nationalities through the universalized connections of family, and particularly redemptive love between parents and children. The primary cinematic bridges across the film's geographic and political borders include its narrative structure, especially the nonchronological order of its plot; visual and sound editing links across the story lines; and point-of-view shots and close-ups that focus on the characters' bodies to elicit the viewer's empathy, a border crossing between self and other.

The film offers various narrative, visual, and sound bridges that function as counterpoints to the borders it depicts. While the scene cuts in *Babel* are often jarring, they contribute to a puzzle-like achronological plot structure that invites the audience to forge at first glance seemingly elusive connections across characters in Japan and Morocco, Mexico and the United States, to make narrative sense of the film. These connections require a forging of the viewer's participation and affective investment. *Babel* also uses scene transitions as bridges across the cuts. This is the case with the match-on-action cut discussed at the beginning of this essay. The sound of the film even more strikingly offers aesthetic bridges across characters and locations. Features of the sound that highlight these connections include the use of J cuts and the powerful score by Gustavo Santaolalla. The recourse to sound presents an alternative to the focus on language, since the film presents language as often failing to communicate effectively or truthfully for characters or in the media. Sound offers an alternative to the failures of exegetic discourse.

On one level, the sound bridges in *Babel* add to the disorientation of the abrupt visual cuts for the viewer because the connections between the audio and video are at first unclear, but they also stitch together the visual jump cuts, inserting an aural continuity across the scenes and thus projecting underlying connections across superficially disparate locations and characters. In one early sound bridge, after the Moroccan brothers learn that the police are looking for the suspected terrorist shooter, it is bedtime and the two lie down with eyes open wide, contemplating the trouble they will face if and when they are discovered. The silence of the rural setting is suddenly transformed by the sounds of static and then a *cumbia* on Santiago's car stereo from the next scene. This sound bridge creates a transition for a sharp visual cut, bringing together two very different spaces and narrative points. Yet the imposed connection—not just placing of the two scenes one after the other but also using the audio bridge—may force the viewer to link the two scenes more closely. These sound bridges are an integral part of the film's constructed borderlands, and such bridging functions as an in-between space that exists only in the space of the film.

Santaolalla's compositions are another unifying element, used not only to set the mood of the film but also to highlight the affective connections between the stories. In several scenes the music takes over, drowning out voices and diegetic sounds even across visual cuts, creating an overarching sound motif that connects across the borders between characters. The music itself displays influences from the various locations of the film, incorporating the distinctive sounds of the oud, a Middle Eastern stringed instrument, and elements from Latin American musical genres. The score is often melancholic, spare, and almost plaintive. Toward the end of the film, Santaolalla's score takes up an increasing portion of the soundscape as the diegetic sounds fade. The score arches across visuals of Amelia's deportation, a memory of the two Moroccan brothers playing on the mountaintop, and the transportation of Susan's ailing body by helicopter. By overwhelming the diegetic sound, the score encourages affective rather than discursive connections between the scenes as each differently focuses on the suffering of characters in distress. Diegetic sound returns with the Joneses' arrival at the hospital as they are bombarded with questions from reporters and we hear diplomats giving official statements on the helipad. Music and sound throughout the film become an alternative language through which the stories become connected across the differences that are apparent in the babel of languages in the film. The language of officials, including law enforcement officials, government agents, and media, promotes suffering, violence, and misunderstanding, while the other parts of the soundscape, particularly the sound bridges and score, further a space of connection.

Another alternative form of communication the film embraces is that of the speaking body. In her sustained analysis of the function of borders, Anzaldúa famously describes the U.S.-Mexican border as an "open wound," linking the land to the body and national borders to violence enacted on the body. In *Babel* the body is the site that displays most clearly the effects of borders. The body is also the site of a potential overcoming of those divisions, as the fragility of the characters' bodies forces encounters with and reliance upon others, overcoming their personal and physical isolations. These bodies are manifested to the viewer via a representation of diverse sensations. The characters in the film scream and cry, are naked, fall, are injured, become dehydrated and dirty, are physically restrained or imprisoned, faint, bleed, and die. These representations of (often abject) bodies in *Babel* rely heavily on the senses, a feature Laura U. Marks locates in "intercultural cinema" that focuses on embodiment and the senses to access alternative forms of knowledge and memory.[10] Though Marks's analysis focuses on noncommercial productions, her work offers a useful lens for approaching *Babel*, especially in her discussions of embodiment and "haptic visuality." *Babel* works to sensitize the viewer in part through this invocation of the senses, presenting characters embodied by these senses with whom the audience may more readily empathize.

Butler suggests that media-shaped desensitization leads to an acceptance of the violence of war, while recognition and empathy toward the other may shift public opinion against war. She explains this mechanism as follows: "Those we kill are not quite human, and not quite alive, which means that we do not feel the same horror and outrage over the loss of their lives as we do over the loss of those lives that bear national or religious similarity to our own."[11] If the U.S. wars in Afghanistan and Iraq and U.S. military and intelligence operations around the globe aimed at curtailing terrorism have been facilitated by a rhetorical representation of the other as less recognizably human because of the threat he or she is believed to pose, then an emphasis on shared humanity through the recourse to affective experience may have the potential to erode support for those wars and policies that inflict violence upon those deemed threatening and other. For Butler such a change can happen through photography. About the censorship of the images of the torture U.S. military personnel committed against prisoners at the Abu Ghraib military prison, Butler states, "It seems to me that those who sought to limit the power of the image in this instance also sought to limit the power of affect, of outrage, knowing full well that it could and would turn public opinion against the war in Iraq, as indeed it did."[12] Butler here projects a faith in the ability of images to move the public, and this is a faith that *Babel* shares.

Babel encourages affective affiliations with characters that U.S. audiences, particularly, are shaped to view as unworthy of recognition, let alone empathy, including Mexican immigrants and Arabs. It is toward this end, for example, that the film opens in Morocco. *Babel* interrupts a U.S. audience's expectation that Arab characters in film will be terrorists by portraying two children rather than adults. Children are more likely to be understood as innocent, and that view is fostered further by representing these children in a film with children and adolescents from other nations. In this way, *Babel* encourages the audience to view characters in their age and familial roles rather than their national categorizations. It is not always successful; this identification falters in the character of Chieko, who does not visually appear to really be an adolescent (the actor was in her mid-twenties when the film was shot), or in the fact that viewers may have a hard time putting names to the characters because of the disorienting nature of the film and so may categorize them by nationality anyway.[13] Nonetheless, the film captures the power of the emotions of the characters, and

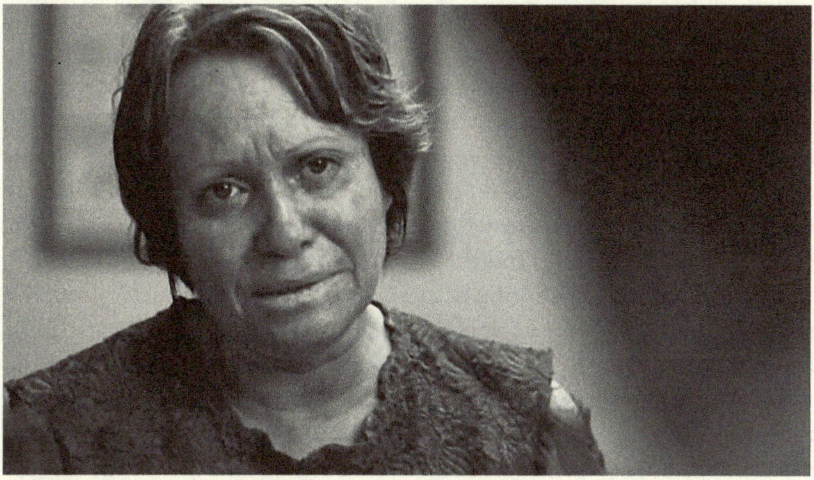

FIG. 5.1 *Babel* (2006): "I made a life here, sir." A close-up of Amelia pleading her case with a Border Patrol agent after being detained.

particularly their suffering, in the strong physical performances of the actors. The empathy that the film forwards is one rooted in a recognition of the bodies of the characters.

In his review of *Babel* for the *New York Times*, A. O. Scott explains that "it gives nothing away to note that every story in *Babel* ends in tears."[14] Scott's estimation rightly points out that the characters display affect in very visible ways. Nowhere is this as clear as in the representation of the characters' tears. The frame holds unflinchingly on close-ups of the characters' faces as they cry. The most notable close-ups are those trained on Amelia during her deportation (see figure 5.1), and on Richard as he speaks to his son on the phone from the hospital where Susan is receiving care for her bullet wound, though almost all of the main characters cry during the course of the film. The close-ups of the crying faces do not allow the audience to look away from the grief suffered by the characters, including even those whose losses First World inhabitants are trained to look beyond. The close-up frame puts the audience face-to-face with the other.

The point-of-view shot is another technique that encourages empathic viewing in *Babel*. By using point of view, the film invites the viewer not just to look *at* the other, as with the close-ups, but rather to look *as* the other. Several times, the film takes on the point of view of Chieko. In addition to positioning the camera in line with Chieko's gaze, in these shots the diegetic sound disappears, attempting to depict her auditory experience too. This occurs, for example, during a scene in which Chieko goes to a dance club with friends. The establishing shots show a packed club with bright screens, strobe lights, and a loud disco mix playing. As the camera takes on Chieko's perspective, the sound disappears suddenly, in noticeable contrast to the loud music. This contrast aims to place the audience in a position to approximate Chieko's experience here, and thus empathize with her, feeling her pain at another frustrated attempt to connect with a boy and her friends, leading to a sense of further alienation and betrayal. In *Babel* the body functions as a bridge in the sense that it creates the opportunity for empathy, suggesting a way to access the experience of another and cross the border between self and other.

The film also models affective border crossing between characters from different nationalities. One example of this is the interaction between Richard Jones and Anwar, the Moroccan tour guide. Anwar attempts to help Richard and Susan after the shooting, bringing them to his home village of Tazarine, where they await an ambulance to take Susan to the hospital. Anwar brings them to a healer woman who helps ease Susan's suffering, and he also brings a veterinarian who is able to stitch Susan's wound as a temporary measure. He sits with Richard in the space of the small room where they tend to Susan and wait. After Anwar's young daughter brings tea for the men, the two begin a conversation. Anwar asks if Richard has children, so Richard shows the guide the pictures of his son and daughter that are in his wallet. Anwar asks "Just two?" and when Richard confirms, implores, "You should have more." The audience knows that Richard did have another son who died before the trip to Morocco. Richard changes the subject, asking how many wives Anwar has. Anwar replies with a laugh, "I can only afford one." This scene models the film's goal of finding common ground among characters who are divided in many ways (by race, nationality, religion, and class) in emphasizing the universalized human experiences of parenthood and loss. At the same time, it shows how much cultural presumptions sparked by difference and ignorance have the capacity to shut down that exploration.

On Happy Endings

While *Babel* models the possibility of connection in an increasingly atomized world, it is by no means utopian. The borders between the characters, particularly the concrete physical and political ones, do not melt away in power or significance. This reflects the film's skeptical view of globalization; a "small world" is not always a better one for the characters in the film, multiplying instead the opportunities for exploitation and violent oppression for the benefit of a few. This is evident in a scene toward the end of the film in which a snippet of a Japanese news report about Susan's release from the hospital plays in the Watayas' high-rise apartment. Against the image of Susan leaving the Casablanca hospital with her arm in a sling, the subtitles for non-Japanese speakers translate the reporter's words: "The American people finally have a happy ending after five days of frantic phone calls and handwringing." The international media's reductive label of a "happy ending" ignores the emotional turmoil of the experience. Even if we read as happy Susan's survival and regained closeness with Richard, the proclamation of that happy ending is deeply ironized in the film. The facile narrative closure of this label masks the deep *unhappiness* created by the U.S. government's long reach in punishing those believed to pose a threat to the Joneses' happiness, leading to killing, deportation, and presumably imprisonment. In *Babel*, borders and the uneven state power to which they bear witness decide who will have a "happy ending." The film ends not with a utopian vision of globalization as a great equalizer but a vision of equal human value despite the iniquities sown by globalization.

While some critics have viewed the foreclosure of a happy ending for the characters from Mexico and Morocco as a sign of the conservatism of the film,[15] Julie A. Minich suggests that the ending is realistic, "demonstrat[ing] how violence is, indeed, experienced much more harshly by the poor, the racialized, and the inhabitants of the Global South."[16] She argues convincingly that the four story lines' endings "collectively reveal . . . that the best possibility for imagining a more democratic and just global society lies in affirming the value of marginalized identities."[17] This point is consonant with my reading of the film as representing the real and unequal effects of global borders while suggesting alternatives through its aesthetic choices. Change is imagined by the film as possible only in the ability of the audience to empathize with others whose happy endings are not considered in the popular discourse represented by global media. The film's narrative and cinematic techniques insist on the equality of the characters despite their vastly unequal experiences and fates, suggesting González Iñárritu's optimism regarding the ability of film to shift audiences' affective response to those deemed threatening and other, especially in the United States.

González Iñárritu has continued to experiment with ways to encourage empathy through cinema and related media. His 2017 art installation project, *Carne y arena* (Flesh and Sand), was the first virtual reality (VR) exhibit to screen at the Cannes Film Festival, and shortly afterward won an Academy Award for Special Achievement. Those experiencing this work enter on their own, passing through three spaces. The first mimics a room in the detention centers nicknamed *hieleras* (freezers) and the participant waits in the cold room barefoot after being instructed to remove his or her shoes; this room contains real collected artifacts from the desert in the form of found shoes lost or discarded by crossing migrants. The participant then enters a large space with a dirt- and rock-covered floor meant to resemble a desertscape and is outfitted with a VR headset. The VR experience immerses the participant in a scene in which migrants cross. It is meant to be primarily realistic, and the participant can interact with characters by walking up to them, listening to them, or even watching a character's dream sequence. The participant can sit next to or even walk through the characters, seeing their internal organs and hearing their heartbeats. While VR is still limited, this new frontier suggests enticing possibilities for immersion and the invocation of empathy. After the participant has walked with migrants in the VR experience, in the final room of the exhibit individual screens show close-ups of the migrants whose experiences were mined for the composite sketch of the undocumented migration process presented in the VR portion. This room encourages the participant to look directly into the face of the other, just as the previous rooms attempts to have the participant walk in the literal and figurative shoes of the migrants whose lives they are meant to contemplate in this work. This project may be viewed as an extension of the experimentation González Iñárritu begins in *Babel*, focused on the ways in which cinematic techniques can facilitate identification and empathy across the borders of nation, citizenship, language, race, and class.

Notes

1 PBS *Frontline*, "Mapping the Black Sites," n.d., http://www.pbs.org/frontlineworld/stories/rendition701/map/.

2 After his "crossover" to Hollywood, González Iñárritu became only the second Mexican (or Latin American of any nationality) to win the Academy Award for Best Director, and he did so twice (in 2015 for *Birdman* and in 2016 for *The Revenant*). The director's first Academy Award in this category came just a year after his friend and colleague Alfonso Cuarón earned the honor in 2014 for *Gravity*.

3 Gloria Anzaldúa, *Borderlands/La Frontera: The New Mestiza* (San Francisco: Aunt Lute Books, 1987), preface (n.p.), and 3.

4 Ibid.

5 Tierney argues that "for all its radical politics *Babel* still ends on a politically and racially conservative note: the privileged (white) family is saved/rescued and instead it is the (dark-skinned) inhabitants of the Third World who suffer or die"; Dolores Tierney, "Alejandro González Iñárritu: Director without Borders," *New Cinemas: Journal of Contemporary Film* 7, no. 2 (2009): 114. Marina Hassapopoulou also points out that "*Babel*'s penchant for female victimization exposes an underlying conservatism when it comes to gender roles"; Marina Hassapopoulou, "*Babel*: Pushing and Reaffirming Mainstream Cinema's Boundaries," *Jump Cut* 50 (2008), http://www.ejumpcut.org/archive/jc50.2008/Babel/text.html. On the personal level, González Iñárritu has continued to speak publicly on issues of discrimination and political demonization in the decade since *Babel* was released. For his criticism of U.S. president Donald Trump's comments on Mexicans and immigrants, see Alejandro González Iñárritu, "Alejandro Gonzalez Inarritu's LACMA Speech 'Undocumented Dreamers,'" *Variety*, November 8, 2015, https://variety.com/2015/scene/vpage/alejandro-gonzalez-inarritu-undocumented-dreamers-immigration-lacma-1201636134/.

6 Tierney, "Alejandro González Iñárritu," 112.

7 Wendy Brown, *Walled States, Waning Sovereignty* (Brooklyn, N.Y.: Zone, 2010), 20.

8 Carla Marcantonio, "Border-Crossing the Global Imaginary: *The Bubble* and *Babel*," in *Global Melodrama: Nation, Body, and History in Contemporary Film* (New York: Palgrave Macmillan, 2015), 102–103.

9 Judith Butler, *Frames of War: When Is Life Grievable?* (New York: Verso, 2009), 47.

10 Laura U. Marks, *The Skin of the Film: Intercultural Cinema, Embodiment, and the Senses* (Durham, N.C.: Duke University Press, 2000).

11 Butler, *Frames of War*, 42.

12 Ibid., 40.

13 Hassapopoulou notes the fact that critics at the time of the film's release defaulted to national references, and that "it is hard to see beyond the nationality of the characters. Thus, most *Babel* reviews in the United States refer to the characters as 'the Mexican nanny,' 'the Moroccan father,' 'the Japanese girl' instead of their scripted names. At the same time, critics persistently refuse to identify Pitt and Blanchett by the names of the characters they play, and refer to the two actors' performances instead (which might suggest that their star texts make it hard for viewers to see them as characters rather than actors)." Hassapopoulou, "*Babel*."

14 A. O. Scott, "Emotion Needs No Translation," *New York Times*, October 27, 2006, http://www.nytimes.com/2006/10/27/movies/27babe.html.

15 See Tierney, "Alejandro González Iñárritu"; and Marcantonio, "Border-Crossing," which argues that "the film ultimately concludes by putting all of its characters back in the national spaces where they 'belong'" (80).

16 Julie Minich, "Rehabilitating Neoliberalism: Disability Representation in the Films of Alejandro González Iñárritu and Guillermo Arriaga," *Journal of Popular Culture* 48, no. 5 (2015): 986.

17 Ibid., 987.

6

Challenging European Borders

Goran Paskaljevic's *Honeymoons*

ANITA PINZI

Goran Paskaljevic's internationally awarded film *Honeymoons* (Medeni mesec, 2009) portrays the journey of two couples that attempt to reach the European Union (EU) by leaving Albania and Serbia for Italy and Austria, respectively. The two couples never meet onscreen—a cinematic decision that multiplies the struggle of movement that migrants endure—but their stories unfold similarly, informed as they are by parallel personal struggles with their families and communities, and by the same desire to look for a better life in the EU. For instance, both couples, the Albanian Nick and Maylinda and the Serbian Marko and Vera, take part in wedding celebrations that become grounds of articulation for familial tensions; both challenge ethnic biases that still inform social relationship between Albanians and Serbs in the aftermath of the 1998–1999 Kosovo War; both have received regular travel documents to legally reach Austria and Italy; and, despite that, both are stopped at the frontier and detained. This unexpected migratory destiny is due to a terrorist attack in the neighboring region of Kosovo that has led to the deaths of two Italian soldiers of the NATO Kosovo Force. This cinematically constructed event takes place in the historical aftermath of the Kosovo War, which saw Albanian and

Serbian ethnic groups opposing each other in the Albanian speaking territory of Kosovo and was appeased by the intervention of NATO forces in the spring of 1999. That tragedy constitutes the historical backdrop of Paskaljevic's film, and the fictional murderous attack represented in it has a double consequence for the unfolding of the plot of the film. On a national level, the inciting attack leads the Albanian and Serbian communities to blame each other for the attack, exposing a resilient nationalism and ethnic tensions that are far from being resolved. On an international level, the attack leads European law enforcement forces to equally suspect both Albanian and Serbian rebel groups, a suspicion that leads to the tightening of inter-European border controls for people migrating from both countries. The two couples therefore, despite having regular travel documents, are caught in the gears of border patrolling, and are eventually stopped at the Italian and Hungarian borders, respectively. Their journey ends, as does the film itself, at the borders of the EU countries, disrupting the characters' plans, crushing their dreams for a different life, and transferring a sense of suspension of time and entrapment of the body to the empathizing viewer, whose perspective is guided by camera movements to align with the characters' perspective.

Drawing from such scholars as Franco Cassano, Iain Chambers, and Sandro Mezzadra, who have theorized contemporary migration in Europe as well as the Mediterranean area and its borders, this chapter discusses the many borders upon which Paskaljevic's *Honeymoons* reflects—a multitude of geographic, ethnic, cultural, political, national, and international thresholds that stand between people, communities, and countries—in order to bring out the film's multilayered work: first, it criticizes national ideological separations; second, it exposes and opposes the absurdity of the progressive control and exclusion that is consumed at the outer border of the Europe of the Schengen Area; and third, it constitutes itself as an active force in challenging both ideological separation and political borders, being as it is a concrete example of intellectual and artistic collaboration across ethnic, linguistic, and cultural divides. The film is indeed the result of the first postwar artistic collaboration between Albanian and Serbian production companies, employing Albanian and Serbian actors and crossing multiple borders to take part in numerous international film festivals. As Paskaljevic has stated in multiple interviews, the film seeks to trace a viable path to overcome ethnic tensions while crossing cultural and geopolitical borders. For this explicit intent, *Honeymoons* was aptly included in the Human Rights Watch Film Festival in New York City in 2010.

Honeymoons, for its engagement with both Balkan history and European borders, can find a place among the contemporary European cinematography studied by scholar Mike Wayne in *The Politics of Contemporary European Cinema: Histories, Borders, Diasporas*. Wayne analyzes European film and filmmaking from the 1980s onward, and his work reflects on the deep interconnections of European cinema and the macrohistorical events that Europe underwent in that period, such as the fall of the Berlin Wall and the subsequent fall of communism in the Eastern bloc. Reviewing *Honeymoons*, produced a few years after Wayne's publication, allows us to extend the historical intersections with cinema to include the Balkan wars and their legacy vis-à-vis the cultural and political shaping of the area, and its negotiation with a growing EU.

Though in 2002 Wayne noted that European cinema seemed to be "a category with little content . . . because the *national* borders within Europe have historically been the prime mode in which social, economic, political and cultural life has been organized," he also underlined the need to reflect on the relationships between national histories that depended on the "increasingly porous borders that 'contains' them."[1] Wayne's research was therefore guided by the cultural and political transformations that the Schengen Agreement—signed in 1985 by the ten states then part of the European Economic Community, and by the subsequent Schengen Convention in 1990—was progressively bringing to Europe, particularly the softening and disappearing of borders and border control within the political union. *Honeymoons*, which looks at the Europe of the Schengen Area, chooses instead to focus on the paradox that Schengen has generated; the removal of internal borders has corresponded to a fortification and militarization of Europe's outer border, a paradox that has led journalist Gabriele del Grande to speak about Europe in terms of a fortress.[2] In addition to this, Paskaljevic's Balkan perspective brings to the foreground another paradox, indicating how the outer border of the EU cuts across the geographical body of Europe, so that European travelers are "not European enough" to move across the Schengen Area.

As stated, the film reflects on a multitude of thresholds, be they economic, cultural, ideological, or political, that stand in the way of a pacific understanding between families, communities, and nations. The first level of relationship that is disrupted is the familial one. Both couples are invited to attend the weddings of members of their respective extended families. The two events, which take place in Tirana and in a nameless Serbian village, respectively, symbolically anticipate the "honeymoons" to which the title of the film refers; the journeys of love, freedom, and advancement that the two couples are anticipating in their journey to the EU. In a parallelism that shapes the entire film, the two weddings reveal themselves as equally complex social events, where interpersonal, ideological, and economic divides emerge and fester in a series of clashes between characters. The unity that a wedding is supposed to celebrate is in Paskaljevic's film overturned by a multiplicity of degrees of separation.

The celebration of the Albanian wedding requires Nick and Maylinda, along with his parents and her in-laws Rok and Vevo, to travel from their village in the mountains to the center of the capital, Tirana. The city is a hectic place, and skyscrapers, traffic, and international retail stores brands have altered its face. The camera follows the father, Rok, and his family as, disoriented, they look for their relatives' place until they give up and resolve to call a taxi. The tall buildings of the city center make them raise their eyes toward the sky, and the camera reproduces their perspective, amplifying the verticality of the city with a low-angle shot of the stairwell of the building where Rok's nephew lives. This is the twelfth floor of a modern building, the material proof of the new capitalist economy and the Westernization of the country that followed the fall of the communist regime. Between the two branches of the family a concrete distance has grown, one that opposes the rural, modestly dressed, raki-drinking, and former political prisoner Rok to his urban, well dressed, whisky-drinking, and politically well-connected nephew. They inhabit two worlds divided by economic, social, and political position.

The nuptial festivity reveals additional degrees of social separation, stressing the opposition between the old wealthy and powerful families of Tirana and the new wealth to which Nick's extended family belongs. For the guests sitting at Nick and Maylinda's table, the family of the affluent relative is still considered peasant-like and vulgar, despite its prominent economic position and the political connections it is consolidating through the wedding of its youngest son to the daughter of a government minister. In addition, the family criticizes the married couple's plans to go to Paris for their honeymoon as a bourgeois choice. Paskaljevic seems in this way to remark on the negative impact that the rapid capitalist and consumerist shift in postcommunist Albania has on social and personal relationships. The almost two decades that have passed between the fall of communism in Albania in 1991, and the year in which the film was produced, 2009, have witnessed a reshuffling of the political and economic hierarchy of the country, one that, as Paskaljevic seems to suggest, has created occasions for social division.

Similarly, ideological, economic, and personal divisions, as well as lack of communication, characterize the Serbian wedding that Marko and Vera attend. Leaving the capital Belgrade, of which only a few rundown tall buildings and a convivial courtyard are shown, Vera and Marko travel to a nameless village that is Vera's hometown. Vera explains to her newly married husband that her father and her uncle had a quarrel a long time ago due to their opposite political positions and due to history that favored her uncle's party over her father's. This is the reason why the two brothers, though living on adjacent properties, hate each other. Their ideological and emotional separation is cinematically marked by a fence and a locked gate that divide the two properties.

Paskaljevic's camera treats this gate as a site of major conflict. On the threshold of the gate, usually locked but now provocatively open because of the wedding, traditional celebratory elements such as shooting bullets in the air or drinking raki are shifted to weapons. Vera's father indeed shoots in the air, not to celebrate but to interrupt the wedding and to move accusations of disrespect and disinterest toward his rich brother, who has organized this magnificent celebration as a display of wealth and a provocation. Still on the gate, Vera's father smashes a bottle of raki to the ground, openly rejecting his brother's peace offering. Ultimately, in the same physical space, the familial conflict is exacerbated by the disowning of Vera, rejected by her father for attending the wedding of his "worst enemy" and for having married Marko without her father's approval.

While articulating these familial tensions, the two weddings also become social occasions to delve into ethnic biases. An Albanian photographer at the wedding in Tirana harshly criticizes the hosts for playing Serbian music, and he is quick to attribute to the Serbs the recent attack in Kosovo where two Italian soldiers have been killed. Similarly, a Serbian barman, backed by a group of aggressive and nationalist youngsters, naturally accuses Albanians of responsibility for the attack. These crucial, though short, scenes significantly tap into the history of the region and the legacy of the Kosovo War, putting the accent on the permanence of biases that run through communities and inflame ethnic hatred.

Paskaljevic is critical of ethnic biases, which the filmmaker has discussed in several interviews that he has given and which the film itself openly opposes. This critique is articulated in *Honeymoons* at the diegetic level by the two main male characters. Both Nick and Marko speak against the popular discourse of reciprocal accusation between Albanians and Serbs and appeal to facts in order to debunk false and discriminatory assumptions. Both note that the police are still investigating the attack and argue that responsibility cannot yet be ascribed to either Albanian or Serbian groups. Their ideological neutrality and rational approach to the event clash with the biased and emotional popular belief, exposing a general refusal of parts from both communities to reflect on their own responsibility vis-à-vis the ethnic and historical tensions in the area.

The clash moves from a verbal to a physical level. While Nick is involved in a minor physical altercation with the photographer, Marko is openly targeted by a group of motorcyclists who provoke him and ultimately beat him up. The scene of the attack is rendered with three long takes—Paskaljevic's predominant technique—where the handheld camera moves along and among the group of people, reproducing the long chase. Through this cinematic move, one that forcibly places the viewer among the attackers and against the victimized Marko, the film seems to alert the audience to the constant risk of individual and collective responsibility vis-à-vis ethnic tensions and discrimination. The viewer is indeed forced to align his or her perspective with the attacker, and therefore compelled to emotionally and ideologically reject that representational space assigned by the camera.

Marko responds passively to the attack, as he chooses not to fight back and keeps his hands in his pockets. While at first his choice comes across as an assertion of peaceful resistance to violence, which aligns well with his rejection of violent and accusatory language against Albanians, the cello music at the end of the scene reminds us that he is a musician and he is most of all protecting his hands for his future musical performance. This scene zooms in on Marko's hands, making them both the symbol of his chance to go to Austria and a premonition of the challenges to do so.

The desire to go to the EU, and the hope for a better life that comes with it, is primarily a way out from the failure of personal and social relationships that the two couples experience in their home countries. To exit the constriction of the family ties, Nick and Maylinda escape in secret, this way asserting that the right to their journey cannot be negotiated. This narrative trope recalls sociologist Sandro Mezzadra's argument in his work *Diritto di fuga* (The right to escape). Discussing the right to the act of fleeing, Mezzadra makes the point that the migrant's defection from despotic realities, the act of subtracting herself from the conditions of material and symbolic deprivations, is what constitutes the subjective and subjectifying dimension of migration. Mezzadra's theorization of migration disrupts the idea of a migrant as a "soggetto debole," a weak subject.[3] Maylinda, who is represented as the quietest and most remissive of the four characters, and who is by tradition confined to an existence of waiting and nonagency, decides instead to flee and follows Nick across the sea, becoming the subject of agency that Mezzadra describes.

The representation of the two couples' journey, by boat and by train, respectively, makes the film's attention shift from the familial and intranational level of division experienced by the four characters, to a political and international level, focusing as it does on the border between the Balkans and the EU. Paskaljevic's narrative becomes openly interested in the political representation of the border, and the dynamics of exclusion that inform that space, almost entirely marginalizing the concept of border as natural barrier. Only two are indeed the occurrences where natural frontiers are represented. The first instance is to be found in the opening panning shot of the mountains around the town of Kükes, in the north of Albania, a vast extension of impervious peaks and steep valleys that form the natural border between Albania and the Albanian-speaking territory of Kosovo. The rocky beauty of the mountainous border, underlined by the pink sky of a lyrical sunset, portrays a border that has solely a natural and contemplative role. A second naturalistic moment is to be found when Nick and Maylinda are on a ferry toward Italy. The camera frames them on the deck of the ferry, finally free to hug each other and laugh in the wind. In the background, the line of the horizon is blue and peaceful, and the Mediterranean Sea is a physical liquid space before their destination, a docile space that is easy to cross. As with the opening shot of the mountains, the Mediterranean is here briefly represented merely in its natural element.

These are isolated moments in the otherwise political role that *Honeymoons* assigns to the border. It is in particular the Mediterranean Sea portrayed as a place of loss and death that comes across as the most challenging to the idea of unity that the EU promotes. Since the beginning of the film, the viewer is informed about Ilir, Nick's brother and Maylinda's fiancé, who went missing three years earlier in the shipwreck of a rubber boat illicitly crossing the sea toward Italy. Ilir's migratory trajectory and his tragic fate recalls the trend of Albanian migration across the Otranto Channel toward Italy during the 1990s, a marine crossing that started in 1991 with the arrival to Bari of the mercantile ship *Vlora*, transporting twenty thousand Albanians and continued throughout the decade. In that span of time, another Albanian vessel, the *Kater I Radës*, sank in 1997 after a collision with the Italian military ship *Sibilla*, killing 108 people and joining a high and growing number of shipwrecks that have been occurring in the Mediterranean Sea since then.[4] Paskaljevic's narration of Albanian migration is inscribed in that recent historical time, marked by tropes of illegality and danger, making Ilir's death at sea as the symbolic starting point for a reflection on what migrants have endured to reach Europe.

At a stylistic level, Paskaljevic chooses not to represent Ilir's shipwreck onscreen; his death is instead brought up in a conversation between Nick and Maylinda, as they plan their own voyage across the same sea. On one hand, the absence of the shipwreck from the screen creates a temporal and spatial distance that transforms the event into a historical one, locked into the past. On the other hand, and contrarily, its screen absence also actualizes it, making Ilir a haunting presence. Ilir's body was indeed never found, creating a suspension of life in which Ilir's family is trapped. In absentia, Ilir still inhabits the spaces and lives of the people that he left behind; his picture hangs from the wall, his suit is guardedly preserved by his mother Vevo, who believes he might be alive, and Maylinda is required by tradition to wait for him while she is instead harboring reciprocated feelings for Nick.

Doubly absent, from the screen and from the diegesis, is Ilir's dead body, lost at sea, which thus ascribes to the Mediterranean the role of a cemetery without graves. This is a trope that links *Honeymoons* to an existing and growing group of border narratives about the Mediterranean as a deadly space, including such works as Edmund Budina's film *Lettere al vento* (Letters in the wind, 2001), Natasha Shehu's novel *L'ultima nave* (The last ship, 2001), Giovanni Maria Bellu's reportage *I fantasmi di Portopalo* (The ghosts of Portopalo, 2004), and Gianfranco Rosi's documentary *Fuocoammare* (Fire at sea, 2016), to mention a few examples of Italian artistic and documentary production.

The trope of the absent dead body also recalls Jacques Derrida's claims in *Of Hospitality* that the absence of physical space in which to pray and a precise location in which to find a tombstone makes mourning impossible, "a mourning deprived of weeping."[5] Though Paskaljevic makes weeping possible, as Ilir's mother Vevo is able to cry for her lost child, mourning still remains suspended because death cannot be experienced as final without a body or a grave. The consequence of this is that the lives of the characters experiencing the absence of Ilir's body (dead or alive) remain suspended between the longing of hope and mourning. The aura of death pervades the whole family, transforming, as Nick comments, the entire household into a grave, one in which its inhabitants are frozen in time, in a static and uneventful existence.

To leave behind the country and the legacy of his dead brother, who had traveled illegally and on an improvised rubber boat run by criminals, Nick plans to migrate to Italy across the same sea with his beloved Maylinda, but with valid visas from the Italian embassy of Tirana and on a proper ferry. Similarly, Marko and Vera in Belgrade prepare for their own legal journey to Austria. They are heading to Vienna, where the Vienna Philharmonic has summoned Marko, a cello player, for an audition. Thanks to the orchestra's invitation letter, Marko and Vera have obtained their visas. Travel documents are in this way central elements to both couples' migratory journeys. Paskaljevic's choice to deal with the well-planned and organized journeys of migrants who have been vetted and have received legal travel documents seems to contest the widespread international media discourse on migration toward the EU, which tends to deploy a language of illegality, emergency, and unchecked invasion. However, the two couples' journeys unfold with difficulties despite their documents, and ultimately terminate on the border, showing how legality and illegality cease to be distinct categories when the migrant's place of origin is flagged as insecure and their reality crashes against the rules of international border control. *Honeymoons*, by reproducing the same outcome of detention of migrants and inhospitality despite the legality of the characters' migration, accentuates the paradox that is intrinsic to the political structure of the EU and its security programs, a paradox according to which internal mobility clashes against hardened checkpoints at the external borders.

When Nick and Maylinda arrive at the Italian port, it is indeed characterized by a display of state forces, and the first image of Italy that the migrants and the viewer have is of the border police, who arbitrarily stop Nick with the accusation of having a fake visa and then detain him with the intention of verifying his connections to Kosovo. Similarly, Nick and Vera, soon after crossing the Hungarian border, are asked to leave the train on which they are traveling and are taken to a police station to verify their documents. With these events, *Honeymoons* reframes the journey of freedom of the two couples according to what Iain Chambers theorizes as modernity's "unfreedom" of movement. In his work *Mediterranean Crossings: The Politics of an Interrupted Modernity* Chambers argues that the Mediterranean area, under the logic of movement control that characterizes all contemporary borders, is transformed into a space of profound "unfreedom" where "the very right to travel, to journey, to migrate today increasingly runs up against . . . borders, confines, and controls."[6] Since both the male characters are connected to Kosovo—Nick used to cross the border to reach a telephone booth (something that was absent in his village), and Marko happened to be born in Kosovo when his father was in the military—they are wrongly suspected to be involved in the murderous attack and the two men's freedom and right to migrate is militarily revoked at the border.

Insisting as it does on the presence and armed role of the border police, *Honeymoons* represents a militarized border, openly recalling Franco Cassano's discussion of borders as frontlines. In his work *Il pensiero meridiano* (The meridian thought, 1996), Cassano goes back to the Latin etymology of the term *frontiera*, the Italian term for border. Originating from the Latin *frons frontis*, the term opens to a double meaning, indicating at the same time the "frontal" relation between people who can observe and mutually understand each other and the tension and conflict between subjects that are different. While it can be argued that the first meaning of the term is implied through the couples' journeys "facing" one another in the structure of the film, it is mostly the second meaning, of opposition, that *Honeymoons* is interested in, a meaning channeled in the military word *fronte* (front line) that indicates a space in which the military presence trumps any possibility of recognition and knowledge of the "other."

Iain Chambers similarly references the patrolling of borders, which, according to his analysis, is a practice that reveals "the essential violence on which the authority of the modern state ultimately depends to secure its legitimacy."[7] Aligning with this perspective, *Honeymoons* links the military presence to the violence exercised on migrants by state authorities. Police physically violate both Nick and Marko, so that their bodies become the ground on which control and detention practices are performed: Nick is handcuffed, stripped naked, physically searched for drugs, and finally detained indefinitely; Marko is immobilized by handcuffs and detained as well.

The trope of violent treatment of the migrant body at the border recalls sociologist Sandro Mezzadra's description of the bodies of migrants as the major example of the dialectic of borders. In *Diritto di fuga* he underlines the extent to which the political and military forces at play in the Mediterranean space act on migrant bodies. Reading the body as a map inscribed by dynamics of power, he states, "i loro corpi esibiscono le ferite e le lacerazioni inflitte dalla quotidiana riaffermazione, in guise molteplici, del dominio dei confini stessi" (their bodies exhibit the wounds inflicted by the daily reaffirmation, in multiple ways, of borders' supremacy).[8] Paskaljevic's camera, though not exhibiting bodily lacerations or wounds, tilts down from Marko's face to his hands, which have been tied up and are now aching and shaking. If we theorize a symbolic linkage between hands and agency, Marko's wounded hands stand for his impossibility to act, as well as his future in Vienna, which is now shaky and uncertain like them.

Beyond remarking on the centrality of the body in a migratory and border situation, Mezzadra also refers to the porosity of borders insofar as people have a chance to pass through the tight controls performed by the police. While Mezzadra talks about the possibility of undocumented migrants getting through the net of border control, *Honeymoons* reframes the trope of porosity along the gender divide. While Nick and Marko are arrested, Maylinda and Vera are admitted without additional inspection. Yet being separated from their partners makes them vulnerable and exposes them to the risk of abuse and exploitation. Maylinda, who does not speak any Italian, is compelled to trust a fellow citizen who promises to help her but who eventually robs her of her money and abandons her in the middle of the road. Vera is instead vulnerable because she is pregnant. Though their vulnerability is not explored further, *Honeymoons* encourages here a reflection on the concrete danger and exposure that international rules might generate when protecting the safety of some people at the expenses of the safety of others.

It is exactly to safeguard Europe and its people that Nick and Marko are detained. Their detention rooms, temporary jails where people remain until their documents are processed and their future decided by the authorities, gather people from different countries, re-creating a symbolic microcosm of shared destinies. From a diegetic point of view, the jail space provides the occasion for brief but revelatory interactions between the two main characters and other migrants. Nick speaks to a fellow Albanian citizen who is ironically convinced that his visa cannot be fake because he has paid a thousand euros for it, and who accuses Italians of being racist against Albanians because they put them in jail with blacks. Marko speaks with a Romany who claims that his people should be granted asylum because of the discrimination they undergo at the hand of the Serbs. With the irony woven into the conversations, *Honeymoons* uses these short stories to map once more cultural and ethnic biases, prevarications, and incommunicability that cut across different communities.

The space of the jail, and the likelihood of ending up in a detention camp—a possibility that the Romany man reveals to an incredulous Marko—ties *Honeymoons*' narrative to the discussion of European prisons and camps as an administrative response to migration, one that uses concentration, isolation, and detention as necessary aspects of migration management. Author Rutvica Andrijasevic underlines how the construction of camps is funded by European countries, Italy among them, both inside and outside of the European borders.[9] In this way, detention camps become crucial spaces for the general redefinition of the external European border, which is indeed displaced and delocalized beyond its geopolitical map. The film only indicates the camp as a possible risk, but this hinting at a future of detention extends the trope of vulnerability from the female to the male characters; they are all equally made vulnerable by the rules of the border.

Honeymoons ends with the two men still in jail, and the two women waiting for them: Maylinda at the harbor and Vera at the train station. The camera, through dolly-in and zoom-in movements, places the viewer in close proximity to these two characters as well as the emotions of sorrow, anxiety, and consternation that are inscribed on their faces. These camera movements induce the viewer to feel a deep empathy for the characters, and in the final scene, the viewer is brought to identify completely with a character's point of view. The scene starts with a close-up of Marko's face that is turning on one side to look toward the window. The camera accompanies this motion with a pan shot toward the window, reflecting Marko's gaze. The pan shot keeps going until Marko is completely out of the frame and the viewer is left alone in front of the window's bars, a prisoner herself. The alignment of the viewer with the character is here complete. The camera keeps moving, though, forward this time, until the bars on the window too disappear from the frame and the viewer can only see the horizon outside the window. This motion forward reinstates a sentiment of hope to the narrative, with the camera breaking free from the space of the jail, conveying a wish for a borderless world.

Yet while the viewer is experiencing this renewed hope for freedom, the landscape outside the jail window is crossed by a cargo train that passes at full speed on the same railroad from which Marko and Vera have been detained hours earlier. Delivering its final image and its final message, the film captures what sociologist Saskia Sassen has indicated as the contradiction of globalization. As Sassen notes, globalization is the primary engine of movement of goods and capital around the world, corresponding with a correlated movement of labor forces. But while goods can freely move across borders, the movement of people is hindered by national and international politics.[10] *Honeymoons*' last image emphasizes exactly this contradiction that lies at the heart of the globalized world and reaches its highest degree of injustice at the border.

As Paskaljevic has stated on multiple occasions while presenting his work at film festivals in New York, Toronto, and Venice, and as corroborated in the interview that accompanies the distributed DVD, *Honeymoons* intends to show the illogical and absurd stance of borders, toward which the filmmaker has a keen aversion. In Paskaljevic's words, *Honeymoons* is a work of "revolt" against the logic of separation and exclusion that characterizes the outer border of Europe. His film exposes that separation, investigating it on a multiplicity of levels, from the relationships within and between communities in the postwar Balkans to the relationships between the Balkans and the EU. The regional ethnic tensions join global forces, both economic and political, to transform the Mediterranean area into a space of exclusion and rights violations.

Besides affirming this position with narrative themes and camera movements, the making itself of Paskaljevic's film aims to denounce and overcome tensions across symbolic and concrete borders. Being the first postwar artistic collaboration between Albanian and Serbian crews, coproduced and cofunded by both countries, the film's production itself stands as a strong and positive symbol of conflict resolution, making cinema surge to a primary role in the reconciliation between peoples in the Balkans. If this noble mission necessarily comes to terms with objective difficulties related to the distribution and circulation of the film in the Balkans and in the rest of Europe, it is nonetheless confirmed by Paskaljevic in an interview on the occasion of the fifty-fourth Valladolid Film Festival, in which he states that his Tirana unit "had some prejudices [to work with Serbs] but after a couple of days they started to cooperate and in the end it was very emotional, [they] even shared some tears."[11] Furthermore, while Paskaljevic's mobility across the European borders was facilitated by his role as a renowned international filmmaker, the participation of the film in several international film festivals has served as a concrete tool for the actors to cross European borders for the first time in their lives. While *Honeymoons* stresses the deep separations intrinsic to the many borders it discusses, it ultimately challenges them and functions as a tool of cultural, linguistic, and geographic crossing.

Notes

1 Mike Wayne, *The Politics of Contemporary European Cinema: Histories, Borders, Diaspora* (Chicago: University of Chicago Press, 2002), vii; emphasis in the original.

2 Gabriele del Grande's blog *Fortress Europe* maps the human cost of crossing the outer European border, and above all the Mediterranean Sea. See Gabriele del Grande, *Fortress Europe* (blog), http://fortresseurope.blogspot.it/.

3 Stefano Mezzadra, *Diritto di fuga. Migrazioni, cittadinanza, e globalizzazione* (Verona, Italy: Ombre corte, 2001), 19.

4 Albanian writer Natasha Shehu based her novel *L'ultima nave* (2001) on the sinking of the *Kater I Radës*.

5 Jacques Derrida, *Of Hospitality*, translated by Rachel Bowlby (Stanford, Calif.: Stanford University Press, 2000), 111.

6 Iain Chambers, *Mediterranean Crossings: The Politics of an Interrupted Modernity* (Durham, N.C.: Duke University Press, 2008), 3.

7 Ibid., 5.

8 Mezzadra, *Diritto di fuga*; my translation.

9 Rutvica Andrijasevic, "From Exception to Excess: Detention and Deportations across the Mediterranean Space," in *The Deportation Regime: Sovereignty, Space, and the Freedom of Movement*, ed. Nicholas de Genova and Nathalie Peutz (Durham, N.C.: Duke University Press, 2009), 147–165.

10 Saskia Sassen, *Guests and Aliens* (New York: New Press, 1999).

11 Goran Paskaljevic, interview by Jorge D. González, November 2009, http://www.cylcultural.org/cine/seminci/2009/Goran_Paskaljevic_honeymoons.htm.

7

Remapping the Borderlands in *¿Quién diablos es Juliette?*

ELENA LAHR-VIVAZ

Carlos Marcovich remaps borders and border cinema alike in his 1997 film *¿Quién diablos es Juliette?* (Who the hell is Juliette?), signaling the porosity of borders and the interconnectedness of those who live in what might be called, following Gloria Anzaldúa, the transnational borderlands. In her seminal *Borderlands/La Frontera: The New Mestiza*, Anzaldúa writes that while borders are intended to delineate, borderlands demonstrate the fundamental undeterminability of space divided: "Borders are set up to define the places that are safe and unsafe, to distinguish *us* from *them*. A border is a dividing line, a narrow strip along a steep edge. A borderland is a vague and undetermined place created by the emotional residue of an unnatural boundary. It is in a constant state of transition."[1] Anzaldúa writes of the U.S.-Mexican borderlands at the same time that she makes clear that she intends the term to be used more generally: "the Borderlands are physically present wherever two or more cultures edge each other, where people of different races occupy the same territory, where under, lower, middle and upper classes touch, where the space between two individuals shrinks with intimacy."[2] Tracing the ties between Cuba, Mexico, and the United States in *¿Quién diablos es Juliette?* Marcovich offers an alternate cartography of the borderlands and intimates that a new, archipelagic paradigm is necessary to more fully understand the complexities of the transnational present, in which long-standing divisions between one nation and another, as well as between nation and diaspora, no longer hold.[3]

On its release, *¿Quién diablos es Juliette?* played to widespread acclaim in Europe, Latin America, and North America. The film won prizes at the Havana Film Festival, the Sundance Film Festival, the Guadalajara Film Festival, and the Cartagena Film Festival, among others, and received the Silver Ariel at Mexico's 1998 Ariel Awards.[4] In the film, Marcovich employs a decidedly tongue-in-cheek tone to foreground the complexities of life in Cuba's capital during the nation's so-called Special Period in Times of Peace: a time of extreme scarcities following the 1989 collapse of the Soviet Union and the loss of the financial aid that the superpower had long provided.[5] As Esther Whitfield reminds readers in her insightful study of what she terms "'Special Period' fiction," the borders of the nation were redrawn during this time of crisis: "The rhetoric of the Cuban Revolution has always invoked combat, from its battles against illiteracy in the 1960s to the threat of invasion that it sustained long after the Cuban Missile Crisis, but the Special Period brought war closer. In announcing it, the government took a series of stringent remedial measures usually reserved for wartime." When these measures did not suffice to right the troubled economy, the government turned to "two new and previously unthinkable sources: remittances and tourism."[6] Both approaches marked a sharp departure from previous policy, and both again redrew national borders, this time in favor of a greater flow of bodies and capital from abroad. Indeed, while the regime of Fidel Castro had long decried tourism—and the dollars it generated—as an ill of capitalism, this quickly changed, and in 1990, Castro went so far as to paint a rosy picture of Cuba as a welcoming destination for tourists: "I envision the entire highway system north of Villa Clara, Ciego de Ávila, and Camagüey lined with hundreds of hotels."[7] The new governmental tack did help to fill national coffers, but at the same time led to deepening divisions between those Cubans able to benefit from increased access to dollars and the spending power that this enabled, and those forced to rely on the national peso, with its limited currency.[8]

Marcovich was fascinated by Cuba, which was increasingly featured in glossy photo spreads in global markets in the 1990s and publicized, albeit indirectly, by films such as Wim Wenders's *Buena Vista Social Club* (1999).[9] In 1991, the director traveled to Havana for the first time, and in 1993, he returned to film a music video for singer Benny Ibarra's "Tonto corazón" (Foolish heart).[10] The video was initially to feature solely Ibarra and a twenty-three-year-old Mexican model named Fabiola Quiroz. Marcovich changed his mind, however, when he met a fifteen-year-old Cuban, Yuliet Ortega, who strongly resembled Fabiola. Struck by the pair's likeness, he decided to add Yuliet to the video as Fabiola's double: "*la niña que fue* una cotizada modelo mexicana" (*the little girl who once was* a sought-after Mexican model).[11] After wrapping the video,

Marcovich returned to Mexico to shoot the 1994 feature film *El callejón de los milagros* (Midaq alley) for director Jorge Fons, starring Salma Hayek. Then, in 1995, he "returned [to Havana] to create Juliette's story."[12]

¿Quién diablos es Juliette?—the film that results from Marcovich's decision to "create Juliette's story"—has been promoted "as a documentary, a fiction documentary, and most tellingly a mockumentary because of the way the characters mock themselves and their different life circumstances."[13] In the film, Yuliet (identified as Juliette in the title) seeks to come to terms with her fraught family history, as does Fabiola, who is again depicted as her double. Yuliet has not seen her father since he departed for the United States when she was six months old; Fabiola has never met her father. Both protagonists have been beaten by the women who raised them, and Yuliet reveals that she has been raped by a man in her neighborhood. Piecing together these stories of familial loss and personal trauma through interviews with the protagonists, as well as their family and friends, Marcovich sets most of the film in Cuba, but also includes sequences set in the United States and Mexico. Fabiola lives and works in New York City, for instance; Yuliet's father lives in New Jersey; and Yuliet travels to Mexico, where Marcovich has arranged for her to meet with the head of a modeling agency and, to Yuliet's surprise, also with her father.

In limning the connections between Cuba, Mexico, and the United States in his film, Marcovich points to the limitations of prevailing images of Cuba as an island nation frozen in time and suggests the need for a more nuanced understanding of the island as one of a number of interconnected spaces belonging to a transnational borderlands. In line with Brian Russell Roberts and Michelle Stephens's cogent argument in "Archipelagic American Studies and the Caribbean," this transnational borderlands space might be described as archipelagic, offering "a vision of bridged spaces rather than closed territorial boundaries."[14] Envisioning Cuba as part of a wider, transnational archipelago reifies the importance of Anzaldúa's seminal work on the limitations of dividing lines marked on maps. At the same time, it also contests what Roberts and Stephens describe as the privileging of the continental over the insular: "much of anti-insular sentiment is the effect of a discourse with a fundamentally *continental* logic, pitting a continental and cosmopolitan universalism against more island-bound creole forms, and thereby rationalizing Euro-American domination of island spaces."[15]

Untethering the borderlands from any single border in rendering it as archipelagic, Marcovich demonstrates the limits of borders as "dividing lines" and points to the need for a cartography that accounts for the sea changes of the space of the borderlands, which remains, by definition, "in a constant state of transition."[16] As I further argue in the remainder of this chapter, the director doubles down on this archipelagic untethering of space in a concomitant unmooring of filmic and spoken language: calling into question the ability of the classical documentary to convey the unvarnished truth through his use of techniques associated with the mockumentary, Marcovich uses wordplay, doubling, and slippage between identities to suggest the need to recognize the borderlands as an archipelagic constellation of interconnected spaces. Suggesting in the film that the *actual* (here and now) is but an *actuación* (act), Marcovich signals the impossibility of clear demarcations between people, places, and performances and demonstrates, by extension, the need for a decentered, archipelagic remapping of borderlands as well as border cinema.

Mockumenting Havana

Drawing on the techniques of the classical documentary to chronicle the exigencies of the Special Period in *¿Quién diablos es Juliette?* Marcovich also utilizes these techniques to draw attention to the ongoing impact of another key moment in Cuban history: the Mariel Boatlift of 1980, in which Yuliet's father departs Cuba for the United States.[17] The events that led to the boatlift began on April 1, 1980, when five Cubans entered the grounds of the Peruvian embassy seeking asylum. By April 6, some ten thousand more Cubans had joined them, also seeking asylum. After asylum seekers had remained on the embassy property for two weeks under extremely precarious conditions, Fidel Castro announced on April 20 that those who were able to find sponsors could leave for the United States from the Cuban port of Mariel. Approximately 125,000 people ultimately departed. The exodus of the Marielitos in the boatlift marked the nation's historical consciousness, with families divided and borders between the nation and its diaspora simultaneously challenged and reaffirmed. In *¿Quién diablos es Juliette?* the traumatic impact of the loss of the Marielitos is underscored in the further familial loss that follows shortly thereafter: Yuliet's mother commits suicide, setting herself aflame in apparent heartbreak.

At the same time that Marcovich employs the style of the documentary to point to the historical lines that divide, the director also signals the tangled familial and national roots that problematize borders of all stripes. In the case of Yuliet's family history, the young protagonist long holds her father responsible for her mother's death. Yet as the film progresses and the story is pieced together through the testimonials of different family members, including Yuliet's father, the cause-and-effect relationship that Yuliet believes to exist between her father's exile and her mother's demise is shown to be more complicated. Yuliet's mother, in fact, has taken up with another man after her husband's departure, and it is her new lover's threat of abandonment that causes her to *darse candela* (literally, "to give herself candle"—i.e., to set herself aflame).

The ambiguities of borders (and borderlands) are further underscored in Marcovich's use of a mix of media and methods in his film. For Santiago Herrera, Marcovich remains "faithful" to the documentary:

> Recurre a todas las herramientas funcionales y formales para decir lo que quiere, pero con todo ello le sigue siendo fiel al género documental, porque le es fiel a una historia real que no vuelve a inventarse, porque no hay un guión con palabras que no provengan o estén por fuera de la verdadera historia de Juliette, porque es la realidad la que brinda los momentos dramáticos, así hayan sido propiciados por la misma película; en este momento la película lo que hace es documentar los efectos de su propia puesta en escena—por ejemplo el encuentro con el padre o con la directora de la agencia de modelos.
>
> He turns to all functional and formal tools to say what he wishes to say, but with all that he remains faithful to the genre of the documentary, because he is faithful to a real history that does not invent itself, because there is not a script with words that do not come from, or that are outside, the true history of Juliette, because it is reality that provides the dramatic moments, which the film itself has paved the way for; in this moment what the film does is to document the effects of the staging itself—for example the meeting with the father, or with the director of the modeling agency.[18]

At the same time that Marcovich employs the techniques associated with the documentary in his interrogation into *quién diablos* (who the hell) Yuliet is, however, he also mixes media and genres in a challenge to the strict borders often held to pertain between genres. In addition to the aforementioned interviews and documentary-style footage of Cuba, for instance, Marcovich incorporates sequences from the "Tonto corazón" video and video shoot, as well as clips from *El callejón de los milagros* and interviews with Salma Hayek, the star of that film.

In mixing media and genres, Marcovich also turns to the mockumentary: a genre that pokes fun at traditional documentary techniques, and, in so doing, calls into question documentary film's indexical relationship to reality. In *¿Quién diablos es Juliette?* he utilizes the mockumentary in his inclusion of a series of clearly orchestrated "mock" interviews that complement (even as they also subvert) the film's traditional, documentary-style interviews. One sequence, for instance, begins with a shot of a hand holding a potato knocking on a door. The door opens to reveal Yuliet, who bursts into laughter when she sees the potato: "Soy tu papa" (I'm your papa [potato]).[19] Portraying Yuliet's father as a *papa* (potato) rather than a *papá* (father) then becomes a running joke that is repeated throughout the film, prompting laughter on the part of the protagonists while simultaneously calling into question documentary film's ability to truly identify the full meaning of either *papá* or—in an era of chronic food shortages—*papa*. In a similar vein, Marcovich asks, tongue in cheek, if Fabiola's father Marco is in fact a *marco* of a different sort. Hence a shopkeeper who is asked for Marco points to a collection of *marcos* (frames); a man questions if Fabiola's father could perhaps be "Marcos, ¿el de la selva Lacandona? (Marcos, the Zapatista from Chiapas?); and a bus is shown emblazoned with the words "Marco Tours."[20] In these instances the director again points to the limited ability of documentary (or mockumentary) film to provide a frame—a *marco*—through which reality might be captured in all its complexity.

In employing mockumentary techniques such as these throughout the film, Marcovich does not remain fully *fiel* (faithful) to the documentary, as Herrera maintains.[21] Rather, as Geoffrey Kantaris argues, the director questions the boundaries between both genres and spaces; in *¿Quién diablos es Juliette?*, as in Marcovich's subsequent film *Cuatro labios* (Four lips, 2006), there is

> un enfoque reflexivo sobre los procesos mediáticos . . . ambas películas cuestionan las fronteras genéricas entre el cine documental y el cine de ficción, al tiempo que ocupan unas coordenadas espaciales también inestables al ubicarse más bien en el lugar de los flujos mediáticos que en algún sitio cartográfico de referencia empírica.
>
> a reflexive focus on media processes . . . both films question the generic frontiers between documentary and fiction cinema, at the same time that they occupy spatial coordinates that are also unstable, locating themselves more in a place of media flows than in a cartographic place of empirical reference.[22]

Untethering documentary film's supposedly indexical relationship to reality, Marcovich further signals the untethering of "coordenadas espaciales" (spatial coordinates) through his portrayal of the Cuban-Mexican-U.S. borderlands as archipelagic, a grouping of spaces that are simultaneously separate and interconnected.[23] Yuliet's father calls his children frequently from New Jersey, overcoming—at least aurally—the nominal divide between island and diaspora; Yuliet and Fabiola travel relatively readily between Cuba and Mexico; and Fabiola works as a model in Cuba, Mexico, and the United States. Almost all of the spaces portrayed in the film, moreover, are themselves archipelagic: Cuba is comprised of thousands of islands, inlets, and keys; New York City encompasses the island of Manhattan, Staten Island, part of Long Island, and various islands associated with each of its five boroughs; and Mexico includes, among others, the floating islands of Xochimilco. The protagonists' transnational, archipelagic itineraries, furthermore, mirror Marcovich's own: the Argentine-Mexican director travels from Mexico to Cuba to film *¿Quién diablos es Juliette?*, and the film is produced with a mix of transnational funding from Mexican actress Yolanda Andrade, Betaimagen Digital, Estudios Churubusco Azteca, the Hubert Bals Fund of the Rotterdam Festival, the Instituto Mexicano de Cinematografía, and Resonancia. In mockumenting life in Havana during the difficult years of the Special Period, Marcovich thus points to the complexities of pinning down the coordinates of the transnational borderlands and signals the need to rethink both borders and border cinema to better account for the realities of what he portrays, to use Anzaldúa's words, as "a vague and undetermined place . . . in a constant state of transition."[24]

Doubling Down

Intimating that the *diablo* is in the details when it comes to borders, be they national, familial, or generic, Marcovich doubles down on his message in a series of double entendres that he includes in the film. For one, the director employs wordplay to signal the plurality, rather than the univocality, of meaning—and, by extension, the flexibility, rather than the finality, of dividing lines etched on earth and marked on family trees. In so doing he untethers signified from signifier and questions once more the fixed nature of borders. In conjunction with this wordplay, Marcovich portrays his protagonists as mirror images of each other: as doubles. With the protagonists assuming multiple identities, each of which overlaps to some extent with the others, the director again detaches signified from signifier, and signals the need to rethink borders and boundaries as interconnected and archipelagic rather than separate and divided.

The film's opening sequence evidences the wordplay that pervades the film and signals the first doubling of its protagonists. Here Yuliet, shown standing on the Malecón wrapped in a towel, introduces herself to spectators: "Soy Yuliet. Tengo dieciséis años. Vivo en ciudad de la Habana en San Miguel del Padrón. Tengo un papá que vive en los Estados Unidos." (I'm Juliette. I'm 16 years old. I live in Havana, Cuba in San Miguel del Padrón. I have a father who lives in the U.S.) The film cuts to black, and the title appears on the screen ("¿Quién diablos es Juliette?"), then cuts back to Yuliet, who contests the spelling of her name: "Mi nombre se escribe con Y, con U, con L, con I, con E, y con T." (My name is spelled: Y - U - L - I - E - T.) Yuliet repeats her claim, and the film stops and appears to rewind, as it might on a VCR, to the title screen. The title is then changed twice—first to "¿Quién diablos es Yuliet?," then to "¿Yyyyy yyyyyyy yy Yyyyyy?"—before a single word fills the screen: "¿Yuliet?" The film then cuts back to Yuliet, who laughingly proclaims her approval: "¡Exacto! Esta es tremenda bobería, ¿me oyeron? Pero esta no es broma mía, es del director." (That's it! We're serving up a big farce here, you hear me? That's the director's joke, not mine.)

As the opening sequence makes clear, Yuliet (the sixteen-year-old *habanera* from San Miguel del Padrón) and Juliette (her onscreen persona, as interpreted and informed by the director) serve as doubles, with each reflecting—albeit imperfectly—the other.[25] Yuliet's agency in the crafting of her onscreen persona, moreover, is shown to be somewhat constrained by the director's vision of who she is: "Yuliet has a voice in claiming her name and language, yet her assertion is manipulated by the foreign director who could have put *Yuliet* in the title. Her agency is performed."[26] The uneven power dynamics between director and protagonist are underscored by Yuliet's attire in the sequence. Appearing onscreen for the first time in the film, Yuliet is here shown clad in a towel, under which she appears to wear a bathing suit. Standing on Havana's famed seaside promenade, the Malecón, and dressed for the beach, Yuliet recalls transnational tourism's promise of the island as a tropical paradise replete with the pleasures of what Kamala Kempadoo aptly describes as "sun, sea, and sand."[27]

Doubled in Juliette, Yuliet is further doubled in Fabiola, the Mexican model cast in Ibarra's "Tonto corazón" video, as well as in *¿Quién diablos es Juliette?*[28] The two protagonists are portrayed as doubles through their shared experience of familial loss, as well as their close physical resemblance, which is repeatedly highlighted in the film. When Fabiola explains why Yuliet is in the "Tonto corazón" video, for instance, she states summarily, "Yuliet está en el video porque se parece a mí." (Yuliet is in the video because she looked like me.) The singer Benny similarly says of Yuliet's participation that "Se pareciera tanto a Fabiola, que hubiese una conexión, tan no probable." (She would look so much like Fabiola that there would seem to be some connection. Maybe something kind of improbable.) Highlighting their resemblance, in one sequence first Yuliet and then Fabiola holds up a picture showing half of each protagonist's face joined together, as though to suggest that the two could indeed be one.

Portraying Yuliet and Fabiola as two halves of a whole, Marcovich suggests the need for a new framework to better take into account the complexities and connections of the borderlands: a framework that, as discussed in the opening section of this chapter, might be construed as archipelagic. As Roberts and Stephens write, such an approach would contribute to an effort to "frame the wider planetary archipelago (that is, the world's islands of the sea) in a truly decentered and unbounded, meta-archipelagic vision that contrasts with both the continent and the insular state. Closer to home, this model conceives of the American hemisphere itself as, paradoxically, an island-system as much as a continental system of states."[29] It would also contribute to what Elaine Stratford, Godfrey Baldacchino, and colleagues describe as the tendency to consider island spaces as separate rather than connected; they note that there are "particular limitations that arise from tenacious considerations of relations of land and sea, island and continent/mainland. . . . Largely missing from these labours have been ontologies that illuminate island spaces as mutually constituted, coconstructed and inter-related."[30] An archipelagic framework thus serves to highlight the connections and continuities that tie the protagonists and spaces of the borderlands together rather than the divisions that separate them.

The importance of an archipelagic paradigm that is "decentered and unbounded" is underscored in Marcovich's portrayal of the protagonists as self-described *putas* (whores).[31] Asking spectators to critically reflect on the borders often imposed between individuals based on their provenance, the protagonists' doubling in this case calls into question the easy distinctions established between one profession and another: "Marcovich shows that the clean rhetorical lines that mainstream discussions on the sex industry seek to draw are impossibly inadequate to the task. His work repeatedly asks what the difference is between a young girl being a model or a *jinetera*, a sex worker. We may wonder also about the distinction among film producers, sex tourists, and those who merely seek to sample an exotic culture and all of its fruits."[32] The nuances of this "distinction" are particularly evident during the Special Period, when many Cubans, including Yuliet, opt to work as *jineteras* to access the dollars-only economy fueled by the tourist industry. As Yuliet explains, speaking of herself in the third person, her choice is purely economic: "Por necesidad, pero no porque le gustó. Porque había lo que ella quería, pero que no lo podía comprar, porque no tenía dinero. Entonces, tenía que acostarse con italianos." (Because she had to, not because she liked it. There were things she wanted, but couldn't buy, because she didn't have any money. So, she had to sleep with the Italians.) Shown lying in bed in this sequence as she speaks, crisp sheets pulled up to her bare shoulders, Yuliet's appearance highlights the availability of her body to those willing and able to pay.

Both Yuliet and Fabiola avow and disavow their identity as *putas* at different points in the film, signaling that the term is multifaceted and that it shifts in meaning as it moves through the transnational archipelago. When Yuliet ruminates on the film's possible ending, for instance, she self-identifies as a *puta*, stating that she will die "de puta pero no de hambre" (from whoring, but not from hunger).[33] When an elderly black woman tells her that she is "la más puta de todas" (the biggest whore of all), however, Yuliet objects, replying, "¡No soy ninguna puta!" (I'm no whore!) Yuliet further points to the nuances in the term in describing her relationship with the tourists she describes as the "italianos" (Italians), and detailing that it includes more than sex: "Me fui a Guanabo, con unas amigas mías, a la playa, bueno, para encontrar italianos. Entonces encontramos italianos . . . y nos hacemos amigas de ellos. Y después, todo el tiempo estuvimos con ellos. Entonces estábamos viviendo en su casa, y eso. Y vamos a lugares con ellos. Comíamos con ellos. También había que singárselos para que ellos te den dinero, porque si no, no te daban nada, pero bueno." (I went to Guanabo beach, with some girlfriends, to hunt for Italians. So we found some Italians there, and made friends with them. After a while, we were staying at their house, and all that. We hung out with them. We ate with them. But, you also had to screw them to get any money, otherwise you got nothing.) As she talks, shots of Yuliet are interspersed with shots of young Cuban women and tourists on the beach, intimating that the experience she describes is far from unique.

In both accepting and rejecting an identity as a *puta*, Yuliet points to the arbitrary nature of the sign and, in turn, to the inherent fragility of borders and boundaries constructed on the basis of nominal difference. This is reinforced in Fabiola's similarly shifting stance regarding her own identity as a *puta*.

During a sequence shot in New York City, a man who seems to be homeless interrupts to tell spectators that "I know this whore [Fabiola] ever since she was two years old. . . . The bitch is a hooker, man." In this case, Fabiola responds with a question, followed by a laugh: "How he knows I'm a hooker?" In another instance, Fabiola seems to identify both herself and Yuliet as *putas*. Marcovich has arranged for Yuliet to travel to Mexico, and Fabiola has just learned that Yuliet's passport and travel permit are ready. Looking into the camera, Fabiola offers her approval: "Yuliet ya va a poder salir y todo. Chíngale. Una puta más suelta por el mundo." (Yuliet will be able to leave and all that. Holy shit! Another hooker loose in the world.) In this instance the artificiality of borders between one individual and another, and the nuances of identities in the transnational, archipelagic borderlands, is once again signaled by the fact that Yuliet will meet in Mexico with the head of Glenda Modelos, the company that represents Fabiola, and that her future work as a model is key to her ability to live "suelta por el mundo" (loose in the world). Fabiola works as a model in a career that is portrayed as prestigious; Yuliet works as a *jinetera*, in a career that is portrayed as motivated by economic necessity. Yet both women use their bodies for money as *putas* "loose in the world"; the similarities between the two protagonists, and their doubling in the film, suggests that any borders between them and their careers are artificial and arbitrary. This is underscored in the film in the insertion of a sequence from *El callejón de los milagros* in which the protagonist, played by Salma Hayek, realizes that while she has been promised a career in modeling, she has instead been tricked into working as a prostitute. The sequence plays again as Yuliet meets with the head of Glenda Modelos and decides that she does not, after all, wish to follow in Fabiola's footsteps.[34] Once more upending the traditional distinction—and related hierarchy—between model and prostitute, Yuliet decides to continue as a *jinetera* in Cuba rather than find herself forced into work as a *puta* masquerading as a model in Mexico.

Actualizando the Archipelagic Borderlands

Characterizing the borderlands as a space of multiple, at times overlapping, identities, Marcovich points to the need for a new, more archipelagic mapping of space in *¿Quién diablos es Juliette?* Such a mapping, the director intimates, would of necessity transcend the binaries often inherent in critical and cartographical renditions of nations as divided, by walls or by waters, and would take into account the realities of the lives of borderlands inhabitants, who are, as Fabiola states, "loose in the world" rather than tied to a particular place and time.

Marcovich's emphasis on the need for such a remapping is signaled in the film by the frequent slippage between the words *actuar* (to act) and *actual*

(actual, present, here and now). In general terms, this slippage is representative of the film's broader focus on the difficulties of accurately capturing reality through documentary:

> Siempre ha habido también un desfase entre la ficción y la referencia en el núcleo del debate sobre el documental (y también en la práctica); desfase . . . entre lo *actual*, el aquí y ahora, la famosa definición que da John Grierson del documental como "el tratamiento creativo de la actualidad" . . . y el verbo *actuar*, la puesta en escena de lo actual.
>
> At the center of the debate over the documentary [and also in practice], there has also always been an imbalance between fiction and reference; an imbalance . . . between the *actual*, the here and now, John Grierson's famous definition of the documentary as the "creative treatment of the present" . . . and the verb *to act*, the staging of the *actual*.[35]

Considered in conjunction with the film's rendition of the porosity of borders, the wordplay here also points to the fact that current cartographies are insufficient to accurately capture the nuances of multifaceted identities of the borderlands, which are, at the end, a constantly shifting performance: an *actuación* of the *actual* rather than an accurate portrayal of the *actual* itself.

The slippage between *actuar* and *actual* is highlighted throughout the film, as Yuliet repeatedly attempts to say one, only to say the other instead, due to her Cuban accent and the resulting lack of differentiation between the letters *l* and *r*. The first sequence in which the slippage is foregrounded occurs immediately following a shot in which Yuliet's grandmother explains, "Soy Obdulia, la abuela de Yuliet. Cuando era joven, quería ser actriz." (I am Obdulia, Yuliet's grandmother. When I was young, I wanted to be an actress.) The film cuts from a shot of Yuliet's grandmother in front of one of Havana's colonial-era buildings to a head shot of Yuliet on the Malecón. Yuliet then states, "Actual. Actuar. Actuar" (Pelform? Perform).[36] Drawing attention to the connections between the two words even as she seeks to distinguish between them, Yuliet's repetition of *actual* and *actuar* is on one level an example of the wordplay often featured in the film: a cue for spectators to chuckle, as they might when the knock at Yuliet's door reveals her *papa* (potato) rather than her *papá* (father). Yet the comments offered by Yuliet's grandmother on what she describes as the Stanislavsky acting method suggest that the slippage might also have an additional level of meaning. Following a cut, the grandmother is shown standing in her kitchen, where she states, "Bueno, el método es, hacer llorar a las personas cuando hay que llorar, y cuando hay que reír, es reír. . . . Es un cambio brusco de . . . llorar a reír." (Well, the method is, to make people cry when they have to cry, and laugh when they have to laugh. . . . It's about making mood changes between laughing and crying.) As the protagonists simultaneously act and showcase the *actual* exigencies of the Special Period, spectators may well feel inclined to both laugh and cry, as the Stanislavsky method would encourage them to do.

The second sequence in which the slippage between *actuar* and *actual* is foregrounded occurs following Fabiola's meditation on the unknown identity of her father, who, her mother has confessed to the camera, is a Canadian archeologist named Marco. Following a series of shots playing with the possibilities of the word *marco* (as picture frame, tour bus name, or guerrilla fighter), the film cuts to Yuliet. Silhouetted as she sits by the water, Yuliet once again attempts to differentiate between *actual* and *actuar* in her pronunciation: "Al-tuar . . . Al-tuar . . . Ac-tual . . ." (Actless . . . ? To act? Ac-tu-arl, actual . . .) Following a cut, Fabiola is shown silhouetted against a darkening background. Visually highlighting the connection between the two protagonists by showing them each in silhouette, Marcovich also foregrounds the murkiness of the distinction between *actuar* and *actual* in Fabiola's recounting of how she and Yuliet met when she came to Cuba to film the music video with Benny.

In the third sequence in which the slippage between *actuar* and *actual* is highlighted, Yuliet stands by the side of a road and states, "Alc-tual. Muy mal. Alc-tu-al" (Pelfolm. Pel-fo-lm).[37] The film then cuts to a young girl who, standing in front of a building wall, offers a lesson in the correct pronunciation of the rolling *rr* in Spanish: "R con R cigarro, R con R barril, rápido cruzan los carros alzando del ferrocarril." ('R' like in cigar! 'R' like in barrel! The ram ran right down the rolling ridge.) After the young girl's singsong recitation of this well-known tongue-twister, the film cuts to Yuliet, who proceeds to repeat the words in a chorus of her own: "Actual. Actual. Actuar. Actuar. Actuar. Actuar. Actual." (Actual. Actual . . . actuar . . . perform.) Underscoring the performative nature of this litany, she then follows up with a question: "¿Qué más me tengo que decir?" (What else do I have to say?) The film then cuts to a shot of Don Pepe, a retired banker who is featured as a supporting cast member in the film. As Don Pepe walks quickly along the Malecón, a crew member walks beside him, holding a microphone to capture his words: "Actuar, actuar, actuar, actuar, actuar, actuar, actuar, actuar."[38] Considered in conjunction with Yuliet's prior recitation and query, Don Pepe's repetition of the word *actuar* underscores the performative nature of the protagonists' participation in the film, as they are asked to *actuar* in the *actual*.[39] More generally, the repeated slippage between *actuar* and *actual* in the film signals Marcovich's characterization of identities as ever-shifting performances. For, as the open query of the film's title suggests, it is impossible to fully document the *actual*. Indeed, as Cubans perform their identities for tourists anxious to catch a glimpse of a nominally authentic present amid the ruins of the past, *actual* and *actuar* become largely indistinguishable.

In much the same way that individual identities are shown to be *actuaciones* in *¿Quién diablos es Juliette?*, the repeated references to the porous borders of the nation destabilize the idea of Cuba as a nation and culture that might be contained within strictly defined borders and point to the need for a greater understanding of the interconnected, archipelagic space of the *actual* borderlands. Considered from this vantage point, it is significant that a key sequence shortly before the film ends occurs on one of the small floating islands of Xochimilco, where Marcovich has arranged, unbeknownst to Yuliet, for the protagonist to meet her father during her trip to Mexico. Yuliet's father is shown stepping off a flower-festooned boat, dressed formally and carrying a bouquet of flowers; he approaches Yuliet, who has already arrived. At first Yuliet does not recognize her *papá*; when she does, she asks him why he did not go to Cuba: "¿Por qué no fuiste a Cuba?" Her father responds that another space was necessary for them to meet: "Porque tuve que venir acá." (Because I had to come here.) Underscoring the fact that *acá* is neither here nor there, the director moves from the handheld cameras that he has used throughout much of the film to an aerial shot as Yuliet insists that she and her father talk alone. In this instance, writes Santiago Herrera, "no le están 'vedados' el uso de la grúa o del helicóptero como en aquella escena de Juliette y su padre cuando aparece una imagen aérea que se aleja y los deja a los dos abandonados en una pequeña isla rodeada de árboles" (the use of the crane or the helicopter is not prohibited, as in the scene with Juliette and her father, when an aerial image appears and leaves the two abandoned on a small island surrounded by trees).[40]

In shooting the small island of Xochimilco from above, Marcovich draws attention to the connections between land and water, and, in turn, to the interconnectedness of the nations that rim the Gulf of Mexico and form a larger, archipelagic constellation. As Stratford, Baldacchino, and colleagues write, archipelagos are assemblages that, like the constellations, come into focus based on the connections established between them:

> The significance of the assemblage is ontogenic: it is not simply a gathering, a collection, a composition of things that are believed to fit together. Assemblages act in concert: they actively map out, select, piece together, and allow for the conception and conduct of individual units as members of a group. Deleuze & Guattari . . . use the example of constellations: assemblages of heavenly bodies that, like Orion the Hunter, take on one (or more) recognizable forms only when their wholeness arises out of a process of articulating multiple elements by establishing connections amongst them. An archipelago is similar. . . . Perhaps, at least as conceptual manifestations, archipelagos are fluid cultural processes, sites of abstract and material relations of movement and rest, dependent on changing conditions of articulation or connection.[41]

As though to underscore the need for the recognition of the connections between islands the aerial shot of Xochimilco then dissolves into a shot of the Havana skyline, as seen from the water. As one island dissolves into another, Marcovich signals the need for an expanded understanding of a transnational, archipelagic borderlands comprising interconnected islands that together form part of a larger archipelagic constellation.

In *Borderlands*, Anzaldúa writes of the border as an open wound: "The U.S.-Mexican border *es una herida abierta* where the Third World grates against the first and bleeds. And before a scab forms it hemorrhages again, the lifeblood of two worlds merging to form a third country—a border culture."[42] In the *actual*, Marcovich suggests, the borderlands continue to evidence the characteristics described by Anzaldúa as a result of a long history of worlds grating against each other and bleeding. At the same time, the director shows, the coordinates of the borderlands in the here and now are not fixed, but are scattered through space, forming an archipelagic constellation of land and sea and pointing to the connections, rather than the divisions, between the individuals and spaces featured in the film and the water that surrounds them.

Notes

Unless noted otherwise, translations from the Spanish are my own.

1 Gloria Anzaldúa, *Borderlands/La Frontera: The New Mestiza* (San Francisco: Spinsters/Aunt Lute, 1987), 3, emphasis in the original.

2 Ibid., preface [n.p.].

3 This chapter expands on the incisive extant analyses of the film's blurring of boundaries between individuals (Martin 2006, Suárez 2011) and genres (Herrera 1998, Kantaris 2015), at the same time that it suggests an alternative, archipelagic framework in which to consider Marcovich's characterization of transnational space.

4 Lucía M. Suárez, "Consuming Cubanas: *¿Quién diablos es Juliette?*" *Cuban Studies* 42 (2011): 156.

5 The exact duration of the Special Period, which Fidel Castro announced in January 1990 (Whitfield 2008, 3), is subject to some dispute.

6 Esther Whitfield, *Cuban Currency* (Minneapolis: University of Minnesota Press, 2008), 3, 6.

7 Fidel Castro, quoted in Vincenzo A. Perna, "Selling Cuba by the Sound: Music and Tourism in Cuba in the 1990s," in *Sun, Sea, and Sound: Music and Tourism in the Circum-Caribbean*, ed. Timothy Rommen and Daniel T. Neely (Oxford: Oxford University Press, 2014), 47. As the aid long received from the USSR demonstrates, Cuba was never as isolated as it often seems in the popular imaginary.

8 As detailed in Zurbano (2013), differences in access were often (though by no means always) tied to race.

9 For an overview, see Suárez (2011).

10 As of this writing, the video is available on YouTube; see Benny [Ibarra], "Tonto corazón," https://www.youtube.com/watch?v=x6kbiqA7ZgY.

11 Santiago Herrera, "¿Qué diablos es ficción y qué documental?" *Kinetoscopio* 9 (1998): 46, emphasis added.

12 Suárez 2011, 159. Suárez offers a valuable overview of the increasing commercialization of Cuba in the 1990s, arguing that in *¿Quién diablos es Juliette?* "Marcovich foregrounds how women and geographic sites are rendered interchangeable and expendable, but he also allows for an interpretive possibility through which the ambivalence and multiplicity of meaning and the sexualized representation of poor women's bodies and lives in different international settings might be reviewed" (2011, 156). Kantaris similarly suggests that the film "pone en entredicho los lazos entre cultura y territorio al tiempo que hace hincapié en las desiguales relaciones de poder involucradas en la mercantilización . . . de las culturas a través de los medios de comunicación" (calls into question the ties between culture and territory at the same time that it emphasizes the unequal power relations involved in the media's . . . commodification of cultures) (2015, 630).

13 Suárez 2011, 159, 156. In *Introduction to Documentary*, Bill Nichols underscores the "diversity of the films that make up the documentary tradition" (2001, 20) and offers a useful overview of what he describes as documentary's six "modes": poetic, expository, observational, participatory, reflexive, and performative (32–33). Following Nichols, Marcovich might be considered to make particular use of the reflexive mode, which "calls attention to the assumptions and conventions that govern documentary filmmaking," and the performative mode, which "emphasizes the subjective or expressive aspect of the filmmaker's own involvement with a subject" (Nichols 2001, 31, 32). Marcovich might also be considered to make use of the techniques associated with mockumentaries, which, Nichols writes in a parenthetical comment, "adopt documentary conventions but are staged, scripted, and acted to create the appearance of a genuine documentary as well as leaving clues that they are not. Part of the pleasure they provide lies in how they let a knowledgeable audience in on the joke: we can enjoy the film as a parody and gain new insight into taken-for-granted conventions" (2001, 17).

14 Brian Russell Roberts and Michelle Ann Stephens, "Archipelagic American Studies and the Caribbean," *Journal of Transnational American Studies* 5, no. 1 (2013): 14.

15 Ibid., 4. Roberts and Stephens add that "continental logic's construction of island-space as quintessentially *bounded* also has evoked the island in terms particularly useful to imperial nationalism and the politics of sovereignty. . . . An archipelagic American Studies seeks to understand how the trope of the island functions as the pivot point of these two seemingly contradictory discourses" (2013, 4). At the time that Marcovich released his film, both discourses referenced by Roberts and Stephens were used to describe Cuba. The island nation was simultaneously characterized as an improbably sovereign Revolutionary state and a fruit ripe for the picking: an exotic tourist destination promising beautifully ruinous buildings, pristine beaches, and welcoming residents.

16 Gloria Anzaldúa, *Borderlands/La Frontera: The New Mestiza* (San Francisco: Spinsters/Aunt Lute, 1987), 3.

17 For an overview of the important role of the documentary in Cuban film history, see Chanan (2003).

18 Herrera 1998, 47. Herrera goes on to note the difficulties of determining the film's precise genre: "No se trata aquí de decidir qué es, si ficción o documental. ¿Dónde están las fronteras? Qué diablos es ficción y qué documental?" (It is not a question of deciding what it is, fiction or documentary. Where are the limits? What the hell is fiction and what is documentary?) (1998, 47).

19 Translations of film dialogue are taken from the English language subtitles on the DVD released by Facets Video.

20 Marcovich might be another potential Marco.

21 Herrera 1998, 47.

22 Geoffrey Kantaris, "Desreferenciar lo real: Paisajes mediáticos en los documentales de Carlos Marcovich (*¿Quién diablos es Juliette?* y *Cuatro labios*)," *Revista Iberoamericana* 81, no. 251 (2015): 630. Kantaris notes the applicability of Nichols's "performative mode" in the context of *¿Quién diablos es Juliette?* (629), but argues that there is a need for a new term, "desreferenciar" (to dereference), to "conceptualizer la referencialidad en la forma documental en el cine" (conceptualize the referentiality in the documentary form in cinema) (627):

> Esta suspensión de un referente flotante, su tendencia a esfumarse en el mismo momento en que se amarra a la "vida real" o se fundamenta en "la naturaleza," es el proceso que quiero resumir con mi uso del término "desreferenciar." . . . [E]s un término usado todos los días por los programadores de computadoras. . . . En los lenguajes de programación orientados a objetos, "desreferenciar" es la acción de buscar la semántica específica referida por un identificador, de acceder a la estructura de datos hacia la cual apunta una referencia. . . . [M]e interesa la ambigua suspensión de la referencia, en el mismo acto de fijar los datos que representa, que sugiere este término.
>
> This suspension of a floating reference, its tendency to disappear en the precise moment in which it is tied to "real life" or is based on "nature," is the process that I wish to sum up with my use of the term "dereference." . . . [I]t is a term used every day by computer programmers. . . . In programming languages oriented toward objects, "dereference" is the action of searching for the specific semantics referred to by an identifier, of accessing the structure of information toward which a reference points. . . . I am interested in the ambiguous suspension of the reference, in the very act of determining the information that it represents, which this term suggests. (638)

23 Ibid., 630.

24 Anzaldúa 1987, 3.

25 The director makes no pretense about his ability to capture either protagonist fully.

26 Suárez 2011, 166.

27 Kamala Kempadoo, *Sexing the Caribbean: Gender, Race, and Sexual Labor* (New York: Routledge, 2004), 20.

28 Yuliet is also doubled in Alma, the character played by Salma Hayek in *El callejón de los milagros*.

29 Roberts and Stephens 2013, 13.

30 Elaine Stratford, Geoffrey Balcacchino, Elizabeth McMahon, Carol Farbotko, and Andrew Harwood, "Envisioning the Archipelago," *Island Studies Journal* 6, no. 2 (2011): 124.

31 Roberts and Stephens, 2013, 13.

32 Suárez 2011, 164.

33 Yuliet speaks of herself in the third person in this instance.

34 Deborah Martin notes that Yuliet's decision to remain in Cuba points to her resistance: "And clearly the plot hinges on the idea of Yuliet's leaving Cuba, on the directorial and spectatorial assumption that this is her desire. So by returning, she thwarts the director's plans, flouts our expectations and ultimately resists the path that has been neatly laid out for her. Of course, her return may also be interpreted as a resistance to Western capitalism, in which she would become involved as a model" (2006, 349).

35 Kantaris 2015, 628.

36 The English subtitles often seek to capture the linguistic slippage and wordplay of the Spanish through creative (mis)spellings.

37 A translation of Yuliet's self-reflective "Muy mal" (Very bad) is not included in the English subtitles.

38 No English subtitles are provided here.

39 The slippage between *actuar* and *actual* is highlighted in other instances as well.

40 Herrera 1998, 47.

41 Stratford et al., 124.

42 Anzaldúa 1987, 3.

8

Crossing through *el Hueco*

The Visual Politics of Smuggling in Colombian Migration Films

JENNIFER HARFORD VARGAS

The Colombian band Mojarra Eléctrica opens the first song on the soundtrack album for the border-crossing film *Paraíso Travel* (Paradise Travel) singing the words "por el hueco" before proceeding to voice the speaker's plans to migrate to New York City.[1] Colombians colloquially describe crossing undocumented into the United States as going *por el Hueco*, which translates as "through the Hole" or "through the Gap."[2] I propose that the term *el Hueco* is a conceptually rich trope that captures both the time and place where migrants cross geopolitical borders undetected as well as the complex process of entering into and subsequently navigating life as undocumented subjects in the United States.[3] The routes migrants traverse *por el Hueco* to access the United States extend throughout Latin America, and these routes are desperate and resourceful responses to exclusionary policies. Holes are deliberately opened when authorized routes of entry are closed, and when one hole is closed by border security, others are sought and created elsewhere. Going through a *hueco* in the border, then, entails exploiting a temporary gap that presents an opportunity as well as enacting shifting strategies to pass under the radar of the state. It necessitates exposing and strategically negotiating loopholes in the formal structures, institutional arrangements, and policing apparatuses that mediate and regulate national geopolitical boundaries. Maneuvering *el Hueco* involves not only agency and opportunity; it also entails being confined and limited in one's spaces of movement and access to resources. This chapter explores the dual aspects of the term's double entendre as hole/gap to underscore both the limitations and opportunities presented by the trope.

The Colombian metaphor of *el Hueco* provides a fruitful new trope for Latina/o/x studies and border studies, one that is directly rooted in the experience of undocumented migration and that complements "the guiding metaphor of Latino Studies: 'la frontera,' the border."[4] As journalist Germán Castro Caycedo explains, many Colombians lack the resources to migrate to the United States through official channels, so they come "por 'el hueco,' es decir, en forma clandestina a tráves de la frontera con México, desde Bahamas en bote o en avión, e incluso algunos por Haití" (through "el hueco," that is, clandestinely over the border with Mexico, from the Bahamas in boat or airplane, and even via Haiti).[5] María Elena Cepeda estimates that four million Colombians live in the United States and that 40 to 50 percent of this Colombian population is undocumented.[6] Colombian undocumented migrants use varying modes of transportation and journey via multiple routes that extend throughout the Caribbean, Central America, and Mexico to access the United States. In her theorization of the Gulf of Mexico as a "Latino-Anglo border system," Kirsten Silva Gruesz has demonstrated how the gulf region provides border studies and Latina/o/x studies a fresh perspective on "the reified map of the land border, *la línea*."[7] I contend that, like the gulf, *el Hueco* is a "distinctive kind of border zone," but its distinctiveness does not lie in a specific topography, geographic location, or geo-political space.[8] Rather, it lies in the border-crossing sites and tactics that can be collected together under the expression *por el Hueco*, as well as the undocumented subjectivity that emerges from *el Hueco*. I am especially interested in theorizing *el Hueco* as a metaphor for undocumented migration rooted in this extended geography—one that connects the Caribbean, Central America, Mexico, and South America—and based on the dual signification in English of *hueco* as a hole and a gap.

The term *el Hueco* interrogates the nation-state's hegemonic border and its naturalized status. The United States imagines its borders to demarcate a sovereign, fixed, and bounded territorial space. Highlighting holes, gaps, breaks, and hidden sites of entry, the border from the perspective of *el Hueco* is a tension-filled geography of political, social, and legal space that subjects differentially navigate. Shifting attention from the border as a site of exclusion to *el Hueco* as a site of fraught access enacts a critical shift in the discourse used to imagine the border. This is similar to the critical shift enacted by the trope of *la frontera*, or the borderlands, deployed by Gloria Anzaldúa, as both tropes expose the border's unstable and constructed nature. The trope of *el Hueco* works in tandem with the trope of the borderlands in fashioning an alternative national cartography demarcated not by natural, static, and stable boundaries but by gap-filled, fissured, and porous margins. Yet, in differentiation from the borderlands, *El Hueco* focuses exclusively on the process of undocumented migration by shedding conceptual light on the spaces entered clandestinely to escape border security apparatuses and on the daily undercover negotiations essential to living and working undocumented within the nation-state.

Though the borderlands and *el Hueco* are doing similar conceptual work, *el Hueco* is a Colombian metaphor for undocumented migration that is not the product of the U.S.-Mexico contact zone nor generated out of or delimited to the spatial imaginary of Greater Mexico.[9] This is crucial for multiple reasons. Given the dominant focus on the U.S.-Mexico border in the U.S. political imaginary and the stereotype in the public sphere of undocumented migrants as impoverished Mexicans, it is pressing that Latina/o/x studies contest these oversimplified views by considering Latin American migration from a comparative perspective that accounts for different national groups, modes of crossing, socioeconomic classes, and geographic sites of entry. Moreover, not only does *el Hueco* map a relationship to countries in the Caribbean, Central America, North America, and South America that are involved as crucial sites of passage, it is both a "geographic and metaphorical space."[10] Though subjectivity can be fashioned anew in the borderlands—as Anzaldúa and other Chicana/o/x scholars and cultural producers have so poignantly demonstrated—the subjectivity that emerges from *el Hueco* is not necessarily one that is multiple or mestiza. For crossing through *el Hueco* produces a death of legal subjectivity and a burial of one's social and national identity. As a trope for undocumented migration, *el Hueco* highlights the very painful and visceral effects that entering without authorization has on migrant subjects, even as it holds out the possibility of forging a new, transnational identity and of reconfiguring restrictive notions of citizenship. In addition, U.S. Colombian cultural production is just starting to be mapped in Latina/o/x studies, so attending to *el Hueco* helps contribute to this burgeoning subfield and thus to expanding such studies, as well as border studies.[11]

In this chapter, I examine how film as a medium can visually capture *el Hueco* by focusing on two Spanish-language films—Joshua Marston's *Maria Full of Grace* (2004) and Simón Brand's *Paraíso Travel* (Paradise Travel, 2008)—that depict undocumented migration from Colombia to the United States.[12] Both films dramatize the issue of smuggling: drug smuggling in the case of *Maria Full of Grace* and human smuggling in *Paraíso Travel*. I analyze the trope of smuggling in the films to bring into tandem focus two different kinds of vulnerable populations: impoverished female drug smugglers and undocumented migrants. The smugglers and migrants who are the protagonists of both films are, in Lisa Marie Cacho's terms, "permanently criminalized people."[13] Cacho argues that "the criminal, the illegal alien, and the terrorist suspect are treated as obvious, self-inflicted, and necessary outcomes of law-breaking rather than as *effects* of the law or as produced by the law. When law targets certain people for incarceration or deportation, it criminalizes those people of color who are always already most vulnerable and multiply marginalized."[14] Films that figure Colombians as drug mules and illegal aliens run the risk of reinforcing the erroneous but pervasive stereotypes in the United States that Colombians are all involved in the drug trade and that undocumented migrants are all criminals who deserve to be deported.[15] Such stereotyping and criminalizing obscures how U.S. immigration law and neoliberal capitalism are fundamental structural problems and that the demand for drugs and low-wage labor in the United States shapes the flow of products and people in the Americas. I unpack the multiple valences of smuggling in *Maria Full of Grace* and *Paraíso Travel*, tracking the various kinds of material goods, bodies, and narratives that are smuggled within and into the films.

Overall, my analysis of the films attempts to fill a *hueco* or gap in border studies and in Latina/o/x cultural studies by using the films to sketch some of the contours of the Colombian undocumented migrant imaginary. I consider how these two Spanish-language films contribute to what this volume terms "border cinema," exploring what the border and border cinema look like from the perspective of *el Hueco*. I am ultimately interested in what we might gain from comparatively studying the visual and narrative discourses forged by Latina/o/x American migrants of various national origins to critically interpret border-crossing experiences.

Smuggled Narratives

Maria Full of Grace follows María Álvarez, the titular seventeen-year-old pregnant protagonist, as she decides to become a *mula*, or drug mule, in order to make more money than what she is making at a flower plantation.[16] She learns from Lucy, another drug smuggler, how to properly swallow latex-wrapped pellets of cocaine or heroin. Stopped by immigration authorities in New York City who believe she is carrying drugs in her stomach, María is released when they find out that she is carrying a baby. The female smugglers are taken by the drug traffickers to a hotel room, where they wait together to excrete all their pellets; Lucy becomes gravely sick from a pellet that bursts in her stomach, and María awakes to see blood all over the bathroom. Terrified, she and her friend and fellow smuggler Blanca flee the room and go in search of Lucy's older sister Carla, who lives in Jackson Heights, Queens. María befriends Carla, who is noticeably very pregnant and tells María that she has stayed in the United States to give her baby a better life than what would be possible in Colombia. Lucy and Blanca eventually return the drugs to the traffickers, and after learning that Lucy's body was cut open and the drug pellets extracted from her stomach by the traffickers, María uses some of the money she made to pay for Lucy's body to be returned to Colombia. On their way to the airport, María holds a sonogram image of her baby with the date of her next appointment, and right before she is supposed to board the plane back to Colombia, she turns and walks away from the gate—and presumably toward a new life in the United States, which she thinks will give her child the best chance.

Film critics and scholars situate *Maria Full of Grace* within the genre of the narco-film and laud it for its humanizing and realistic depiction of drug smuggling. The film depicts the process of making drug pellets and learning how to swallow them properly, and it exposes the physical dangers of this manner of smuggling drugs, but absent are the stereotypical tropes of the narco-film genre typified by films and television shows such as *Scarface*, *Miami Vice*, *Blow*, and *Narcos*. According to Michelle Rocío Nasser, the narco-film genre is characterized by a great deal of violence, a hypermasculine and ruthless drug lord, a submissive hypersexualized trophy wife, and copious amounts of white powder and green bills.[17] In contrast, *Maria Full of Grace* depicts drug smuggling through a wide-eyed teenager whose name evokes the Virgin Mary, and the drug lord is a paternalistic elderly man with a cane. The film is also very quiet, with little music, relying primarily on facial expressions and minimal dialogue. Though it eschews the materialistic and sensationalistic excesses of the narco-film, it surreptitiously introduces a subplot that celebrates and romanticizes the United States.

While *Maria Full of Grace* is ostensibly about drug smuggling from a Colombian perspective, the film smuggles under the cover of the narco-film genre a celebration of the American dream and American exceptionalism, at the same time that it traffics in the illusion that it is a Colombian film. The dialogue is entirely in Spanish and, with mostly nonprofessional actors and handheld camerawork, it has a documentary feel. Despite the fact that HBO funded most of the film, it won a number of foreign-language awards at film festivals in the United States, eligible because the Colombian government contributed some funds. Yet the film is written and directed by Anglo-American Joshua Marston, who had a friend translate his English script into Spanish, with the explicit intent of educating U.S. audiences and humanizing the dangers of the drug trade.[18]

The film also traffics in the traditional migration narrative that scripts the United States as the site of freedom, hope, and economic possibility, using the sisters Lucy and Carla as vehicles to voice the American dream. While in Colombia, María asks Lucy what the United States is like. Lucy, smiling for the first and only time in the film, tells her that everything is "demasiado perfecto" (too perfect). Later, in New York, when María tells Lucy's sister Carla that she is going to return to Colombia, Carla, who is pregnant and assumes a motherly role in this scene, responds, "Usted no va a regresar, mi niña." (You are not going to go back, my child.) Tears run down her face as she tells María that the reason she stays in the United States is for her son because "él tendrá muchas más oportunidades" (he will have so many more opportunities) in the United States. Carla laments "la situación" in Colombia, which is how Colombians colloquially and euphemistically refer to the civil conflict and poverty of their country. The film thereby "enforces a dichotomy that places the concepts of safety, prospect, and hope together with America into one category and poverty, danger, and despair together with Colombia into another category without highlighting the bias of such a categorization."[19] The scene positions Carla as a model mother and moral guide for María. This is subtly reinforced by the camera angle as viewers are positioned in María's sightline looking up at Carla's face, which is lit by the glow of a bedside lamp; a silver decoration that depicts a mother holding a child in her lap hangs next to the lamp. At the same time, the scene sets up the United States as the only site where María has any hope of achieving economic mobility and stability, implying that if she wants to be a good mother she needs to forgo being a mule and become an undocumented migrant.

In the final scene of the film, we witness María choosing to stay in the United States rather than returning to Colombia. As she walks down the airport terminal toward the exit, an advertising sign hangs on the wall behind her. The communications and technology company Intel provides the moral lesson the film is smuggling in the background: "It's what inside that counts" (see figure 8.1).[20] The words advertise several messages: What is "inside" María is her baby and it is her baby's future that counts, so María must logically remain in the United States, where her unborn baby will be assured of having a better future. What also "counts" is economic mobility and monetary success, which are "opportunities" Carla tells her are only available in the United States for her unborn child. Ironically, this message is being propagated by a multinational corporation founded and headquartered in the United States, one that produces many of its parts overseas and has been accused of violating various laws and regulations in the United States and internationally; this links Intel to the exploitative flower plantation that employed María in Colombia, exposing how neoliberal capitalism shapes María's life on both sides of the border. Furthermore, given the title of the film and its allusion to the Virgin Mary, the "what's *inside* that counts" sets the audience up to read María as full of grace or being an essentially morally good person who is honest, well intentioned, and determined to have a better financial future but is trapped in a morally compromising situation as a result of being poor and a woman in Colombia.

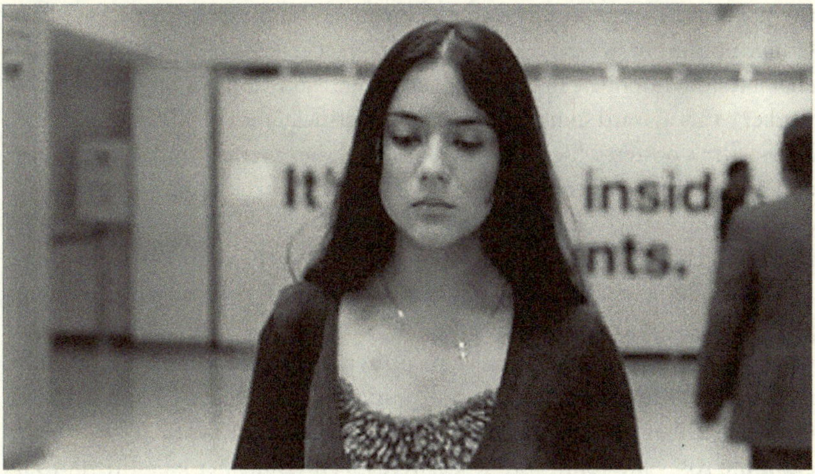

FIG. 8.1 *Maria Full of Grace* (2004): "It's what's inside that counts."

In this way the film sets up María's body as both the site of desperation and the source of redemption. Though María fills her body with drugs, she is also filled with the grace of a child. Indeed, two eerily parallel images of women's body cavities establish this link. In a scene earlier on in the film, María spots a doctor and an immigration official at the airport looking at an X-ray that reveals the cocaine pellets inside a fellow female smuggler's stomach. The film plays on the idea of the state's penetrating gaze with the threat of being subject to the surveillance technology of the X-ray machine, but even though she is detained by the state, María is miraculously saved from being X-rayed because she is pregnant. In a scene later on in the film, María undergoes a sonogram and tears up when she sees the image of her baby on the screen. In each scene, a doctor points at the visual image that exposes what is inside the woman's body. María uses her body and the *hueco* in her stomach to smuggle the drugs; though María's original intention was not to migrate *por el Hueco*, the film suggests that if she instead focuses on what is now inside her—a child—she will choose to be an undocumented migrant in the United States. María is redeemed from her illegal drug smuggling by two subsequent sacrifices: first, she sacrifices part of the money she earns to send Lucy's dead body back to Colombia, and second, she sacrifices returning to Colombia and remains in the United States. That is, María is able to attain grace by abandoning that illicit and corrupt path for the straight and narrow path of the hardworking mother laboring for her baby's future.[21]

The film is built around a linear sequence of events, and this conventional chronological plot development structures María's character development within a conventional ideological narrative that situates the United States as the site of both opportunity and redemption. The film, as Florencia Cortés-Conde points out, relies on a "classical three-act structure."[22] It scripts María's character development in terms of her progression from an oppressed flower worker to a wayward smuggler and then a sacrificial mother. This is reinforced by the film's poster, which depicts María with her eyes turned toward heaven and her mouth open to receive not the body of Christ but a white pellet of cocaine. The tagline "Based on 1,000 true stories" suggests that María's story represents that of all drug smugglers, trafficking in the testimonial genre that positions María in a figuratively synecdochic role vis à vis female drug smugglers; her story is a part of the "1,000" true stories which comes to stand for the whole of them. Yet the film sets María up as the exception. She begins the film laboring in a rose plantation amid pesticides. Her local Colombian boss refuses to let her go to the bathroom when she feels sick, and then forces her to clean the roses she vomits on; María refuses and quits her job. The film suggests that though María is one among many laborers, she is the only one to resist her exploitation, and from the outset this situates her within a U.S. narrative tradition that celebrates individualism as heroic. Moreover, as Cortés-Conde argues, "US ideology, inscribed in the narrative of [*María Full of Grace*], sees constraints on individual aspirations as the driving force that leads to crime, and offers an environment where upward mobility is possible as the corrective context that reestablishes social order."[23] María's inability to find a decent job drives her to become a drug mule, but when Don Fernando, a generous Columbian ex-patriate who helps people in the community, tells her he can help her find a job in New York and Carla tells her the United States will provide her the economic opportunities to help care for her child and her family in Colombia, María buys into the U.S. ideology the film is smuggling into her story line. Unlike her friend Blanca, who returns to Colombia and presumably back into the drug trade, María forgoes that route in favor of the American dream. The film endorses this narrative in its final frame as María is surrounded by an aura, aglow with possibility and hope and filled with a determined faith symbolized in the cross around her neck and the halo of light surrounding her. Blurred around the edges, the film's final shot prevents it from tackling the harsh reality that María is stepping into with her choice to remain in the United States as an undocumented pregnant teenager who does not speak English and has little formal education or job skills—and the attendant challenges she will face as a result.

The final shot also underscores how the film blurs the larger transnational and neoliberal socioeconomic and sociopolitical structures that shape María's individual choices. The film begins with María visually situated as one among many women working in the rose plantation named Amorosa (which translates as "loving" in English but, given the industry, is also a pun meaning "I love rose"). The film sets up the rigid Colombian boss at Amorosa as the symbolic source of María's unhappiness, since the rose plantation is her only opportunity for employment in the village. While the plantation endangers the women's health and violates their labor rights, its agricultural production is tied to transnational neoliberal trade agreements; the film gives no concrete sense of these agreements between the United States and Colombia or of the U.S.-funded Plan Colombia and its dire effect on Colombia's economy and environment or the civil conflict it brought to the nation.[24] Instead Amorosa merely functions as the setting for the conflict between María and her boss, which develops the plot by establishing María's need for a new job to make money, with no indication of the harmful effects of pesticide spraying on Colombian agricultural workers, industries, and the natural environment as a result of Plan Colombia. Though viewers with knowledge of Latin America's long history of reliance on export-oriented economies whose capital flow has been manipulated and controlled by the United States and U.S.-owned multinational corporations may recognize how Amorosa is embedded in this history, the film does not give any of this historical or economic context, so it runs the risk of reinforcing the stereotype of Colombia as an impoverished country rampant with drug running.

In one scene set in Jackson Heights, Queens, toward the end of the film, María walks down the street and past a flower vendor trimming rose stems, which reminds us that we in the United States consume the flowers that María and the other women labor to cultivate, but the film's overall one-sided portrayal of the supply side of the drug and flower industries helps reinforce the traditional migration narrative that the film smuggles into the story. More subtly, as María walks around Jackson Heights, at two different points signs with "Bravo" hover over her, as if to celebrate her fierce determination and bravery; indeed, several of the meanings of *bravo* in English include "to be brave," "to be fierce," and "good job." The film suggests that María's determination and the American dream will save her from the poverty and corruption of Colombia's drug trade. The United States is shown as a too-rosy site of hope and mobility rather than as deeply implicated in the economic market and political forces that drive María's decision to go through *el Hueco* and remain in the United States as a poor, undocumented, pregnant teenager who will encounter great obstacles.

Smuggled Bodies

María Full of Grace represents the female body as the site of innocence that is corrupted by Colombia and then redeemed by the American dream. In contrast, *Paraíso Travel* visualizes the American dream as a seductive illusion, using the hypersexualized female body as a site through which to interrogate rather than reinforce the American dream. Unlike *María Full of Grace*, which only reveals itself as an undocumented migrant narrative in its conclusion, *Paraíso Travel* opens with protagonists and lovers Marlon Cruz and Reina having recently arrived in Queens.[25] The film revolves around the themes of undocumented migration and young love/lust. The main story line follows Marlon's journey after he goes out to smoke a cigarette, runs from the police who approach him for throwing the cigarette on the ground, and becomes hopelessly lost. While he obsessively searches for Reina over the period of a year, the film follows Marlon's integration into the local Colombian and Latin American migrant community in Jackson Heights. This story line is frequently interrupted by flashbacks that reveal how Reina seduced Marlon into accompanying her to the United States and chronicle how the two made their way clandestinely from Medellín, Colombia, to the United States *por el Hueco*.

In order to migrate *por el Hueco*, Marlon and Reina must pay someone to guide them; what they encounter, unsurprisingly, is an elaborate structure of exploitation. Scholars use the term *migration industry* to describe the whole apparatus that makes undocumented migration feasible; this extends from travel agents to labor recruiters and from human smugglers to document forgers, who in this case are hired by Paraíso Travel, the "travel agency" that gives the film its ironic title. The scantily dressed woman who works for Paraíso Travel sells the aspiring migrants an easy vacation-like trip across Central America and Mexico where they will take a "viaje fluvial," or trip via river, and stay in "resorts." The reality is much bleaker. Along the route they encounter motel workers and bus drivers extort additional fees from them, provide them with cramped sleeping conditions, and threaten them with abandonment and violence. At one point a bus driver in Mexico demands a bribe, and since they do not have any more money, a woman traveling with them named La Caleña pays for them to continue by doing the man a sexual favor. At another point they cross over a dangerous river between Guatemala and Mexico holding onto a flimsy rope, with their belongings in trash bags, only to stumble shaken to the ground and get attacked by thieves who steal all their money, sexually molest the women, and shoot one man dead. The migrants' experiences crossing *por el Hueco* are not exceptional; in fact, many undocumented migrants crossing through Central America and Mexico fall victim to robbery, beatings, rape, and abandonment at the hands of so-called coyotes, gangs, Mexican police, and U.S. Border Patrol officials.

I am particularly interested in how the film visually renders their coming through *el Hueco* and crossing over the U.S.-Mexico border as a kind of burial. In order to be smuggled into the United States, the migrants hide inside hollowed-out logs in the back of a long truck. The camera cuts between shots from within the logs, which are sealed shut, and shots of the migrants being forcefully yanked out of the logs after they cross over the border; within one log we witness Marlon's point of view and hear his panicked screams, and outside the logs, we see the clearly shaken migrants coughing and throwing up. The jolty handheld camerawork mimics the migrants' disorientation. The space of the log resembles that of a coffin (dark, narrow, enclosed), making the crossing *por el Hueco* into a burial of sorts. This metaphorically enacts the kind of legal death that Marlon and Reina undergo as they enter the United States. Lisa Marie Cacho argues that undocumented migrants are subjected to what she and other scholars have termed "social death"; immigration law creates a "permanently rightless status" that makes these migrants "*ineligible for personhood*" because they are "subjected to laws but refused the legal means to contest those laws as well as denied both the political legitimacy and moral credibility necessary to question them."[26] The film visually captures this social death as the undocumented migrants lay in the wooden cemetery. The coffin-like experience of the *hueco* symbolizes the burial of the migrants' previous national identity and social location. On a less symbolic and more literal level, one unnamed man dies in the log, likely from suffocation or a heart attack. The border-crossing scene ends with the camera focused on the bereft wife mourning loudly as she embraces her husband's corpse.

But before the border-crossing scene ends, the camera pans outward to show Marlon walking away from the man's lifeless body to approach Reina who stands a short distance from the truck, physically but also emotionally distancing herself from the group. Reina, facing the audience with the tragedy behind her in the background, smiles broadly and declares that the worst is over because they are in the United States now (see figure 8.2). Her joyous reaction at having arrived safely in the United States is tempered by the widow's forlorn wails of grief and the bleakness of the sky behind her. The tonal contrast evident between the foreground and background in this single frame is unsettling. Unlike the airport scene in *Maria Full of Grace*, in which María chooses to become an undocumented migrant to provide a supposedly better life for her unborn child in front of the Intel advertisement that celebrates her choice, *Paraíso Travel* refuses to endorse Reina's individualistic choices. Given that the film has positioned Reina as the embodiment of the desire for the American dream, this scene forcefully raises the question of the deadly costs of believing in such dreams.

Marlon later experiences another kind of death as he wanders for an immeasurable amount of time, half starving and utterly filthy, until he stumbles upon a restaurant that, ironically, is named Mi Tierra Colombiana (My Colombian Land). When Marlon is kicked out of the restaurant for trying to eat leftover food, he sits immobile across the street, desperately staring at Mi Tierra Colombiana. Marlon's spatial separation from this symbolically nationalist space captures how he is a doubly nationally alienated subject who does not legally exist in the United States but also no longer lives in Colombia. He is, to use Mai Ngai's term, an "impossible subject." Ngai writes, "Immigration

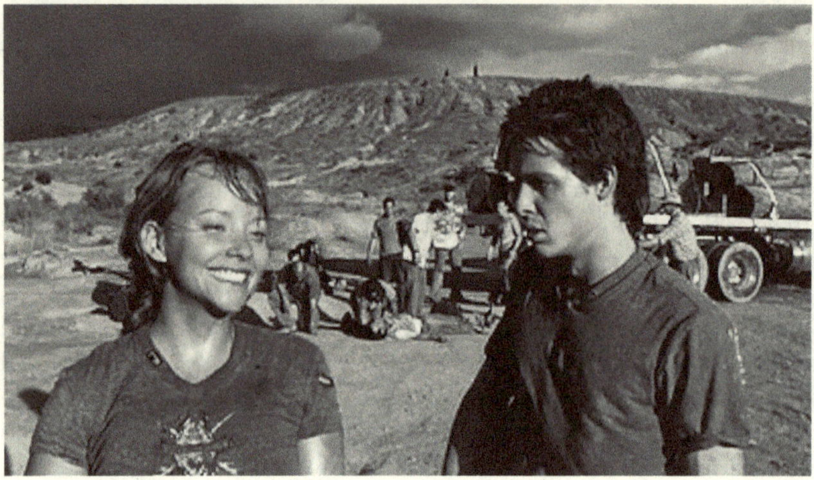

FIG. 8.2 *Paraiso Travel* (2008): Reina's American dream.

restriction produced the illegal alien as a *new legal and political subject*, whose inclusion within the nation was simultaneously a social reality and a legal impossibility—a subject barred from citizenship and without rights. . . . The illegal alien is thus an 'impossible subject,' a person who cannot be and a problem that cannot be solved."[27] Marlon exists in a legal gap or hole that simultaneously generates his nonexistence as a rights-bearing subject. The expression in Spanish *está hueco* to indicate that something is hollow or empty also captures how undocumented migrants are stripped of their subjectivity and rights, forced to occupy a hollow citizenship as they chase the empty American dream. When Doña Patricia invites Marlon Cruz into the restaurant to bathe and introduces him to a community of fellow migrants, he—in another border-crossing of sorts—crosses the threshold into a new life. Appropriately moving away from the paradigm of the nation-state, the film figures Marlon's reincorporation into Colombian land, so to speak, as entering into a transnational space of belonging based not on passports but on shared cultural affinities, affective kinship ties, and cultural citizenship.[28]

We can thus interpret *el Hueco* as a kind of tunnel that not only functions as a burial space but also as a kind of birth canal, suggesting that the death of one (legal) subjectivity can result in the birth of another (transnational) subjectivity. While Marlon's crossing through *el Hueco* transforms him into an "impossible subject," it is from precisely this social location that Marlon is, as time passes, able to forge a new identity and enact shifting strategies to pass under the radar of the state. As Marlon and his friend Giovanny gaze out at the New York cityscape from a rooftop, Giovanny tells Marlon, "Mirálo bien. Ese es el monstro que vas a tener que domar. (Take a good look. This is the monster you are going to have to tame.) José Martí's famous 1895 declaration, "Viví en el monstruo y le conozco las entrañas—y mi honda es la de David" (I have lived in the monster, and I know its entrails—and my sling is that of David) takes on new significance in this scene.[29] Martí metaphorizes the United States as a monster and the migrant Latin American as living within its entrails.[30] Crucially, in *Paraíso Travel*, an undocumented migrant produces and shares his reading of the city as a monster with a fellow undocumented migrant. But, as the film suggests, undocumented migrants who live in the belly of the beast have different relations to the structures of power than those who are here with documents. For Marlon and Giovanny there is a distinct danger in provoking the monster (the danger of being deported), and this threat modifies their approach to life in the United States. That is, Martí claims he is a David figure ready to fight the monster of U.S. imperialism with his slingshot, whereas *Paraíso Travel* focuses more on the crushing, restricted living space of the entrails. Being undocumented modifies Marlon's habitus and forces him to undertake a different kind of labor. Giovanny takes Marlon from the rooftop to "el muro" (the wall), where he introduces him to the stark reality of being a day laborer. Marlon learns how to participate in this poorly compensated informal economy because, as Giovanny tells him, migrants must stand in line and labor to find happiness, especially if they have come through *el Hueco*.

The crafted and commodified myth of the United States as "paradise" is evoked in the "Paradise Awaits" sign that Marlon and Giovanny sit under on the rooftop. The commercial advertisement is rooted in exoticization and sexual undertones, with the women's silhouette evoking Reina's seduction of Marlon into migrating to New York and the seductive illusion of the American dream. In stark contrast to this paradisiacal image, Marlon first stays in the basement of Mi Tierra Colombiana, then in a space for drug addicts, and then in a dilapidated tenement occupied by squatters. He rents a bed from Roger Peña, a scheming stutterer who is into S&M photography and who uses his dog Demon to help steal clothes. Roger befriends Marlon but makes him pay, so to speak, by posing for photographs when Marlon cannot afford the rent. Marlon not only relies on the informal economy for jobs and for a place to sleep, but his search for Reina is reliant on informal networks rather than official channels. As Giovanny tells Marlon, as far as the United States is concerned, Reina does not exist. And as Doña Patricia explains to him, to find a missing person you would normally consult hospitals, morgues, and the police, but because Marlon and Reina came through *el Hueco* and do not have any documents, he does not have access to these resources.

The contrast between the fantasy of socioeconomic success and life in *el Hueco* is highlighted later in the film in a montage that features images of Marlon working as a food deliveryman and audio clips of the radio announcements that Marlon pays for in his search for Reina. The song by the band Mojarra Eléctrica that was mentioned at the beginning of this chapter, which is entitled "*El Hueco*," plays in the background over the montage. The lyrics voice the desire to achieve the American dream:

Adios me voy (por el hueco)
me voy pa' Nueva York (por el hueco)
para volverme rico (por el hueco)
yo quiero un carrito (por el hueco)
que sea rojo (por el hueco)
que sea un Ferrari (por el hueco)

Goodbye, I am leaving (through *el Hueco*)
I am going to New York (through *el Hueco*)
to become rich (through *el Hueco*)
I want a car (through *el Hueco*)
let it be red (through *el Hueco*)
let it be a Ferrari (through *el Hueco*)

The upbeat lyrics, which sing about making it big in New York City, hover as an auditory counterpoint to the montage of Marlon cleaning bathrooms and biking around to make deliveries; the expression *por el Hueco* repeated by the chorus in a slightly more quiet tone at the end of each line of the song hauntingly reminds the listener of the limitations on economic success for undocumented migrants.[31] When Marlon finally does find Reina at the end of the film, she is living in a trailer park with her alcoholic mother and her infant daughter. She has lost the mysterious allure of her different colored eyes and now has two brown eyes and a tattoo on her breast; she is working as a prostitute to make ends meet. Paying the Paraíso Travel agency to go through *el Hueco*, Marlon and Reina hope that "Paradise Awaits" them in the United States, only to find that life in the United States is not what they dreamed.

While *Paraíso Travel* usefully critiques the illusion of the American dream that tantalizes many Latin American migrants, it accomplishes this, in part, through the problematic hypersexualization of Reina. Reina seduces Marlon into accompanying her to the United States by putting photos of New York City and the money she steals to pay for their journey down her pants and between her legs, promising Marlon that they will consummate their relationship once they are in the United States. Reina represents "the seductive power of the American Dream. She is its manifestation in Colombia: obsessed with the opportunity America promises, convinced of the hopelessness of life in Colombia, and deeply seductive in her narrative about the possibilities of life in the United States."[32] Marlon quickly learns that the idealized image of the prosperous life Reina constantly told him they would have is an illusion. The film contains a double romance narrative in which Marlon is lured by his desire for Reina and Reina by her desire for the American dream, but both turn out to be failed romances. Marlon's accidental physical separation from Reina is traumatic, but it serves as a catalyst for him to develop alternative forms of attachment and thereby, by the end of the film, to no longer desire Reina or believe in the myth of the American dream. While the film ultimately provides a useful reimagining of national identity, it is important to note that its plot development centers on the migration experience of its male protagonist and its narrative resolution is based on Marlon's growth, which comes at the expense of Reina's character development and reinforces the well-worn tropes of the female seductress and the gendering of the nation as a female.

Instead of achieving monetary riches, Marlon's new life is rich with the network of Latin American migrants of various national origins who help him rebuild his life in the United States. As a result of his social location as an undocumented subject and the friendships he establishes in Queens, Marlon comes to live out national belonging differently. His citizenship is no longer tethered to state sanctioning or the geopolitical boundaries of the nation-state; instead it is based on the action of caring affectionately for others and creating intimate ties. As he creates kinship through *el Hueco*, Marlon's actions gesture toward an affective sense of belonging that is not based on the singular nation-state or on a single (heterosexual) relationship but rather on a more diffuse set of attachments. This affective citizenship is a feeling and a state of being. María Elena Cepeda's spelling of "imagiNation" to highlight how it functions as "both noun *and* verb," or as "a collective activity embedded in a definite sense of place(lessness)," aptly describes the more expansive sense of Colombian identity and cultural citizenship that the film puts onscreen.[33] Marlon's experiences of social death in the United States are counterbalanced by his experiences of a tight-knit migrant collective that functions as a community of sentiment, and this, in turn, gives rise to an alternative vision of belonging.[34] The film thus reimagines national affiliation by depicting that it need not be restricted to the nation-state; rather, it can extend transnationally and intersubjectively.

Alternative Signs of Belonging

Maria Full of Grace relies on a conventional narrative structure that is chronological and moves from South America to North America, and the film ultimately reinforces an idealistic view of the United States. *Paraíso Travel*, in contrast, is built around three different temporal modes through which events unfold; as such, the film is not strictly chronological in its temporality nor strictly south-to-north in its geographic spatiality. These various temporalities, interspersed throughout *Paraíso Travel*, and the migrations northward and southward create a simultaneous and shifting movement between national spaces, which highlights the transnational subjectivity of undocumented migrants. The images that accompany the film's credits also scramble geographic spaces, going from the bus in Mexico in which the driver extorts money from Marlon, Reina, and their fellow migrants, to the truck and the logs they hide in to cross the U.S.-Mexico border, to the river they waded to cross from Guatemala into Mexico, to the cityscape of New York City, which then gets turned into a snow globe. This closing image of New York City as a snow globe highlights the idealized (and white) image many Latin Americans are sold of the United States. The neon red sign "Paraíso Travel" that opens the credits fades into "Pais," which translates as "Country" or "Nation," indicating that we need new signs (pun intended) to signify the alternative forms of national belonging for undocumented migrants.

Given the current slew of anti-immigration laws, discriminatory policies, and xenophobic discourse surrounding undocumented migration to the United Sates, it is ever more pressing that we be attuned to the differing contours of undocumented migrant imaginaries.[35] It is imperative that we challenge the negative hegemonic metaphors associated with Latina/o/x migrants and citizens because such a stigmatizing discourse, which Leo Chávez has encapsulated in what he terms the "Latino threat narrative," only serves to reinforce their domination, racialization, and marginalization.[36] The metaphor of *el Hueco* is part of a larger set of what Otto Santa Ana calls "insurgent metaphors," which Latina/o/x migrants and citizens are constructing to contest the dominant negative construction of undocumented migration.[37] The structural and ideological conditions that produce undocumented migration and its attendant social death necessitate radical transformation. In the meantime, the knowledge and metaphors that undocumented migrants (and their allies) use to describe and interpret their existence as impossible subjects contribute critical paradigms for documenting migrant lives and border-crossing experiences in the Americas.

Notes

Unless otherwise indicated, all translations from others' works and of film dialogue are my own.

1 Mojarra Eléctrica, "El Hueco," track 1 on *Paraíso Travel*, Codigo Music, 2009.

2 The term is more frequently written as "*el hueco*," but some authors use "*el Hueco*" or "*El Hueco*." I choose to capitalize *el Hueco* as a proper name in order to distinguish it from the common noun *el hueco*. Colombian newspapers use the term when they report on Colombian undocumented migration to the United States, and the prolific Colombian journalist Germán Castro Caycedo interviewed a number of Colombians who journeyed *por el Hueco*, publishing a nonfiction book; see Germán Castro Caycedo, *El hueco* (Bogotá: Editorial Planeta Colombiana, 1989). For an analysis of representations of *el Hueco* in Colombian

border-crossing novels and album artwork, see Jennifer Harford Vargas, "The Undocumented Subjects of el Hueco: Theorizing a Colombian Metaphor for Migration," *Symbolism: An International Annual of Critical Aesthetics* 17 (2017): 31–53.

3 When referring to the U.S. policy toward migrants, I use the term *immigration* because that is the term employed by the state. However, I prefer the terms *migrant* and *migration* to *immigrant* and *immigration* because they accommodate a number of different trajectories, goals, and statuses rather than the fixed destination with the eventual acquisition of citizenship implied by the term *immigration*.

4 Juan Flores, *From Bomba to Hip-Hop: Puerto Rican Culture and Latino Identity* (New York: Columbia University Press, 2000), 212.

5 Castro Caycedo, *El hueco*, 20. Note that Castro Caycedo chooses not to capitalize the article or the noun (i.e., "el hueco").

6 María Elena Cepeda, *Musical ImagiNation: U.S-Colombian Identity and the Latin Music Boom* (New York: New York University Press, 2010), 32. Cepeda's estimates are from 2018 or earlier, so these numbers are likely higher today. Cepeda relies on various sources for her data because, as she and other researchers point out, errors in the 2000 U.S. Census resulted in a very inaccurate count of the U.S. Colombian population (Cepeda, *Musical ImagiNation*, 178). Unfortunately, the 2010 U.S. Census and more recent studies, such as those released by the Pew Research Center and the Migration Policy Institute, still appear to underestimate the number of Colombians in the United States.

7 Kirsten Silva Gruesz, "The Gulf of Mexico System and the 'Latinness' of New Orleans," *American Literary History* 18, no. 3 (2006): 470.

8 Ibid., 490.

9 Coined by Américo Paredes, "Greater Mexico" is the collection of Mexican culture and Mexican-origin people extending beyond the national boundaries of Mexico.

10 Monica Perales, "On *Borderlands/La Frontera:* Gloria Anzaldúa and Twenty-Five Years of Research on Gender in the Borderlands," *Journal of Women's History* 25, no. 4 (2013): 164.

11 To date, Cepeda's book is the only full-length work on the cultural production of U.S. Colombians. Most work on U.S. Colombians has emerged in the social sciences; for exceptions to this, see Michelle Rocío Nasser de la Torre, "*Bellas por naturaleza*: Mapping National Identity on U.S. Colombian Beauty Queens," *Latino Studies* 11, no. 3 (2013): 293–312; Juanita Heredia, "South American Latino/a Writers in the United States," in *The Routledge Companion to Latino/a Literature*, ed. Suzanne Bost and Frances R. Aparicio (New York: Routledge, 2013), 436–444; Suzanne Oboler, "Introduction: *Los que llegarón*: 50 Years of South American Immigration (1950–2000)—An Overview," *Latino Studies* 3, no. 1 (2005): 42–52; and Silvio Torres-Saillant, "Pitfalls of Latino Chronologies: South and Central Americans," *Latino Studies* 5, no. 4 (2007): 489–502.

12 *Paraíso Travel* is based on the novel by Jorge Franco, *Paraíso Travel* (Bogotá: Editorial Planeta Colombiana, 2001); the English edition is *Paradise Travel*, translated by Katherine Silver (New York: Farrar, Straus and Giroux, 2006).

13 Lisa Marie Cacho, *Social Death: Racialized Rightlessness and the Criminalization of the Unprotected* (New York: New York University Press, 2012), 6.

14 Ibid., 4.

15 Additionally, they play into the "double discourses of criminality" in which "Colombians are associated with widespread criminal organizations and 'illegal' border crossings." Ariana Ochoa Camacho, "Living with Drug Lords and Mules in New York: Contrasting Colombian Criminality and Transnational Belonging," in *The Immigrant Other: Lived Experiences in a Transnational World*, ed. Rich Furman, Greg Lamphear, and Douglas Epps (New York: Columbia University Press, 2016) 169.

16 Though the film is in Spanish and the titular character's name is María, the title, which is in English, uses the English-language spelling of her name ("Maria," not the Spanish–language spelling "María").

17 As Michelle Rocío Nasser notes, "Colombian men are shown as dangerous, deceitful, money hungry criminals living a lavish life, committed to nothing but their immediate fortune, and ready to kill at a moment's notice," while "[Colombian] women are shown as sultry, loud, insubordinate, yet easily dominated by their violent partners" and are depicted as "trophy accessories" and as "insignificant and voiceless." See Michelle Rocío Nasser, "Tra(n)zando Identidades: Colombian Neighborhoods, Images, and Narratives from Narco-Trafficking to Beauty Queens" (PhD diss., Tulane University, 2008), 86–87.

18 For documentation of these issues, see Florencia Cortés-Conde, "Telling Identities: Crime Narratives for Local and International Markets in *María, Full of Grace* (Marston, 2004) and *Rosario Tijeras* (Maillé, 2005)." *Studies in Latin American Popular Culture* 29 (2011): 80–101.

19 Silvia Schultermandl, "From Drug Mule to Miss America: American Exceptionalism and the Commodification of the 'Other' Woman in *María Full of Grace*," *Journal of American Culture* 34, no. 3 (2011): 286.

20 The advertisement appears in English, and there is also a blue circle with "Yes" in bold white letters on the right-hand side of the sign. In contrast to the signs in Queens, which are in Spanish, here the film ends with a sign that privileges English and the assimilationist paradigm that pressures María to learn English and remain in the United States, affirming her choice with its enthusiastic "Yes."

21 For more on how this narrative problematically "domesticates" female migrants in a global market that exploits their labor, see Margarita Saona, "Migrant Mothers: The Domestication of Latina Images for the Global Market." *Letras femeninas* 34, no. 1 (2008): 125–145.

22 Cortés-Conde, "Telling Identities," 81.

23 Ibid., 86.

24 For a brief historical overview of the political crisis in Colombia and U.S. involvement through Plan Colombia, see Cepeda, *Musical ImagiNation*. Cepeda traces how these have influenced Colombian migration; at the same time, she points out, "The international media's longstanding focus on Colombia's political struggles, while justified, has unwittingly led to a decreased emphasis on the other primary impetus driving mass migration to the United States. . . . In actuality, high unemployment rates provoked by neoliberal economic policies, the socioeconomic disconnects provoked by rising education rates, and an increased familiarity with North American styles of consumption constitute the key immigration 'push' factors for rural Colombians in particular" (28).

25 Unlike *Maria Full of Grace*, which was written and directed by an Anglo-American, *Paraíso Travel* is a Colombian and U.S.-Colombian production. The

novel's author, Franco, cowrote the script for the film with Juan Rendón, and the film was directed by Simón Brand, a Colombian-born filmmaker who has lived in the United States for most of his adult life. U.S. Colombian–Puerto Rican John Leguizamo acted in the film and was a coproducer, and part of the movie was filmed in Colombia.

26 Cacho, 6; emphasis in the original.

27 Mae Ngai, *Impossible Subjects: Illegal Aliens and the Making of Modern America* (Princeton, N.J.: Princeton University Press, 2004), 4.

28 For more on cultural citizenship, see Renato Rosaldo, "Cultural Citizenship, Inequality, and Multiculturalism," in *Latino Cultural Citizenship: Claiming Identity, Space, and Rights*, ed. William F. Flores and Rina Benmayor (Boston: Beacon, 1997), 27–38.

29 See José Martí, "Letter to Manuel Mercado," in *Selected Writings*, translated by Esther Allen (New York: Penguin, 2002), 347. In reflecting on Martí's metaphorization of the power relationship between Latin America and the United States as one between David and the giant Goliath, Laura Lomas notes, "Martí's strategy for addressing this difference is to defeat brute force with ingenuity. . . . Such a strategy authorizes the perspective of the dissenting minority deep within the monster's gut, precisely the position that Martí claims he occupied while living in New York." Laura Lomas, *Translating Empire: José Martí, Migrant Latino Subjects, and American Modernities* (Durham, N.C.: Duke University Press, 2009), 221.

30 This provides an interesting contrast to *Maria Full of Grace*, in which Maria uses the *hueco* in her stomach/entrails as a vessel to smuggle drugs.

31 The full version of the song that appears on the film's soundtrack but not in the film itself announces that a group of Colombians were captured while trying to cross el Río Bravo or, as it is called in the United States, the Rio Grande.

32 John D. "Rio" Riofrio, *Continental Shifts: Migration, Representation, and the Struggle for Justice in Latin(o) America* (Austin: University of Texas Press, 2015): 51.

33 Cepeda, *Musical ImagiNation*, 8, 10. For more on cultural citizenship, see Rosaldo, "Cultural Citizenship."

34 I take the phrase "community of sentiment" from Arjun Appadurai, who defines it as "a group that begins to imagine and feel things together." Arjun Appadurai, *Modernity at Large: Cultural Dimensions of Globalization* (Minneapolis: University of Minnesota Press, 1996), 8.

35 Here I am playing on Alicia Schmidt Camacho's term "migrant imaginaries" to highlight the imaginaries of undocumented migrants and to highlight that many of these imaginaries are themselves not documented. See Alicia Schmidt Camacho, *Migrant Imaginaries: Latino Cultural Politics in the U.S.-Mexico Borderlands* (New York: New York University Press, 2008), 5.

36 Leo Chávez, *The Latino Threat: Constructing Immigrants, Citizens, and the Nation* (Stanford, Calif.: Stanford University Press, 2013), 21.

37 Otto Santa Ana, *Brown Tide Rising: Metaphors of Latinos in Contemporary American Public Discourse* (Austin: University of Texas Press, 2002), 295.

9

Toward a *Transfrontera*-Latinx Aesthetics

An Interview with Filmmaker and Artist Alex Rivera

FREDERICK LUIS ALDAMA

Filmmaker and artist Alex Rivera is very much a Latino of his time—and place. Born in New York City in 1973, to Peruvian parents from New Jersey, he was raised biculturally in New Jersey and upstate New York. As much at home with *lomo saltado* as with hamburgers, he grew up cosmopolitan urban *and* tract-home suburban. He was as impressed by Isaac Asimov, Terry Gilliam, George Lucas, Ridley Scott, and John Steinbeck, and with such Latino creators as Lalo Alcaraz, Coco Fusco, Guillermo Gómez-Peña, Los Bros Hernandez, and Gregory Nava. Like many Latinx creators of his generation, he grew up not only bicultural, but *transcultural*. He is of Generation *Transfrontera*-Latinx.

That Rivera was born in New York City in 1973 is significant. He grew up during a sociohistorical epoch when doors were being forcibly opened by Latino activists, creators, and scholars. It was a time when technologies for making video and digital films were becoming less expensive and easier to use, giving the layperson more access to them. This confluence of sociopolitical forces and technological advances cleared a creative space for Rivera once he was in college, where he pursued audiovisual storytelling and documentation of the otherwise marginalized or erased experiences of the everyday struggles and lives of Latinos. As an undergraduate at Hampshire College he acquired knowledge furnished by critical race and class theory and learned the art of do-it-yourself filmmaking. By the mid-1990s technologies for recording and watching film had become cost accessible and self-teachable: expensive, cumbersome cameras and editing machines were a thing of the past, swept aside by lightweight digital cameras and highly sophisticated postproduction computer graphic editing software. He could, as he explains in this interview, access the kind of technology that would allow him to begin to realize his experience and that of countless other Latinxs who were growing up not only *between* multiple geographies (urban and rural, and of the North, Central, and South Américas), cultures, languages, and identities, but also *across* these spaces.

As Rivera honed his filmmaking skills, so too did he witness the proverbial "browning of America," where Latinos became the largest minority in the United States (and the actual majority in the Southwest). During this period, Rivera also grew acutely aware of the sharp discrepancy between demographic *visibility* and sociopolitical *erasure*, that he was living in a country where the dominant racist and classist ideologies drove *actual* policies and practices that sought to eliminate Latinos: the increased militarization and surveillance of the U.S.-Mexican border, mass detentions and deportations of women and children, and the passing of draconian race/ethnic-based identity policing laws, among others. Rivera has lived through a time when mainstream cultural pundits have championed inclusionary practices with such TV shows as *Dora the Explorer* (2000), all while Latinos are being policed, deported, and murdered at the highest rates in history.

Forced from lands and bloated megalopolises, Chinantecos, Guasaves, Mayas, Mixtecos, and Zapotecas risk their lives to survive another day by crossing dangerous borders where they encounter *pandilleros* (gang members) like the Mara Salvatrucha (MS-13), who prey on the innocent, *rateros* (ratmen) who steal from the already superimpoverished, corrupt and violent *migra* (immigration police). Conservative estimates situate the present level at more than ten thousand Latinos who have died crossing the U.S.-Mexican border. With Operation Gatekeeper (California), Safeguard (Arizona), and Hold the Line (Texas) in full swing, more walls have been built, and motion sensors and other surveillance devices have been installed; there are Black Hawk helicopter sweeps, and infrared-equipped, gunned-up sport utility vehicles push people to gamble with extreme odds when crossing one of the planet's most scorched deserts.

Rivera is of his time(s) and place(s). He's a transfrontera-Latinx creator, but one who chooses to dedicate his work to peeling back veneers that attempt to cover who is responsible for the creation of an insufferable, destructive reality increasingly mediated by state capitalist interests where the ebb and flow of lives—and life—across the U.S.-Mexican border and the increased policing of Latinos in the United States serve Monsanto-style global corporate interests.

Rivera chooses to be a socially conscious creator of cultural phenomena, and he does so in ways that take what has come before and build upon it. In his short and feature-length films, for instance, he produces narratives that creatively reconstruct experiences of displacement, exploitation, and struggle that characterize the Latino experience. In this sense, he continues a tradition of Latino filmmaking, as seen in the works of filmmakers from the 1980s and 1990s like Luis Valdez (*Zoot Suit,* 1981 and *La Bamba*, 1987), Gregory Nava (*El Norte*, 1984), and Darnell Martin (*I Like it Like That*, 1994), as well as contemporaries like Peter Bratt (*La Mission*, 2009), Aurora Guerrero (*Mosquita y Mari*, 2012), and Mexican actor and director Diego Luna (*César Chávez*, 2014). In the making of his films he also draws from and enlarges a world cinema with similar preoccupations, such as Cary Joji Fukunaga's *Sin nombre* (Without a name, 2009), Chris Weitz's *A Better Life* (2011), and Diego Quemada-Diez's *La jaula de oro* (The golden dream, 2013). However, Rivera engages world cinema with a difference. In the creating of his socially conscious films (and art installations and dummy websites) he tends to gravitate toward themes and formal shaping devices that foreground the role of technology in today's and tomorrow's society; its role in the lives of everyday Latinos as a tool for self-empowerment (e.g., communication and mobilization) *and* repressive disempowerment (e.g., weapons of surveillance and annihilation). Naturally, the theme of technology attracts Rivera's filmmaking to science fiction as a narrative mode and genre.

Like all aesthetic artifacts, sci-fi narrative is the distillation, then *re-creation,* of a chosen slice of reality to *make new* our perceptions, thoughts, and feelings about that reality. Science fiction creates a blueprint that foregrounds the authority of "scientific knowledge" (in bold scare quotes) and aims to create a new relational experience between the subject (reader, viewer) and object (novel, comic book, film). When the HAL 9000 computer goes crazy in Stanley Kubrick's *2001: A Space Odyssey* (1968), we are given a series of "scientific explanations" as the story progresses. This differs from, say, Julio Cortázar's short story "Axolotl," where the human protagonist transmogrifies into an Axolotl without scientific explanation. In the case of Cortázar, the interpenetration of different ontologies simply happens, whereas in Kubrick's film, the pact established with the viewer is very different; the narrative explains events that Cortázar's narrative might leave as mysteries. Sci-fi is thus a capacious enough genre to allow creators like Rivera to generate diverse relations (or pacts) with their readers and viewers through degrees of "scientific" explanation.

With great intelligence and skill, Rivera uses science fiction to distill from and then reconstruct the building blocks of reality: the contemporary state of labor and capital in the United States and at its southern border. In so doing he also enlarges the science fiction terrain. His short and long sci-fi films add to and expand a corpus that now includes U.S. Latinos like Robert Rodriguez (*Planet Terror*, 2009), but also increasingly those from south of the border; I think of Carlos Salces's *Zurdo* (Mexico, 2003), Esteban Sapir's *La antena* (Argentina, 2007), Fernando Meirelles's *Blindness* (Brazil, 2008); Francisco Laresgoiti's *2033* (Mexico, 2009), Rodrigo Ordóñez Nischli's *Depositarios* (Mexico, 2010), and Diego Ayala's *Conexión* (Chile, 2013). And, like African American creators of Afrofuturist cultural phenomena seek to vitally imagine a future-located subjectivity enriched by selective (progressive) ancestral heritages, so too do we see a similar move in Rivera's work. Taken as a whole, Rivera's films add to and expand the periodic table of global and global-othered science fiction narratives.

Rivera has begun to solve the problem he so eloquently points out (here and elsewhere): the lack of a cinema made by Latinos that reflects on the future of Latinos. In contrast with the many Hollywood-created science fiction films that only imagine futures generated in and through a U.S.-located male whiteness, Rivera's science fiction films and installation pieces give texture to a future that does imagine people of color and how the majority of humanity (barely) lives as exploited and surveilled.[1] Take, for instance, Rivera's installation art: *Memorial over General Atomics* and *LowDrone*, first physically exhibited at the University of California, San Diego, continue to live on via the internet.[2] Rivera takes a technology of surveillance and destruction (drones used to monitor the U.S.-Mexican border *and*, in their scaled-up versions, to drop bombs), strips it down, and reconstructs it with new parts—and a new use: as a cultural object for us to apprehend *and* as a tool with which to make sense of today's reality. With the repurposed drone in *Memorial* he creates an aerial sculpture that combines drone technology with human radial bones; he asks us not only to fly with this repurposed drone to see what is happening at the factory where they create drones of mass destruction but also to think about the radial bones that function to hold its propellers: the laboring arms (or *braceros*) worked to death. Rivera's repurposing of the drone in *LowDrone* similarly asks us to establish a new relationship with the use function of a tech object otherwise used for destruction. Here Rivera combines a model of a vintage lowrider (kicking its wheels out to the edges as blades to the repurposed drone) that one can use to watch the surveyor (*la migra*) as one flies or "hops" back and forth across the wall that divides Mexico (Tijuana) from the United States (San Ysidro). Before entering the *LowDrone* website, you agree to "not hold LowDrone.com responsible for the consequences of my transnational hopping."[3] Rivera calls attention to a U.S.-Mexican border surveillance system that damages and destroys brown lives while maintaining plausible deniability.

We see this same drive to distill, reconstruct, and repurpose objects and subjects that make up our world in Rivera's films. In his first short film, *Papapapá*

(1995), he does so to make new his audience's perception, thought, and feeling about Latino identity. Moving between documentary realist and fictional film techniques, Rivera creates an audiovisual narrative that, as Amy Sara Carroll notes, "code-switches between a presumed real timespace and science fiction."[4] In so doing Rivera asks that his audience make *new meaning* about Latinos like his father, who might live physically in the United States but live imaginatively in spaces south of the border. In other of his short films, we see the making of what Carroll identifies as Rivera's "undocumentary poetics."[5] For instance, he chooses to use a neutral yet Anglo female–identified voice-over narration in *Why Cybraceros?* (1997), whose tone and cadence conveys total ignorance concerning day laborers and migrant workers, to create a huge disconnect with visual images of historical reportage that portrays the violent oppression of said workers. So while this chipper Anglo voice-over narration celebrates the great arrival of a new "cybracero" program that allows for one to *use* Latinos without having to *deal* with Latinos, Rivera asks the audience to hold these two disparate actions in their head: a lighthearted ignorance that perpetuates white privilege and the brutal, actual exploitation of Latino workers.

In his short film *Sixth Section* (2003) Rivera uses the technology of filmmaking to make known how technologies harnessed by a group of displaced Mexicanos known as Grupo Unión (living in Newburgh, New York, but from Boquerón, Mexico) allow for communication and movement of material means (money) across borders in ways that create new, twinned communities: the money sent back to Boquerón has built hospitals, schools, and a baseball field, for instance. Rivera's short film complicates, as Carroll concludes, "facile understandings of displacement because members of Grupo Unión resist assimilation, using their very precarity as political leverage in a rapidly evolving global Mexican public sphere."[6]

In his short film *A Robot Walks into a Bar* (2014) Rivera chooses to set his story *in* the future, where robots now serve the function of today's Latino day laborers—and more. Rivera asks us to keep both the sci-fi technology of the robot and its servile use function with today's exploitation of Latinos. Yet he also gives us a narrative that asks us to overlay sci-fi robots with everyday life for Latinos today (an allegorical palimpsest of sorts). There is a twist: the robot learns how to empathize through its contact with a Latino, now unemployed and unable to provide for his family because of the robot. In solidarity the robot (which refuses to work and holds his fist high in a power salute) stands against exploitation of its self, and its fellow Latinos.[7] In a creative, paratextual move, Rivera also created a dummy website that identifies ways that you can invest in the cybracero technology to have cheap laborers in Mexico cybernetically do work in the United States to create profits. Rivera also includes a tongue-in-cheek warning: that the movie *Sleep Dealer* "is an inaccurate and undeservedly critical portrait of our pioneering business model and is not representational of our business."[8]

Rivera explores both the pros and cons of technology in his sci-fi feature film *Sleep Dealer* (2009). While the narrative largely shows the destructive use of technology (cybernetic technology in the form of drones and brain nodes that allow for the exploitation of Mexican cybraceros manipulating robots on construction sites in the United States), it also shows its positive uses: as a way to connect disenfranchised people and to preserve memories when humankind no longer has the capacity for memory. Rivera asks audiences to hold side by side in their minds these two uses and outcomes. Additionally, as Cordelia Barrera astutely points out, the film works as audiovisual, politicized, witnessed narrative (or *testimonio*) that critiques "a world in which the masculinist gendering of technology threatens individual and collective identity"; for Barrera, it is a film that reveals "broader ideas of environmental racism and issues of social justice on the borderlands."[9] And for Christopher González it is a film that repurposes mainstream sci-fi tropes (virtual technology and body-to-computer interfaces) to "highlight ethical concerns of the undocumented and immigrant labor force in the United States." González notes that Rivera uses, then abuses, the sci-fi genre to create a story about the "the erasure of a willful body and the preeminence of a machine-like mentality—a mechanized consciousness that places the labor value of one's self above all else," and that this erasure "is not simply a sci-fi device."[10]

When a director like Rivera chooses to use the sci-fi storytelling envelope to shape his filmic stories, he is making a decision to participate in a format that can (by convention) take audiences into new worlds with new social relations and new sets of emotion and thought systems. While the potentiality is there, because of the cost of the kind of technologies (computer-generated imagery, green screen, etc.) that allow for this future-set immersion, we have seen few Latinos filmmakers creating in this area. Yet as Rivera shows (and as we have seen in less expensive storytelling modes, such as comic books and alphabetic literature created by Latinos), sci-fi can be an immensely generative space for Latino creators. It can offer, as Catherine Ramírez sums up, a means for exploring "the ways that new and everyday technologies, including their detritus, transform [Latino] life and culture," questioning "the promises of science, technology, and humanism for [Latinos] and people of color" and offering a way to see in a new light "colonial and postcolonial histories of indigenismo, mestizaje, hegemony, and survival."[11] And for Fabio Chee, not only does the genre and its focus on "aliens" resonate powerfully with Latinos, but its construction of hybrid human/machine characters allows us to imagine the hybridity of Latino-ness as an affirming, ontological state that resists restrictive ways of being in the world.[12]

Before wrapping up this introductory overview of Rivera's vision and work, let me mention briefly another of his non-sci-fi creations that rounds out a total sense of his *transfrontera*-Latinx aesthetic: music videos. Rivera has directed several activist-based music videos grown out of his work with the National Day Laborer Organizing Network and the National Immigrant Youth Alliance. The videos variously feature the banda, soul, and rock lyrics and sounds of musicians hailing from all parts of the Americas, like Aloe Blacc, Manu Chao, La Santa Cecilia, and Ana Tijoux. Yet they do so as a palimpsestic overlay to visuals that depict the struggles of real-life day laborers, activists, and family members of deported immigrants. In her analysis of two such music videos, "El Hielo (ICE)" and "Wake Me Up," Rebecca Schreiber demonstrates how Rivera's careful camerawork and point-of-view lensing and editing visually convey the subjectivity of "migrant apprehension and its effects on the everyday lives of undocumented Latina/os."[13] That is, Rivera uses filmic visual shaping devices to create a camera presence that travels *with* the migrant workers, and not one that looks and judges from above or afar. So while at first viewing one might think of these as conventional music videos, on second look, the auditory (music and lyrics) creates a contrapuntal play with the visuals of everyday life for Latinos surviving at the edges of society. Rivera asks his audience to carry both sights and sounds in mind. He asks us to see the ways in which musical lyrics and sounds by activist artists like Manu Chao and Tijoux can intensify but not sentimentalize understanding of the undocumented, detained, and deported.

As Rivera discusses in this interview, his work is sustained by cultural and intellectual spaces, such as universities and museums: from the Guggenheim Museum, the Museum of Modern Art, and Lincoln Center to university campuses that have exhibited, screened, and featured him as a speaker. And yet, Rivera's savvy use of technology (film, music video, the internet, and much more) has ensured that his independent vision and work breathe air beyond these spaces. Indeed, as this interview attests, Rivera is very much a *transfrontera*-Latinx creator who seeks to overcome obstacles to create works that reach the *many* by constantly repurposing and making new, alternate means of dissemination. He's a *transfrontera*-Latinx creator who seeks to open eyes and ears to those draconian laws and inhuman actions that show us the darker side of what it means to be Latino in the United States. He's a *transfrontera*-Latinx creator who shows us how mindful creations can be artful and transformative. In all his work, Alex Rivera invites us—*urges* us—to imagine ourselves in a tomorrow—and the ways we can actively transform this tomorrow to be better and more humane than today.

FREDERICK LUIS ALDAMA: When did this impulse grow in you to want to become a film director—an activist-creator, or *artivist*, if you will?

ALEX RIVERA: When I was fourteen years old, I volunteered to do environmental work on the Hudson River for the Clearwater organization. I met its founder, Pete Seeger. At the time I had no idea who he was, but soon learned of the many ways that he was able to do political and social activism through the making of culture, specifically as a folk musician.

As an undergraduate at Hampshire College in the 1990s, I asked myself, How would an artist like Seeger be an activist today? It wouldn't be picking up the banjo. It would be to harness the power of the media. So I took a lot of classes about the relationship of media and power. And I became increasingly interested in telling stories through the audiovisual medium that could intervene in the world and open up new spaces in the political imaginaries.

I still don't identify as an activist. I have partnered with activist organizations. I hope that the work I create says something provocative and useful about the world. I distinguish between my work that seeks to provoke thought and dialogue to expand the imagination of what is possible *from* on-the-ground, tactile, and tactical activism and organizing of people to push against targets of oppression. The media I do is a *piece* of it, but it's not the same as real bodies in the street.

FLA: While at Hampshire, instead of writing a term paper, you created the film *Papapapá*, where you use the audiovisual devices of film to give shape to your father's story as a Latino *and* the pre-Columbian history of the potato. In many ways, this first film presents an Alex Rivera worldview that seems to have sustained a continuous line through the rest of your film work.

AR: First films are special, creatively and experientially. You're working in multiple vortexes. You have no option but to do something wildly creative. I made *Papapapá* in the mid-nineties. This was riding a wave of enthusiasm for autobiographical documentaries—especially from filmmakers coming from socioeconomic, ethnic, racial, gender margins. There was Michael Moore's chronicling of the material and emotional effects the closing of auto plants had on his family and community in *Roger and Me* [1989]. There was Marlon Riggs doing creating work about being black and queer with *Tongues Untied* [1989]. There was Lourdes Portillo making films about her family and Mexican mysteries and rituals, such as seen in *La Ofrenda: The Days of the Dead* [1988], *Mirrors of the Heart* [1993] and *The Devil Never Sleeps/El diablo nunca duerme* [1994].

I was living in the middle of this renaissance of first-person filmmaking from the margins. It was a form that appealed to me. It was a way of filmmaking that I wanted to actively help shape. So I turned the lens on my own family—specifically focusing in on my dad's journey to the U.S. His wasn't the classic immigration story. His was not a story of immigration that many in our community experienced. It wasn't the story of the brutal awakening of starry-eyed Latino looking for streets of gold and who finds an American *nightmare*, as dramatized in Robert M. Young's *Alambrista* [1977] or Gregory Nava's *El Norte* [1983]. On the one hand, my dad came from the middle class and, once in the U.S., found the American dream materially. On the other hand, there was something missing in his life: a longing for home and language left behind. The TV network Univision became his lifeline to Peru. He'd jack in for six to eight hours of Univision a day. I wanted to capture this in my film—a film that would reflect on those complexities of identity, nostalgia, transborder life that I saw in my dad's lived experience.

FLA: You choose to bring a certain levity, and you give a TV-like shape to *Papapapá*.

AR: I didn't want to convey that his sense of loss was tragic. And I chose to use the form of channel surfing itself so that *Papapapá* would also offer a self-aware, critical reflection on the way we interface with TV and how it becomes a fragmented mediation of reality.

FLA: In your films you seek ways to capture stories like your father's, where Latinos exist *across* cultural and national spaces. For instance, in your documentary *The Sixth Section* [2003], you tell the story of those Latinos that formed Grupo Unión in New York to send money back to Mexico to rebuild the town they left behind. You tell the story of those who create twinned communities that transcend national borders.

AR: In *Papapapá*, *The Sixth Section*, and my films since, you'll see a deep interest in telling the stories of cross-border life and transnationality in the way that Latino immigrants use technology to mediate distance and divisions.

FLA: You've taken advantage of the advances made in filmmaking technology, as with your use of digital imaging to create your stories, and also to clear the space for imagining how we might transform the world tomorrow.

AR: When I began making films in the mid-nineties, digital imaging was widely accessible. It allowed me to explore thematically questions of technology and borders, connectivity and distance. And it allowed me to shape and texture the films themselves. For instance, to visualize this idea of my dad inhabiting a mental borderland *suspended* across North and South America, I used digital imaging in *Papapapá* to visualize a third space that I identify as Virtual Lima in the film; the computer graphics allowed me to share with viewers of the film this imaginary in-between place of my father's suspended identity.

From this moment onwards, I've used digital imaging in my filmmaking for audiences to be able to visualize these liminal spaces and experiences that immigrants and many others embody; after all, we are all just transitory visitors on this planet as we move from light and life to disappearance. I choose to give shape to these liminal spaces as experienced to hyperbolic degrees by Latinos. We're constantly told to be *present* and yet simultaneously told to be *absent*; we are told to exist in one culture and language, and yet we exist within and across languages and cultures.

My films focus on Latinos who live in this kind of vortex or transitional space. And this is a space that can be most accurately visualized through the digital toolbox of morphing and compositing a virtual reality to express how we are a composited, morphed, virtual people. This is to say that for me the digital and visual tool set is really appropriate to describe our experience.

FLA: You're self-trained as a filmmaker.

AR: I've always worked with and learned from my fellow creator friends: musicians, three-D computer graphic programmers, and cinematographers. While I never studied film language deliberately in film school, say, I did study with the Marxist media theorist and experimental video filmmaker Norman Cowie. At Hampshire College I studied media theory, but not film production.

FLA: Elsewhere you mention the influence of films such as *Star Wars*, *Blade Runner*, and *El Norte*. Were there other creators that made you think, Wow, this is someone who has given radical new shape to an experience in ways that opened my eyes, thoughts, and feelings to the world in new ways?

AR: I mentioned Lourdes Portillo and Marlon Riggs already, but to these I would add many of the other pioneering media artists like performance artist Guillermo Gómez-Peña and experimental filmmaker Craig Baldwin. These are all very different artists, but all of them working in spaces that were politically charged, and that were treating the medium itself with reckless abandon, making visual texts that were simultaneously archival and science fictional, all while using elements that were staged to tell a documentary story. They were artists that were very aggressively experimenting with the form and crossing the wires on these circuits in ways that, in theory, you're not supposed to. I love that work. And while there's a lot of really wonderful art being made, I miss the direct attack on form that happens in these artists' work.

Inspired by these artists, you see in my career broadly the mixing, matching, sampling of fiction, science fiction, and documentary. I've never been faithful to any one medium. I'm drawn to the collage.

FLA: Isn't it risky to work within and across genres and mediums—especially as a Latino director, where there's a certain expectation that you should tell the *El Norte* immigrant story, for instance?

AR: I definitely have Latino filmmaker colleagues who react to the expectations that they should tell Latino stories by pushing back and rejecting it. They experience this as a constraint and reject it. I understand that impulse, because when we enter into this creative space of filmic storytelling, we want to feel free to create what we want. But I think that there is no way to escape history and identity in our world. You can't make a film and tell a story without confronting questions of race, and gender, and all those histories that surround our bodies. You can't escape it.

What I've been doing is reconstructing in film some of those parts that make up the whole of the Latino experience. A big part of the recent Latino story is the immigrant experience. And while I've chosen to reconstruct this experience, I do so in ways that also seek to profoundly mess with any preconceptions. For instance, in *Sleep Dealer* I focus on the impulse toward alienation that is inherent in the system of immigration: wanting work without the physical presence of brown bodies. I use the figure of the robot as a worker without a soul and body as an exemplary, glowing, incandescent distillation of this impulse.

I identify as a Latino filmmaker. I play in the sandbox of expected thematics and questions. But once inside that sandbox, I blow it up so as to take us to places that we've never gone before.

FLA: This must be at once emancipating and deeply challenging.

AR: In the U.S. we're trapped inside identities like Latino, but if you pretend they don't exist, you end up reinscribing them. The only way to escape them is to engage with them and *mess* with them. It's this approach that's allowed me to find a creative freedom—and joy in creating.

FLA: You have a tremendous amount of experience with different modes of production and distribution, from documentaries and music videos to feature film. I know that you had difficulties with Maya Entertainment, the original distributor of *Sleep Dealer.* Is your work reaching its respective audiences?

AR: I don't think *Sleep Dealer* has ever fully found its audience. When distributing a Latino-created film, you're dealing with many vectors of the imaginary and of expectation. This becomes even more layered and complex when you break new ground. There hadn't been a science fiction film by and about Latinos. So when *Sleep Dealer* arrived, there were no models in place for it to reach its audiences. Some missteps were made in investment in and placement of advertisements, when and where to open the film, and on how many screens. It didn't do well when it was first released.

Fortunately, *Sleep Dealer* had a really strong festival run. And teachers, professors, and scholars across the country have studied and taught the film, keeping it alive now for over ten years. It's these two communities that form the beating heart of the film's distribution. It did well in festivals, and it's done well in academia.

Sleep Dealer's a film that's infected the discourse and impacted the dialogue in some weird and interesting ways, and we're now working on a TV series based on the ideas of the film. If this becomes a reality, then the ideas of the film will reach a big and broad and pop audience finally. It's Latino themed, but it's a genre picture with big ideas, so it could have as big an audience as *The Matrix* or *Star Wars*. In the African American cultural production system we see countless examples of black culture that become broad American culture and then world culture. There's no reason why this piece of Latino culture could not do the same. It just needs to be produced and handled the right way. I'm optimistic.

FLA: With *Sleep Dealer*, why did you choose to give a science fiction shape to a story of migration, exploitation, material division of Mexico from the U.S. with a gigantic wall?

AR: There's no reason why *not* to use the science fiction genre to tell the story of today. When you work in the abstracted language of the science fictional, where you have the scripted, acted, and performed in an imaginatively limitless way, the story of today can and does take on additional wonderful resonances that take audiences beyond our *today*. When you're working in the language of science fiction, you can create an altered state or a different reality. It lets you take impulses that are normal and natural and make them strange and alien. It can feed audiences' feverish, ravenous hunger, all while intensifying their understanding of exploitive, *alienating* labor relations that have become *naturalized* as commonplace human interaction and practice today. And, once taken into the world of science fiction, where you can exaggerate these exchanges and where employees are now cybernetically plugged-in remote Latino workers, they become very surreal and worthy of contemplation and wonder.

Science fiction has a great power and potential to take the world that seems natural and normal around us and make it absurd and unstable. That's very hard to do in the documentary language or in the journalistic mode. You can tell what *is* through documentary and journalism, but through fiction and especially science fiction you can talk about what *might be* or what *could be*. Science fiction allows you to denaturalize what *is*.

FLA: Elsewhere you say, "We need visions of the future that reflect our multicultural planet. We need thoughtful science fiction more than ever." And you add, "If we can't imagine it, how can we participate in it?"[14]

AR: There are so many different vectors that go into all of these considerations. One vector is around the question of social justice and participation, especially as it relates to formerly excluded, formerly colonized, formerly enslaved, or dispossessed groups. If we take the example of the Latino community, we see that there's been some headway made in terms of participation in literature, in the visual arts, but not in TV and film. In fact, the more expensive the art form, the less people of color you see in it. Our numbers of participation in the production of film and TV are miserably low. Currently in Hollywood, studio films are written and directed by about two percent of Latinos in a city [Los Angeles] that is over fifty percent Latino. So it's really not a question of needing more diversity, the excuse often given by the establishment. It's a question of justice and the fact that the Hollywood film industry is governed by a neoapartheid system that locks us out.

To participate in filmic storytelling we *do* need to be inside that storytelling space of talking about the future. It's this science fictional space that's uniquely powerful. It's a space of dreams and nightmares. Formerly colonized people and marginalized people need to be actively diving into this space to describe *our* dreams and our nightmares. There's a small subset of filmmakers of color who get into storytelling and filmmaking to challenge history's exclusion *and* expand our imagination. But I don't want these filmmakers to only make documentaries or neorealist dramas because they think these are the only ways to confront political injustices. I want to see these filmmakers who have that kind of social and political awareness making the next *Avatar* or the next *Star Wars*. I want to see filmmakers who come into the game with an awareness of colonialism and racism and to struggle to overcome it, and to make the next science fiction blockbuster.

FLA: Other Latino filmmakers, like Robert Rodriguez [*Planet Terror*, 2007] and Guillermo del Toro [*Pacific Rim*, 2013], have chosen the science fiction format to tell their stories.

AR: Robert Rodriguez is a masterful repurposer of core Latino aesthetics and Latino story frames that elevates the B-flick genre. And while del Toro doesn't engage as directly with U.S. Latino themes, nonetheless, you feel the Mexican-ness of his films radiating through his scripts and characterizations. Rodriguez and Del Toro are filmmakers who have an awareness of their identity, of their place inside history. They give innovative, aesthetic shape to their histories, experiences, and memories in ways that refresh, reinvigorate, and expand what we might think of as mainstream cinema.

FLA: In your films, you at once drive hard at giving shape to localized experiences *and* move toward the global.

AR: Everything that is universal today began as something local and particular yesterday. Everything that is mainstream was also once ethnic or racially particular. George Lucas's very particular and local experience as a farm boy growing up in central California is very specific to him, his family, and his views. But these get baked into *Star Wars* and become a kind of universal myth. There's no reason why Latino experiences, our history and memories and our aesthetics, could not also feed into cultural work that could become the next mainstream.

FLA: You also make music videos—a filmmaking art where the visuals traditionally have been used to intensify the music and lyrics, and not to detract or distract. However, we see in your work, such as "Wake Me Up," that the visuals of Latino laborers and deported family members are just as important as the music.

AR: In terms of the music, they were all made in collaboration with an actual activist group, the National Day Labor Organizing Network, that has over twenty thousand day-labor members across the nation. They were one of the groups on the front lines in fighting SB 1070—the harsh anti-immigrant law in Arizona. During this struggle, I met them with other artists, to see what we could do in solidarity in this struggle. We decided to take a song we could give new meaning to through attaching visuals to it. We've done five now. The ones that I think have worked most powerfully are ones where we script a story to accompany the song, and the story gets acted out like a fictional film by actors, and that story runs parallel to the song.

FLA: Where do you come up with the stories that you attach to the songs?

AR: From real, everyday people's lives and life stories. I would write a story based on what I heard. Then I would ask members of the group to perform the story and create a document. These collaboratively created pieces are at once documentaries, true stories embodied by the people who lived it, [and] fictional, crafted and intentional, and yet still music videos. They circulate in systems of music video circulation, such as YouTube and MTV.

My creating of these music videos returns us to the beginning of our conversation and my discussion of Pete Seeger's influence and how songs—purposive culture generally—can challenge and uplift people. I see these collaboratively made music videos as working within this performative and mediative space. I've returned to those roots, but as firmly planted in the twenty-first century.

Notes

1 Mark Engler, "Science Fiction from Below: Alex Rivera, Director of the New Film Sleep Dealer, Imagines the Future of the Global South," Foreign Policy In Focus, http://fpif.org/science_fiction_from_below/.

2 See Alex Rivera, "Installations," http://alexrivera.com/installations; and Alex Rivera, LowDrone: The Transnational Hopper, http://www.lowdrone.com.

3 Rivera, LowDrone website.

4 Amy Sara Carroll, "From *Papapapá* to *Sleep Dealer*: Alex Rivera's Undocumentary Poetics," *Social Identities* 19, nos. 3–4 (2013): 477.

5 Ibid.

6 Ibid., 489.

7 See Matthew Goodwin, "The Technology of Labor, Migration, and Protest," in *The Routledge Companion to Latina/o Pop Culture*, ed. Frederick Luis Aldama (New York: Routledge, 2016), 120–128.

8 Alex Rivera, Cybracero Systems, http://cybracero.com/.

9 Cordelia Barrera, "Cyborg Bodies, Strategies of Consciousness, and Ecological Revolution on the US-Mexico Borderlands," *Chicana/Latina Studies: The Journal of Mujeres Activas en Letras y Cambio Social* 14, no. 1 (2014): 28, 51.

10 Christopher González, "Latino Sci-Fi: Cognition and Narrative Design in Alex Rivera's *Sleep Dealer*," in *Latinos and Narrative Media: Participation and Portrayal*, ed. Frederick Luis Aldama (New York: Palgrave Macmillan, 2013), 223.

11 Catherine Ramírez, "Afrofuturism/Chicanafuturism: Fictive Kin," *Aztlán* 33, no. 1 (2008): 187.

12 Fabio Chee, "Science Fiction and Latino Studies Today . . . and in the Future," in *The Routledge Companion to Latina/o Pop Culture*, ed. Frederick Luis Aldama (New York: Routledge, 2016), 115.

13 Rebecca M. Schrieber, "The Undocumented Everyday: Migrant Rights and Visual Strategies in the Work of Alex Rivera," *Journal of American Studies* 50, no. 2 (2016): 306.

14 "Alex Rivera speaking at Platform Summit 2014," *YouTube*, https://www.youtube.com/watch?v=eHPsmfLdiUs.

10

No-Man's-Land

Shifting Borders and Alternating Identities in Contemporary Israeli Cinema

ANAT ZANGER AND NURITH GERTZ

Fifty years into its occupation of Palestinian territories, Israel has become split within and between borders, cease-fire lines, checkpoints, and walls. Its borders are inscribed in two modes: the first includes demarcated and visible borders of the transference zone, and the second is characterized by invisible yet present borders that have been adopted and internalized. In the national sphere, those borders reflect the perception of a unified society that is enclosed within them—a perception based on harmony between territory, people, family, and army: four elements, each of which represents the others. The prevailing discourse strives to preserve that national unity in the face of external threats, the memory of past traumas, and the danger of anticipated traumas. The stronger the threat to Israeli society and the more powerful the traumas, both past and future, the stronger and more prevalent becomes the myth of a homogeneous Israeli identity, fortified behind borders separating it from Palestinian identity. Yet it is an imagined unity and harmony, and individuals under its patronage cannot merge into and become part of it. Its inherent cracks incessantly expose the national collective in all its weakness. Thus the "separating" border and the "permeable" border are interwoven daily in spheres affecting history, strategy planning, and public consciousness, reflected in a worldview that is implemented in Israel's foreign and domestic policies alike. Adriana Kemp has described this vacillating attitude toward the border as one that bears a "Janus face."[1] The melding of demarcated boundaries and blurred ones finds expression in the space of outlying regions—cease-fire lines and checkpoints.

Stefano Mezzadra and Brett Nielson describe this kind of space: different types of borders drawn in various ways by individuals and groups in transition and in a continual state of change, subdividing and reorganizing space.[2] Such borders enable flow in certain places and blockage in others; they are mobile, elastic, and continually being redrawn. As we shall see, the case of Israel suggests a more specific complexity to this fluidity of borders and relationships between the real and the imagined. The Israeli borders, cease-fire lines, walls, and multiple checkpoints in the occupied territories are far from rigid and fixed, and are rather in constant formation; as Eyal Weizman observes, "a highly elastic political space is often more dangerous and deadly than a static, rigid one."[3]

Giorgio Agamben's "state of exception" frames the occupation as an ongoing process, with no end in sight.[4] This process requires political and military praxes of closure, along with the designation of closed military zones, sterile zones, and firing zones. The state of exception is manifested on one hand by the border's elasticity, and on the other by an increasing need to demarcate borders. Any ethical foundation is abandoned, and the law's flimsiness throughout society's various strata is reflected in the assorted monitoring, regulatory, and enforcement agencies. In this state, considered a "state of emergency" (a term coined by Carl Schmitt),[5] the value of the lives of subjects in democratic countries is abandoned in favor of the rule of law, becoming what Agamben calls "bare life." In a state of emergency, the regime suspends the law, so that its nonimplementation is the primary manifestation of its authority. In other words, this exception is outside the whole to which it belongs, and yet in which it is still included; it is thus located both outside the law and within it, living a bare life. These subjects live in a no-man's-land, where the law that includes does not protect and the rule of law does not apply.

In this chapter we examine how the blurring of borders produces the state of exception that manifests in various spaces: a bus station (*Death in the Terminal* [Mavet Be-Beer Sheva], 2016), the city of Modi'in Illit, located on the border near outlying Palestinian villages (*Beyond the Mountains and Hills* [Me'Ever Laharim Vehagvaot], 2015); a Jerusalem neighborhood separated by a checkpoint from a Palestinian village (*Self Made* [Boreg], 2014); and East and West Jerusalem (*AKA Nadia* [Nadia Shem Zmani], 2015). What all these works have in common is the way in which the no-man's-land between them—which Agamben calls "the camp," Edward Soja calls the "thirdspace," and Gloria Anzaldúa calls the "borderlands"—becomes dominant and suggests a world outside the law, as well as how the films depict borders being drawn, traversed, and violated.[6]

While depicting, traversing, and violating national and familial borders, these films describe a state of abandonment. They present that state, however, as having an inherent possibility for coexistence within borders that separate communities but also conjoin them, that allow for a different relationship between the "singular" and the "plural," to use Jean-Luc Nancy's terms.[7] These films show the multiplicity of borders as a basis for another existence of individuals who have not assimilated into the collective but instead preserve their independence and the option to move between and within communities and groups, thus expressing various facets of their identity, positing an alternative option for a postnational society.

The first part of this chapter examines Shira Geffen's *Self Made* (2014) and Tova Ascher's *AKA Nadia* (2015), which offer fantasies of switched identities and express at the same time a fervent desire for open borders and a fear of them. The chapter's second part examines Eran Kolirin's *Beyond the Mountains and Hills* (2015), which offers a snapshot of contemporary Israel wherein the borders are crossed and the law loses its validity. The final section focuses on Tali Shemesh and Asaf Sudry's *Death in the Terminal* (2016), in which the border built by the national discourse is replaced by a network of borders that traverse identities and link them. This creates cracks in the national unity that is (presumably) built into national borders, suggesting the option for different relationships that are ethical instead of national. As we show, each of these films simultaneously proposes its own alternative to the matter of borders—overlapping, connecting, or disconnecting[8]—while also challenging them.

Fearing and Embracing Open Borders: *Self Made* and *AKA Nadia*

Following Henri Lefebvre, it can be said that Israeli space is in a process of "constant production" or "becoming."[9] From Israel's founding until the present, the relationship between the border and the Israeli collective consciousness has undergone changes. At the same time, the attitude toward the border is always ambivalent, and is never at peace with itself. The "separating" border and the "permeable" border are interwoven daily in spheres affecting history, strategic planning, and public consciousness, reflected in the worldview that is implemented in Israel's foreign and domestic policies. Kemp has described this vacillating attitude toward the border as one with a "Janus face"; however, living in a state where "a line is not a line and a border is not a border"[10] gave rise to a growing need for separating Israelis from Palestinians.[11] At the same time, we can point to a change that has occurred in the collective consciousness and is reflected in Israeli cinema.

Contemporary Israeli cinema focuses on the impossibility of executing this separation, and the cumulative effect of living under "exceptional circumstances" on both sides of the border.[12] Thus, in this cinema we find what Homi K. Bhabha describes as narratives of displacement, dislocation, and exile, in which the distinction has become blurred between the border as a public space of liminality where the "self" faces the "other," and the home as the subject's private space.[13]

Accordingly, we now focus on two films: *Self Made* and *AKA Nadia*, in both of which the checkpoint plays a prominent role. In addition, in both films the checkpoint is situated in a space between "ours" and "theirs," as a facility whose main function is to identify, distinguish, and regulate, thereby presenting the border as a physical manifestation. Yet both films depict the checkpoint's failure to create that separation, offering hybridity as an alternative and, furthermore, the protean borders in the films shift, taking charge of the domestic and familial space as well, and bringing about its disintegration.

The cinematic space of *Self Made* stretches from both sides of the Green Line, from the Jerusalem neighborhood of Ein Kerem, where Israeli artist Michal resides, to Etaca, a furniture manufacturing plant outside Jerusalem, where the Palestinian Nadine works. While the two women seemingly occupy separate worlds, the film links them by means of the protagonists' respective acts in the space, as well as via trucks bearing the name "Etaca" that deliver the company's products from the plant to Jerusalem. The film simultaneously depicts the separate lives of Michal (who suffers from short-term memory loss) and Nadine until their meeting at the checkpoint and the exchange between them. The name Etaca—echoing Ithaka, the place to which Homer's Ulysses longed to return—is a goal as well as a journey. Ithaka, then, is a path symbolizing human inability to return to the same place of the past. While Ulysses extends his stay longer and longer, the two female protagonists in *Self Made* travel to Ithaka and back.

The paths of the two women cross, diverge, and cross again as their identities are switched. When Michal the Jewish Israeli loses her memory, is it her subconscious will that leads her to Ithaka? When Nadine the Palestinian is brought to Michal's house in a West Jerusalem neighborhood that was originally inhabited by the Arab population, is this not her home as much as it is Michal's? The film raises questions regarding what Ithaka is, where home is, and under what conditions they might exist when the path from home to Ithaka passes through a checkpoint.

Hannah Arendt's distinction regarding relationships between the wall and the border are significant for us in the analysis of how these relationships are drawn in *Self Made*, as well as in contemporary Israeli cinema in general.

According to Arendt, "The political realm is guaranteed by two kinds of walls: the wall surrounding the city which defines the zone of the political, and the walls separating private space from the public domain, ensuring the autonomy of the domestic realm."[14] Internal and external borders are crossed several times in *Self Made*, as the public space invades the private. While Michal tries to organize her thoughts and get dressed, or assemble her new Etaca bed, a team of journalists surprises her when they come to interview and photograph her for a German magazine feature on influential women. She does not remember who she is and asks them to leave, but the journalists insist on interviewing her "to clarify the meaning of her art." Meanwhile, the Etaca workers also go in and out of Michal's house at will: they deliver the bed, then bring another bed in its place, all while Michal walks around wrapped in a towel. The chef who arrives bearing prawns ordered by her husband to celebrate their anniversary bursts into the bathroom, and the Skype session with Michal's husband invades the domestic space and with it various other spaces and times. When Nadine enters Michal's house, the journalism team returns; Michal's husband is Skyping her, and neither the journalists nor her husband realizes that she is not Michal, but rather Nadine. The fluidity of the national border thus invades the narrowing distance between home and outside, between one subject and another.

The border is present in the film metonymically, by means of the checkpoint situated in an isolated area. It consists of a booth staffed by soldiers, humming with fences, queues, ID procedures, monitoring, and checking—except that, instead of dividing, it produces "enclaves of hybridity" that constitute meeting points between the two nations. Nadine crosses through the checkpoint daily on her way to work at Etaca. When she seeks to visit her aunt abroad, she is detained. Michal, for her part, goes to see her own art exhibit in order to try and jog her memory, and from there ends up at the same separating wall that she has depicted in her art, and then at the checkpoint. Thus both women are detained at the checkpoint. Michal wraps a scarf around her face, thereby "passing" as a Palestinian. Due to the identity error, a soldier accompanies Nadine to Michal's house, while another soldier sends Michal in the opposite direction, into Palestinian territory. The film thus indicates the failure of both the checkpoint and its checking and sorting mechanisms. Anzaldúa's words in the context of borders and women—who are always on the road and are torn between two borders—take on a local interpretation here: "I, a *mestiza*, continually walk out of one culture and into another, because I am in all cultures at the same time."[15] Thus the checkpoint that is supposed to divide the Palestinian from the Israeli contains the simultaneous duality of both separation and blending.

Over the course of the film the relationship between Michal and Nadine is built upon both contradiction and completion: while each has her path, toward the film's end, the switch occurs, with Michal continuing on Nadine's path, and vice versa. When Michal's bed breaks, the self-assembly Etaca bed that she ordered arrives missing a screw, which is what leads her to Nadine. The path that Nadine walks daily from the checkpoint to work is littered with screws, which she sprinkles on the ground like breadcrumbs to help her find her way. In contrast, Michal has lost her memory following an elective hysterectomy, which she documented in her art. Concerned over losing her grip on reality, she collects scraps of information to orient herself—letters, her works in progress, her exhibitions, and the media are all clues to navigate her path. Michal described her artwork thus: "I collect what others throw away. I remember what they forget." But now it is Nadine who collects what Michal has left behind. Toward the end of the film, Michal unwittingly crosses the border into Palestinian National Authority land, wearing an explosive vest, and it is Nadine who presents Michal's story—which was originally hers.

The first time the magazine crew arrives, Michal is unable to tell her story, incapable of giving the interview in Arabic, despite having claimed she knows the language. The second time, when Nadine is the interviewee (although the crew identifies her as Michal), in fact only she, Nadine, can tell the story. The magazine interview sequence, which plays out twice, raises the same question that Trinh T. Min-Ha poses in the context of speech in the postcolonial world of exile: "Who speaks? What speaks?"[16] Thus *Self Made* questions who tells whose story. Who owns the house in Ein Kerem, and what will be the fate of the national narrative?

The checkpoint in *Self Made* actually reveals its failure to fulfill its declared task, and in the absence of a stable political border, the boundaries of the home and its walls are correspondingly weakened. In this sense, the film challenges Arendt's distinction between the walls surrounding a city and those demarcating the borders of a home that, like the walls encircling a city, transpire to be permeable.

The film *AKA Nadia* might be considered a sequel to *Self Made* in that it suggests how Nadine's life might have unfolded had she continued to assume Michal's identity. *AKA Nadia*'s protagonist is Palestinian Nadia, who leaves her village as a teenager to follow her lover, a Palestine Liberation Organization member, to the United Kingdom, where she goes underground. When the organization is uncovered, she is unable to return home to her Palestinian village and takes on the identity of a young Jewish woman who has died.

Two paths are laid out in *Self Made*, walked by each character who takes up where the other left off, echoing her footsteps until a random meeting between them at a checkpoint. There an identity error leads to their replacing one another. Conversely, in *AKA Nadia*, the story revolves around one woman—Nadia/Maya—with a dual identity: Maya is an esteemed Israeli choreographer residing in Jerusalem with her husband, Yoav, and they are parents of two grown children. She has severed all ties to her Palestinian past, except to her mother, whom she meets with rarely, always ensuring that she remains unseen. Nadia/Maya lives a fictional life that only her mother knows about. Twenty years later, her past is exposed and her fragile existence disintegrates. Because life would be equally intolerable for her in Palestine and in Israel, she flees to London, her city of refuge. The transparency of the filmic space can be misleading, but space, as perceived by Lefebvre, is always a "social" product.[17] In this sense, both films offer a fantasy of identity between the Israeli subject and the Palestinian subject, and at the same time, a narrative of displacement and dislocation points out the fear of fluid borders and the possibility of permeating them.

Against that backdrop are two significant elements found in both films: language and checkpoints. The first is a function in which Nadine the Palestinian in *Self-Made* "passes," like Nadia in *AKA Nadia*, as Israeli. In doing so Nadine refrains from talking: she's silent when she discerns the mistake made at the checkpoint, when a soldier apologizes to her and takes her to Ein Kerem and Michal's house. Thereafter Nadine makes no attempt to change her accent when speaking in Hebrew, the language of the occupier. She neither pretends nor denies her new identity, since the immediate environment identifies her as Michal. For her part, Michal no longer remembers who she is, and does not protest when the checkpoint personnel remove her to the "wrong" side of the checkpoint.

In contrast, in *AKA Nadia*, Nadia as a teenager persuades her lover to take her with him to Britain. She points out the fact that she knows Hebrew, suggesting that his organization can use her knowledge. Over time, as she takes on a Jewish identity, Nadia/Maya adopts Israeli mannerisms, inflection, and cultural references in order to hide her Palestinian identity. As Frantz Fanon has discerned, "To speak means . . . above all to assume a culture, to support the weight of a civilization."[18] Passing, therefore, is defined in *AKA Nadia* as borrowing an ethnic or national identity, whether by the character or the actors.[19]

There is a sequence that appears twice in *AKA Nadia*: the first time in the audio alone, and the second time in the visual channel as well. Yoav describes Maya to a friend as someone who never took an interest in politics. He recounts their first meeting at a party. While all the guests were engaged in an argument concerning the Israeli-Palestinian conflict, Maya was the only one who did not participate. She stood up abruptly, turned up the volume on the music, and started dancing alone. Yoav says that he was mesmerized, could not take his eyes off her, and he joined her dance. The effect of the incident from Yoav's point of view, given by his voice alone, emphasizes his interpretation of it as an emotional reaction on Maya's part to the conflict. Toward the film's end, after Yoav has discovered Maya's true identity, he refuses to come to terms with reality. Maya/Nadia closes all the windows and shuts herself in their bedroom just before leaving home once more. The party sequence is repeated, this time as Maya's flashback, in both the audial and visual channels. Here the dance is presented as a constituting moment that enables entry into the Israeli sociocultural fabric, bringing Maya's acceptance as an Israeli to completion. Moreover, the dance is offered as an alternative to the spoken word, one that has the potential to bring Israelis and Palestinians closer, but is ultimately rejected by the Israeli side.

The second element is the checkpoint as the site of sovereignty within the state of exception. In both *AKA Nadia* and *Self Made*, the checkpoint is situated between West Jerusalem and Palestinian villages on Jerusalem's outskirts. Its function as a mechanism of identification and regulation is suggested several times in *AKA Nadia*. Near the checkpoint, with the wall in the background, mother and daughter sit among the olive trees, eating food cooked by the mother and updating each other about family members whom Nadia left behind, and those whom the mother has never met and who have no idea of her existence. Nadia's mother speaks in Arabic, and Nadia answers her in Hebrew. Nadia's mother tongue positions her vis-à-vis the "language of the colonizer" that she is using. It emphasizes her split identity, and thus again Trinh's query is relevant here: "Who speaks? What speaks?"[20] In the two films we have examined here, the checkpoints and the separation walls serve as a screen projecting the repetitive movement between inside and outside, the domestic and the public space, feminine and national identities, and different languages.

Without a Border: *Beyond the Mountains and Hills*

In the opening shot of *Beyond the Mountains and Hills* we see a group of people, including soldiers, officers, and civilians—some friends, some family, some women, some men—standing at attention, looking at the camera. The performance of an Israel Defense Forces (IDF) entertainment troupe heard in the background lends the shot a military-nationalist hue, which is underscored as the camera pans over the protagonist alongside a picture of the Israeli flag. He raises a glass and toasts "Lehayim!" as the camera lingers on the entertainment troupe. It is a farewell party for David, a career IDF officer who's entering civilian life, and it embodies the desire for family, national, and military unity. This party reflects the perception of a unified society that is enclosed within its national borders, as the national emblems of the army and family reflect and represent each other. Yet the celebration and unity are violated by movements that cross the screen and the entire shot: a soldier crosses the screen from right to left; David's daughter Ifat crosses from left to right, looking gloomy and out of place; and another soldier, crying, stops at the front of the shot, blocking our view of the troupe. The scene presents Israeli society celebrating its unity, while in fact it remains torn, separated by borders both within and without. There is no visible border between the Israeli neighborhood and the Palestinian village. This is the "sieved space" as defined by Gilles Deleuze and Félix Guattari within which invasions, sorties, smugglings, arrests, and assassinations are carried out.[21] The crossover between the two locales is via a no-man's-land, as Agamben defined it—an unpopulated zone where conflicts, invasions, and desires surface.

The unstable and unmarked borders between Israelis and Palestinians reverberate and continue to be reflected in the blurring of the internal, ethical, and familial boundaries throughout Israeli society, discernible in what is essentially the fractured harmony in this depiction of the family, military, and nation. While it focuses on one Israeli family, the Greenbaums—father, mother, son, and daughter—*Beyond the Mountains and Hills* outlines the interaction between the blurring of a territorial border and the crossing of internal borders—filial and ethical boundaries. David, the father of the family, as well as his wife and daughter, are located between two differing orders: the rule of law and what lies beyond it. Thus the events in the film, like its main protagonists, fluctuate between the hegemonic order (of the army, the state, the family) and a new alternative one.

This enables our understanding of the two gazes noted in the opening scene: while David, the father who is celebrating, looks straight into the camera, Ifat's gaze wanders outside the frame. The tension between the two gazes expresses the struggle between the father who wishes to maintain the boundaries of the existing order, even if he cannot manage to do so, and the daughter who tries to dismantle them.

In the final scene, the Greenbaums are on their way to a concert by Shlomo Artzi, one of Israel's most popular performers. On the way, David runs a stop sign, and a police officer pulls him over. After checking David's license, instead of ticketing him, the cop tells him, "Next time, pay attention. Drive safely." What happened to the Greenbaums? Which boundaries did they cross, and where were they not paying attention? When one order ends and is not replaced by another one, a gap forms in which the known rules no longer apply. This is the state of exception where, on the one hand, events, values, and beliefs are not backed by the law, vested interests overtake sensitivity as trust is violated, and betrayals take place both within the family and outside it. On the other hand, this existence outside the law allows an exploration of ethical and moral possibilities that are not sanctioned by the law. It is in this state that the family continues to exist: in a subversion of the external border, and the existence of a no-man's-land in what lies beyond it, reflected by the family that represents Israeli society. The chief protagonists in *Beyond the Mountains and Hills* abandon the principles that guide their familiar fields of meaning—the national and the familial—as though they live where law and order do not reign, when in fact they seek an alternative beyond their borders.

Thus, one morning, David, who has not yet found his place in civilian society after many years of army service, and Ifat, a politically active teenager, are riding in their car. A member of the security forces stops them and reports that a Palestinian operative was shot last night in that very spot. Looking out the car window, David sees an ambulance on the road leading to their neighborhood, and recalls firing his gun into the darkness of no-man's-land the night before. He realizes that it was he who shot the Palestinian, but does not tell. Ifat is also looking out of the window, and sees the dead body. She recognizes it as Ayman, the young Palestinian she had been talking with near her home the night before.

The previous night, Ifat had wandered down the road leading from her neighborhood (one side of a barren, unlit hill) to the no-man's-land, the undeveloped space between her neighborhood and the other side of the hill where Arabic Palestinians live. In this no-man's-land, Ayman invited her to hang out with his friends—beyond the mountains and hills. Although she was curious, Ifat declined his invitation. One family, one event, and two different gazes: David never confesses to his crime, and Ifat does not tell him that she knew the victim. Later David cooperates with the police in order to distract them from the murder he committed. In his and her own ways, both father and daughter have crossed the border between Israel and occupied Palestinian territory. This transgression destabilizes the moral boundaries that have protected the family, creating a chasm between father and daughter, and later on, between husband and wife. And yet it is precisely this calling into question of boundaries that helps their attempts to realize moral, more humane, and authentic values.

In fact, all the protagonists in *Beyond the Mountains and Hills* are searching for a way across their borders. The mother crosses a border when she has an affair with her student; the father crosses a border when he accidentally shoots the Palestinian using his military weapon although he is now a civilian; the daughter crosses a border when she goes to visit that same Palestinian's family. Yet the acts that were supposed to reassure their ethical existence fail to fulfill this purpose. Ultimately, the protagonists who tried to breach the borders and boundaries are left in a no-man's-land, a place of ethical chaos, where intersubjectivity becomes inhuman: the pupil with whom the mother had an affair betrays her; when Ifat goes to Ayman's widow to offer her condolences, the widow orders her out of her home; and the father, who had tried to integrate into civilian life, is left guilty of murder. All three protagonists cross boundaries to experience what they never found within the borders—love, justice, humanity, and friendship. They fail to find them—within their own borders and outside them as well.

Beyond the Mountains and Hills ends with a shot that echoes its opening. David forgives his wife: "No one can convince me that we're bad people," he tells her after she confesses her affair to him. The family reunites, and they drive off to a concert. The police officer who stopped them on the way lets them off with a warning, and the camera rises skyward, then descends sharply into an amphitheater. The family is seated together, swaying and singing along with the music, looking at one another, embodying the unity shown in the opening scene. In the background we hear the voice of Shlomo Artzi, a symbol of the hegemonic "consensus" that "unites" Israelis, singing a song that promises life and love "after the war." Again, like the opening scene, something clouds the cohesion and solidarity: this time it is Ifat's look, wandering away, out of the theater, beyond the screen.

The family is seemingly reunited into the consensus, swept by the false promise of peace that the song offers. Once more, as in the opening scene, this same consensus is perturbed by Ifat's gaze, which stares ahead into what is invisible to our own eyes. Is she reminded of her attempt to help the Palestinian family in hope of answering her own moral calling, and that attempt's failure? Does she realize she was a pawn not just in Ayman's hands but in those of the Israeli security forces? Does she understand that there is no hope of life beyond the boundaries and confines of the nation?

Reframing Israeli Border: *Death in the Terminal*

On October 18, 2015, an armed terrorist entered the Beersheba bus station, shot and killed a soldier, seized the soldier's rifle and, after a gun battle, was shot by security forces. This is the premise of the film *Death in the Terminal*. The event, which occurred at the height of the "knife intifada" after a series of previous attacks, added another link to Israeli society's "chain of trauma." The media exacerbated the trauma by reporting on the attack over and over, each report containing more details on what preceded the attack (the terrorist's recruitment by Hamas, his preparations for the attack) and what occurred in its wake (arrests, reports on the wounded, interviews, testimonies). The story of these events was repeated across newspapers and news sites, ramping up the fear stemming from past traumas as well as those inevitably to come. As usual, the relentless reporting exacerbated Israeli society's post-trauma acting out, without the ability to process it, overcome it, or comprehend the present that replays the past and will be replayed in the future.[22]

The reports of the Beersheba attack demonstrate well the national rhetoric that has taken root in Israeli discourse over recent years. It ignores the fluid borders spidering out over Israeli space and tries to strengthen the national borders of that space, all the while condemning and sidelining anyone deviating from such discourse. Thus it produces an appearance of an intact, unified society confronting a common enemy. These national borders are viewed through the lens of the relentless media, which make sure to show the terrorist over and over alongside the victims, who unify around the various choices: to escape, to protect oneself, to offer help, or to attack back. In *Death in the Terminal* Tali Shemesh and Asaf Sudry document the attack using the same security camera footage that the media used, yet they deliberately blur the borders demarcated by the media between Arabs and Jews, and in their place build other borders—internal, changing, and fluid. These are the borders described and defined by Mezzadra and Nielson, as well as by Nancy.

From the outset, *Death in the Terminal* shrinks the borders of the event in time and space, ignoring what preceded and followed it and, using the security camera footage, focusing solely on what happened at the bus station. Within the borders of the station, the film skips over the terrorist, the shots fired, and the ensuing pandemonium and instead focuses on a single scene: the site of the lynching of an Eritrean migrant who was mistaken by the mob for the terrorist. Thus the entire story, which unfolds over three discrete time periods, as well as the entire space of the bus station, are replaced by a single scene of a single event compressed into limited temporal and spatial borders. Here the "headline event" is upstaged by an event that stemmed from it and was considered merely "a sidebar": the killing of the Eritrean migrant.[23] It is precisely here, inside the shrunken cinematic frame, that the "solid" border dividing Arabs and Jews, and a terrorist and his victims, is blurred and replaced with other borders that separate various human choices: good or evil, empathy or violence.

The editing of the footage reflects the development of the story: the film opens with a shot looking into the entrance of the bus station, cutting to the station corridor, finally resting on the site of the lynching. The director chooses to focus on seven characters, among them an Arab worker, an Eritrean who was a relative of the lynching victim, and five Jews, one a soldier who ran for cover in the restroom and another a nursing student who at first took cover and hid, then later came out of hiding to offer aid to the wounded.

The footage shows the nursing student bending over an injured person and treating him, and in the interview intercut with the footage, she explains why she decided to come out of hiding, despite the danger. In the same locale, we see a security services officer who threw a bench at the injured migrant and kicked him, explaining that he was certain that the injured man was the terrorist. He says that he entered the station after hearing shots fired, as he "couldn't have lived with himself" if he had not done so. Another interviewee had tried to shield the dying migrant from the wild mob, not giving up even after being shoved to the ground and beaten himself. He explains, "I couldn't leave. I had to rescue him. They were tearing him limb from limb. They were destroying their own souls."

The interviewees thus draw elastic, elusive borders in lieu of the presumably solid borders separating the terrorist and his victims. They do not blend into the clear-cut national unity. Each of them is part of the Israeli community that convenes randomly in the station, in the same closed space and at the same departure point: the horror of the attack. While none of them ceases being a part of that threatened community, the border that the cinematic editing builds separates them not from the terrorist but instead from each other as it also separates each of them from the collective to which they all belong. Without ceasing to be part of that collective, they express differing positions and act in different ways, so that they are simultaneously together with all the others, and alone; they are part of the web that Nancy refers to—of the singular and the plural that are not fused—yet are nevertheless linked to each other. Nancy has described this fluidity as a continual motion of coming together and separating, a "melee" of identities that is based not on purity but rather combines the singular with the plural in a looping that runs in many directions. That fluidity positions the people recorded in the film within the boundaries of nation and community, yet simultaneously beyond them. "Cultures, or what are known as cultures," claims Nancy, "do not mix. They encounter each another, mingle, modify each other, reconfigure each other. They cultivate one another; they irrigate or drain each other; they work over and plough through each other, or graft one onto the other."[24]

In his writings on cinema, Gilles Deleuze (1986, 1989) distinguished between the movement-image and the time-image. According to Deleuze, the time-image is prominent in cinema that—contrary to that of the movement-image—shapes protagonists who cannot act in the world, cannot respond actively to a situation they perceive consciously, and so they replace action with watching. Yet while *Death in the Terminal* indeed halts the action, the cessation and the watching testify not to the impossibility of acting in the world but rather to attempts to understand it precisely—in order to act there.

By lingering for a prolonged period on a video framing a small space, *Death in the Terminal* is able to reveal what the unifying story told by the media and based on the movement-image could not show: the simultaneity of actions in the moment. In other words, focusing on the constructed borders of the time-image makes it possible to discern the borders that are dismantling national unity from within. Unlike the movement-image, which in its "empirical" form of time (Deleuze 1986) suggests a chronological succession and elaboration of relationships and events, the film halts in order to peruse the environment, within chaos and confusion, to see various people who made different choices and acted in differing ways, even contradictorily. They could choose to help or to strike out, to heal or to kill, to show compassion or to engage in violence. While these choices divide the various interviewees, the borders between them are fluid and change from moment to moment, and they exist even within each one's behavior and psyche—for example, the security officer who entered the station out of a sense of mission, ready to sacrifice his own safety, and who was ultimately led by his rage and aggression to the lynching, or the case of the bystander who experienced both terror and rage but nevertheless used his body to shield the migrant from the violent mob.

This connection between the individual and the many, the range of choices and actions that *Death in the Terminal* presents and the elasticity of the borders it draws, are related in the formulation of an alternative temporality. Instead of the unidirectional framing of the traumatic national fate movement image that repeats itself in the past, present, and future, an option for another story is proposed, one that offers the potential for a different future with other time paths. The games that *Death in the Terminal* plays with the alternating, accelerating, and slowing camerawork, moving forward and backward, emphasize this potential; the directors halt time, play with it, and direct it to other paths. They thus expose what is hidden in the present: possibilities of another knowledge, another understanding. A Jewish midrash says, "While all is preordained, free will is granted." *Death in the Terminal* is about "granted choices" within which the ethical option is flagged. This means discovering the "nowhere that the law of the other carves out within it."[25]

We might conclude by saying that freezing the time-image and watching a given situation from various angles is what constitutes the basis for the search for differing ways of understanding the world and acting within it—ways to expose other borders, changing and fluid, within shrunken borders of time and place hegemonically represented by the nation and the media. Among these, *Death in the Terminal* attempts to offer possibilities unexplored in the event's backstory or, in Walter Benjamin's words, "fanning the spark of hope in the past," brushing "history against the grain," and thus, if not leading to action, then at least leading to an understanding that enables action—if not today, then perhaps tomorrow.[26]

The films discussed in this chapter reflect Israeli space in its fragmentation, addressing the geography demarcated in Israeli hegemonic discourse. The reverberations of borders, identities, and the ways of breaking them down enable the imagining of an Israeli community that is not a homogenous entity defined by its borders. Rather, these boundaries constitute a challenge, calling upon us to dismantle, cross, and go around them. Whether as visible manifestations or as invisible separations that nevertheless exist, the films discussed here present borders that let us envision what may become a different, postnational, and postheroic community.

Notes

1 Adriana Kemp, "Border, Space, and National Identity," *Theory and Criticism* 16 (2000): 18.

2 Stefano Mezzadra and Brett Nielson, *Border as Method, or, the Multiplication of Labor* (Durham, N.C.: Duke University Press, 2011).

3 Eyal Weizman, *Hollow Land: Israel's Architecture of Occupation* (London; New York: Verso, 2007), 7.

4 Giorgio Agamben, *State of Exception*, translated by Kevin Attell (Chicago: University of Chicago Press, 2005), 1.

5 Carl Schmitt, *Political Theology: Four Chapters on the Concept of Political Sovereignty*, ed. and trans. George Schmitt (Chicago: University of Chicago Press, 2005).

6 Agamben; Edward Soja, *Thirdspace: Journeys to Los Angeles and Other Real-and-Imagined Places* (Malden, Mass.: Blackwell, 1996); and Gloria Anzaldúa, *Borderlands/La Frontera: The New Mestiza* (San Francisco: Spinsters/Aunt Lute, 1987).

7 Jean-Luc Nancy, *Being Singular Plural*, trans. Robert Richardson and Anne O'Byrne (Stanford, Calif.: Stanford University Press, 2000).

8 Mezzadra and Nielson, vii.

9 Henri Lefebvre, *The Production of Space*, trans. Donald Nicholson-Smith (New York: Wiley-Blackwell, 1992).

10 Kemp, 18; Shalev (1985), quoted in Kemp, 22.

11 As Kemp notes, in the 1990s there was a discourse of urgency regarding separation (Kemp, 27).

12 The checkpoint, as depicted in Israeli films of the early 2000s, foregrounds the interaction of territory and national identity, focusing on the injustices suffered by the Palestinians on the one hand and the anguish of the occupier on the other. Prominent examples include Yoav Shamir's *Checkpoint* (Machssomim, 2003), Ram Loevy's *Close, Closed, Closure* (Sagar, 2002), and Avi Mograbi's *Avenge but One of My Two Eyes* (Nekam Achat Mishtey Eynay, 2005). For a further discussion of checkpoints in Israeli films, see Zanger (2005, 2012).

13 Homi K. Bhabha, "Signs Taken for Wonders: Questions of Ambivalence and Authority under a Tree outside Delphi, May 1817," *Critical Inquiry* 12, no. 1 (1985): 151.

14 Hannah Arendt, *The Human Condition* (Chicago: University of Chicago Press, 1998), 63–64.

15 Anzaldúa, 99.

16 Trinh T. Minh-ha, *Woman, Native, Other: Writing Postcoloniality and Feminism* (Bloomington: Indiana University Press, 1989).

17 Lefebvre, 26.

18 Frantz Fanon, *The Wretched of the Earth*, trans. Richard Philcox (New York: Grove Press, 1963), 8.

19 For previous depictions of passing in Israeli cinema of the 1990s and early 2000s, see Carol Bardenstein, "Cross/Cast: Passing in Israeli and Palestinian Cinema," in *Palestine, Israel and the Politics of Popular Culture*, ed. Ted Swedenberg and Rebecca Stein (Durham, N.C.: Duke University Press, 2005). As Naaman, writing also about passing, notes, "The passing device could be seen to highlight the tensions and demarcations between belonging and exclusion in the Israeli social fabric"; Dorit Naaman, "A Rave against the Occupation? Speaking for the Self and Excluding the Other in Contemporary Israeli Political Cinema," in *Israeli Cinema: Identification in Motion*, ed. Miri Talmon and Yaron Peleg (Austin: University of Texas Press, 2011), 257.

20 This sequence contains an intertextual reference to Douglas Sirk's *Imitation of Life* (1954), which presents the conflict experienced by the interracial daughter of a black mother who "passes" as white without anyone around her knowing otherwise. When the mother visits her, she introduces her as her nanny. In this we can also see a visual resemblance between the actress portraying Nadia's mother and the actress who portrayed the mother in Sirk's film.

21 Gilles Deleuze and Félix Guattari, *A Thousand Plateaus*, trans. Brian Massumi (London; New York: Continuum, 1988), 415.

22 On this subject, see the discussion of the Israeli TV series *Fauda* in Gertz and Yosef (forthcoming).

23 In Certeau's terms, a process of switching, abandonment, and finding detours took place.

24 Nancy, 151.

25 Michel de Certeau, *The Practice of Everyday Life* (Berkeley: University of California Press, 1984), 105.

26 Walter Benjamin, *Illuminations*, trans. Harry Zohn (London: Fontana, 1973), 391, 392.

11

The Borders We Cross in Search of a Better World

On Border Crossing in Three of Amos Gitai's Feature Films

YAEL MUNK

The three films discussed in this chapter propose a revision of the Israeli borders not only in physical but also in metaphorical and ethical terms. Considering that Israel is surrounded by borders that cannot be crossed unless a peace agreement is signed (in practice such agreements have been signed with Egypt and in Jordan but, as we can learn from the daily news, these borders remain dangerous), the border issue continues to preoccupy Israel and its citizens today. From the beginning of his career and more particularly after his return to Israel in the mid-1990s, Amos Gitai has investigated borders, their populations, and their inherent dramas in feature films—the most prominent being *Disengagement* (Itnatkut, 2007), which retraces one of the many human dramas caused by Israel's pullout from the occupied Gaza Strip in summer 2005. He directed three trilogies whose added value lies in their being a reflection of the endless situations of conflict in which Israel's citizens remain prisoners of upheavals in its history. In light of this understanding, I would like to propose another horizon of borders that emerges in Gitai's Israeli films—one that does not have to do with the physical space of borders but rather with the borders of the national ethos. These kinds of borders are in fact delineating the recent corpus of Gitai's Israeli films: beginning with *Kippur* (2000), which deals with the filmmaker's personal experience during the Yom Kippur War, which soon became synonymous with national trauma, and ending with his most recent film *Rabin, The Last Day* (Rabin, HaYom Aahron, 2015), which deals in a very complex and subtle way with another national trauma, Prime Minister Yitzhak Rabin's assassination on November 4, 1995. Though these are not physical borders that can be crossed, they represent for each and every Israeli a wound that prevents history from progressing in its natural course. Gitai's choice of borders that span fifteen years in cinematic time (roughly the amount of time that passed between the production of *Kippur* in 2000 and *Rabin, The Last Day* in 2015) is no coincidence.

On Borders and Border Crossing

"A borderland is a vague and undetermined place created by the emotional residue of unnatural boundary. It is a constant state of transition. The prohibited and the forbidden are its inhabitants."[1] These words appear in the opening pages of the feminist poet and activist Gloria Anzaldúa's pioneering borderland study, *Borderlands/La Frontera: The New Mestiza* (1987) and define borderlands as a kind of new identity, one born of the border and referred to today as hybrid identity. Her book's composition is also hybridized; formed from poems, memories, and essays, it traces for the first time the complexity of those lives lived in border zones. Sociologist Nancy A. Naples notes that Anzaldúa's *Borderlands* has been especially influential in its interdisciplinary reach: "In some ways, the broad appeal of Anzaldúa's work is quite surprising given that it is a passionately written semi-autobiographical account that weaves her own struggles as a lesbian of Mexican American descent with poetry and other literary forms."[2] However, another sociologist, Pablo Vila, points to the dangers of considering a borderland to be "any physical or psychic space about which it is possible to address problems of boundaries: borders among different countries, borders among ethnicities . . . , borders between genders, borders among disciplines and the like. . . . This approach not only homogenizes distinctive experiences but also homogenizes borders."[3]

Following this contention, Vila concludes that the subjects who cross borders may be considered as the privileged subjects of history. But the very homogenization of the border-crossing experience prevents them from being such subjects. As opposed to those tourist travelers visiting other places, there are those who are expelled from their territories, those subjects on whom border crossing is imposed, and can thus be considered victims of history. Indeed, although border crossing has always been imposed on these oppressed subjects wishing to survive, it became more acute at the time of World War II, specifically when the Nazis came to power and more and more European citizens found themselves obliged to leave their native land in search of a better world. At the time, border crossing became imposed on individuals as an act of survival. This tendency became even more dominant some decades later, with the fall of the Berlin Wall and the Soviet Union. Suddenly people who were deprived of their most basic freedom began to search for a better world beyond their national borders. This new kind of journey of immigrants who had nothing to lose has inspired a vast number of Western feature films—such as Theo Angelopoulos's *Landscape in the Mist* (Topio sin omichli, 1998), Xavier Koller's *Journey of Hope* (Reise der Hoffnung, 1990), or Stephen Frears's *Dirty Pretty Things* (2002)—challenging Western audiences' capacity, or incapacity, to feel empathy for refugees and migrants.

In the state of Israel, the situation is slightly different because the majority of the country's population are Jewish immigrants that came—and keep coming—to Israel thanks to the Law of Return, a piece of Israeli legislation passed on July 5, 1950, that gives Jews around the world the right to return and the right to live in Israel and to gain Israeli citizenship. But since this law applies only to Jews, it leaves others in vague situations, with no option for establishing a civic status. This chapter deals with legal and illegal border crossers, of Jews and non-Jews, and their desire to reach salvation as represented in the three films of Israel's most prolific filmmaker, Amos Gitai. Born after World War II and after the establishment of the state of Israel in 1948, Gitai has devoted part of his cinematic career to the investigation of concrete and metaphorical border crossings, geographical borders between continents, abstract borders between genres such as fiction and documentary, and symbolic borders between historical events. As the French critic Jean-Michel Frodon contends, "in Gitai's work, the journey is inseparably connected to borders. One travels because there are borders of every kind and state (closed, open, permeable, visible and concealed). *For Gitai, the journey is the form and the border is the question.* [In all of his films] the question of borders plays a central role. Amos Gitai's status as a great artist in the world of filmmaking can be explained by the significance of borders in his work."[4]

After crossing a professional border, straying from his original path as an architect, Gitai began to direct documentaries. At first he created a series of important documentaries for Channel One, the only Israeli television channel at the time, until, after the First Lebanon War in 1982, he decided to leave the country and move to Paris.[5] There he directed films that focused on international themes such as the documentaries *Bangkok Bahrain* and *Ananas*, both from 1984. These films reflect his interest in the new world of border crossings, a world that transfers and trades in objects and human beings. This is in fact the globalized, capitalistic, neoliberal world that seems to place the individual in a relatively inferior position.

Gitai returned to Israel from France in 1994. His first Israeli cinematic project was the ambitious adaptation of Yaakov Shabtai's canonical novel *Zchron Dvarim*. The film, released universally under the title *Memorandum* (Davrim, 1995), tells the story of nine symbolic months in the lives of three adult bachelors in the city of Tel Aviv, desperately looking for meaning in their meaningless existence.[6] In 1990s Tel Aviv, such an adaptation was considered doomed to failure, as no one had ever entertained the possibility of adapting such a canonical work to the screen.[7] In retrospect, this cinematic adaptation can be considered a bold attempt to deal with the deepest myths of Israeli history and society. It also represents the first manifestation of a challenge that this chapter will try to demonstrate: to take border crossing beyond its political implications and try to understand the human dimension of impelled migration. In fact, Gitai's huge cinematic work offers an interpretation of the border as the true landmark of a long and significant journey.

Revisiting Gitai's Trilogies

Gitai has created many film trilogies that together compose an intellectual reflection on major themes in Israeli life: the first one is the Cities Trilogy, which begins with the above-mentioned *Memorandum* (Dvarim, 1995) set in Tel Aviv, followed by *Day by Day* (Yom Yom, 1998) set in Haifa, and concludes with *Kadosh* (1990), set in Jerusalem. The concept informing this trilogy is that each and every city in Israel has its own definitions and characteristics: Tel Aviv bears the traces of the Zionist founding fathers; Haifa, the delicate Jewish and Arab coexistence; and some parts of Jerusalem, the constraints of the Jewish religion. The trilogy investigates the distance between these cities, which are geographically very close to one another but in practice very different in many aspects.

Another Gitai trilogy examines Israeli history, and comprises *Kippur* (2000), which retraces the filmmaker's traumatic experience during the Yom Kippur War in 1973; the period drama *Eden* (2001), inspired by a short story by Arthur Miller that portrays a young woman's relationships with five different men (her father, her brother, her husband, her friend, and an immigrant), told against the backdrop of 1930s Palestine; and finally *Kedma* (2002), which retraces the voyage by a group of Holocaust survivors to Palestine a week before the Israeli Declaration of Independence. This second trilogy was to be followed by a third one that Gitai dubbed the Border Trilogy: *Promised Land* (Ha'aretz Hamuvtachat, 2004), *Free Zone* (Ezor Hofshi, 2005) and *Disengagement* (Itnatkut, 2007).

This chapter proposes a disentangling of the original Border Trilogy to suggest a new one, which reimagines *Kedma*, a film that gives a detailed account of an immigrant group of Holocaust survivors' journey from the ancient European traumatic world to the "promised land" of Israel as the first chapter of the Border Trilogy, to be followed by *Promised Land* and *Free Zone*. In all three films, men and particularly women cross borders for social and political reasons, thus suggesting the possibility that women's border crossing is more frequent and thus more influential historically. The promised land may vary in its nature but always features as the object of desire that stimulates the protagonists' action. The reason for linking these films across two of Gitai's trilogies is first and foremost thematic.

The first film of this regrouped trilogy, *Kedma*, depicts the Holocaust survivors' journey, and their painful encounter with Palestinians at the moment the latter turn into refugees, and is then capped at the close of the film by a philosophical and ideological tirade about the potential interchangeability of historical positions.[8] The second, *Disengagement*, focuses on a national tragedy and one of the most dramatic moments in Israeli history: the 2005 disengagement from the Gaza Strip and the evacuation of its inhabitants. This is not border crossing, but rather impelled internal migration, and the film examines the emotional effects that follow. In this sense it joins two major national traumas that were adapted to the screen: the Yom Kippur War in 1973 that is superbly reconstructed in *Kippur* (2001) and Prime Minister Yitzhak Rabin's assassination that is the basis of Gitai's *Rabin, the Last Day*. These three films retrospectively compose another trilogy that could be named Israel's National Traumas.

Keeping this regrouping in mind, this chapter wishes to investigate the roles and functions borders play in those three feature films that I consider the true Border Trilogy: *Kedma*, *Promised Land*, and *Free Zone*. Though all the three deal with journeys to and from the state of Israel, only the last two can be considered as road movies because of the physical presence of a road. The three films are very different in their narrative; they take place at different Israeli borders and at different historical times. Still, they share a strong common gender denominator: the fact that these borders are crossed by women. With the exception of *Kedma*, in which the main characters are a group of male and female immigrants, the two other films focus exclusively on women's border crossing, a fact that may have political implications as it points to women's capacity to make peace with the enemy. Just as Laila the Palestinian protagonist in *Free Zone* says to her Israeli partner, Hanna: "You will help me, because you're a woman, because you're a mother," designating this common ground shared by women and revealing a potential alliance between Israeli and Palestinian women—as is the case in various peace organizations, such as the Coalition of Women for Peace—that is often ignored in the ongoing Middle East discussions.[9]

Revisiting the Beginning: *Kedma*

Kedma, a Hebrew expression meaning "toward the Orient," is the name of a boat that brought 794 illegal immigrants, all of them Holocaust survivors, to the land of Palestine at the end of 1947. Upon their arrival at the Israeli shore, they were expelled to Cyprus by the British Mandatory Authority that ruled Palestine at the time. Gitai is largely inspired by this episode in the history of Israel but he twists the plot, changing the date of their landing to a week before the Israeli Declaration of Independence. In an interview with film scholar Annette Michelson in 1999, Gitai speaks about the importance of the 1948 War of Independence in his historiographical vision and absentmindedly (or maybe not) describes his project:

> The year 1948 is interesting because of the juxtaposition of the Jewish project and the Palestinian exodus. This is a dramatic project and an extremely complicated one; this [film] I should like to make. I'm starting to think about it. It will be called *Latron*. This was a single battle on the road to Jerusalem. It was the only static battle. Ben Gurion very much wanted to capture this British-built citadel. When the British left in '48, they gave it, together with control of the road leading to Jerusalem, to the Arab Legion. The Haganah made five attempts to capture this point and failed every time. The war of 1948 ended without Israeli control over it, and until 1967 the way to Jerusalem, which I remember as a child, was extremely complicated; you had to meander through mountains, etc. In this battle there were immigrants from Europe, sent straight to the barracks. People died without anyone able to identify them. And there was a linguistic confusion. Because they did not understand the language, they could not understand the commands. They spoke Russian, some Polish, some Yiddish. The commanding officers spoke Hebrew.
>
> A couple of years ago, I came across some diaries of women in the Haganah who had been in Bergen-Belsen; they served as nurses in the battle. This is really powerful material. And add to it the fact that later on, during the war, they displace whole Palestinian villages. The overlapping of . . . well. I shouldn't talk about future projects.[10]

It seems that these ideas made their way into another narrative: the one about a boat of illegal immigrants on their way to Palestine just before Israel's Declaration of Independence. The confusion of languages, their past trauma, and their facing the unknown all create a ground for the delicate human situation that is the basis of *Kedma*'s narrative. Upon their arrival in their promised land, the Holocaust survivors discover the Palestinian refugees who have to leave their homes and their land because that land has now been promised to others: the Jews. The film deals with the tragedy of a twice-promised land and the implications of a long-lasting conflict.

It opens with a caption intended to situate the viewers vis-à-vis historical events—"May 7th, 1948"—a week before Israel's Declaration of Independence. This caption, creating certain expectations in the viewers' minds as to the battles and the violence that might now take place on screen, is immediately contradicted by the still close-up frame of a woman's naked back. As the frame expands, it reveals a man lying on a bed. The woman joins him in an intimate embrace, but when the camera further distances itself from the protagonists, the viewer discovers that this intimate scene is in fact taking place in a crowded space at the bottom of the boat, under the eyes of other frightened immigrants who, like these two, are Holocaust survivors. This formal choice of moving from the most intimate to the most public, from a seemingly private love scene to a general scene of panic, is in fact intended to reveal Gitai's cinematic preferences as will be manifested throughout the narrative: his fixed camera revealing the fixed gaze of those tormented immigrants who fail to hold to one singular point in space. Moreover, the alternating between close-ups and long shots re-creates in the viewer's mind the sense of disorientation experienced by the newcomers.

In a long and continuous tracking shot typical of Gitai's cinematography, the camera moves from the depths of the boat up to the deck, revealing a crowded space in which many immigrants are tightly packed in complete silence. These immigrants, completely alien to each other, are standing still or sitting, exhausted, waiting to see their promised land. The enthusiasm of the Jewish newcomers typical of early Zionist films is completely absent in this sequence.[11] This is expressed not only through the absence of synchronization between the sound and the visual but also by the events on screen: one immigrant vomits over the railing, and another cries in the arms of a friend. Generally speaking, the refugees' body language on the deck indicates that they do not know each other but have just been thrown together for the voyage, for the period of crossing a physical border from Europe to Palestine and a metaphorical one from captivity to freedom. But, as the film will show, while the first kind of border can be crossed regardless of the physical difficulties and dangers, the second one will remain impossible to cross and will inscribe itself on the individual's mind as a further trauma, as beautifully illustrated by Gitai's provocative quotation of Haim Hazaz's story "The Sermon," analyzed further in this chapter.

Gitai's fascination with borders and border crossing can also be identified in the long sequence in which the immigrants reach the shore. While the seemingly chaotic mise-en-scène of these men, women, and children corresponds to a classical Zionist scene of the Jewish immigrants reaching the promised land, in Gitai's film they are neither happy nor excited. While at first sight they seem to be waiting to take part in the Zionist ideological project, their behavior will reveal that they still carry the traumatic memories that are not to be spoken of, as exemplified by the man who mentions the last letter he had received from his mother just before the ghetto uprising, and the question he addresses to a woman—"How did you survive?"—which remains unanswered. This question, referring to the well-known rumor about Jewish women who survived the camps by having sex with the Nazis, does not require an answer. It points to the then common knowledge of women's sexual favors in the concentration camps (which, since then, has been refuted on many occasions). As such it points to another border crossing, the moral one. This is, in fact, Gitai's way of saying that when crossing geographical borders, other borders are often crossed too.

This situation's complexity is further expressed in a superimposed long shot intended to re-create the anonymous travelers' subjectivity. A woman's face in close-up is superimposed on the violent events taking place on the seashore as the clandestine newcomers are confronted by the British soldiers. Her melancholic expression tells the entire tragedy of those displaced subjects who had innocently believed that somewhere a better world would be awaiting. A few minutes earlier, while still on the deck, this same woman was shown in the crowd, reciting the national poet Haim Nachman Bialik's famous poem "To the Bird." Nurith Gertz, Gal Hermoni, and Yael Munk note that this poem, "published in 1912, when [Bialik] was still a young boy in Russia, in the diaspora, expresses his longing for the faraway, unreachable land of Israel. The poem has become an emotional signifier of the Zionist ideology, of yearning by the diasporic for the land of Israel, from the past to the future, from the static place the poet is in onward to the Promised Land."[12] But, in the film's narrative, times have changed and Bialik's dream of the promised land has been transformed into a search for refuge for the persecuted Jewish newcomers (but also a nightmare for the Palestinians who suddenly become displaced people on their own land).

From this point on, the narrative follows the newcomers' attempt to survive in a violent land where Palestinians are still fighting for their rights, fearing the possibility of becoming refugees. Gitai translates this fear explicitly in a scene in which Palestinian refugees come across Jewish refugees. The former are being expelled from their land, while the latter are coming to populate their promised land, which happens to be the same one. They exchange gazes under a meaningful silence, the Palestinians indicating their hatred of the Jews, because of whom they have been expelled from their homes. But the viewer, like the director himself, is fully aware that, this time, borders are crossed not because of individual desires but rather because of international agreements—namely, United Nations Resolution 181, declared on November 29, 1947. The new Jewish settlers, who hardly know where they are going, are being moved around like pawns on the chessboard of history. Their private narrative is unimportant; they are merely numbers in the eyes of those politicians eager to replace the Arab population with Jews. *Kedma* creates an overall atmosphere, at the end of which, as French critic Charles Tesson describes it, "we have the impression of a country comprised of people without a place,"[13] a description that echoes the famous slogan often attributed to the British Zionist writer

Israel Zangwill that has been adopted by Zionist demagogy: "a land without a people for a people without a land."[14]

Kedma reveals the physical and symbolic journey of these Jewish refugees toward their own land, a journey that begins with the physical stepping on the ground and the unexpected encounter with Palestinians and ends with the realization that there are no promised lands for the "victims of history." They expect things to happen for the best; but the more they progress, the more they understand that their dream is far from coming true. At the height of their journey, after having experienced the death of some of their companions in the camps and during their long journey to Palestine, Yanosh, who is also the refugee who was seen making love in the opening scene, stops and gives a strong and moving speech, which is actually quoted from Haim Hazaz's canonical text, "The Sermon," written in 1941. "We have no history!'" he says. "From the day we were exiled from our country, we are a people without a history. . . . We did not create our history, the gentiles did that . . . they created the history as they wished it and in their shape, while we only accepted it from their hands. But this history is not ours, not ours at all! Moreover, I don't respect it . . . I oppose it."[15]

Being spoken in respect to the promised land of Israel/Palestine, the text becomes ironic. Returning to the land of Israel is considered the greatest achievement in Jewish history since the Jewish people were sent into exile upon the destruction of the Second Temple. But the persecuted Jew, who has only just overcome the horrors of the Holocaust and who is now witnessing another form of blind violence in his own land, cannot find any comfort in this new setting. The borders have been crossed, but no better world has been revealed to the displaced Jews of Europe.

In an interview for the art journal *October*, upon the release of the film *Kippur* (2001), Annette Michelson addressed Gitai with the following provocative comment: "You appear to retain a certain sympathy for the Zionist project, which is now the object of a strong, indeed, a radical critique, constructed by the new generation of historians." Gitai, who has long been identified with the radical left wing in Israel, provided the following unexpected answer: "I frequently observe a lack of synchronization between thought in academia—that is, between analytic, critical thinking—and events in the Middle East. We don't have firm territorial boundaries. Israel is a kind of open border on its eastern front since 1967, and it does not have firm cultural and mental borders; it's a fluid situation."[16] In other words, as an intellectual filmmaker, Gitai is fully aware of the border issues in the state of Israel and its reflections on the individual. He knows and acknowledges the influence of borders on the Israeli psyche and still digs into history and actuality in order to reach a more stable ground.

In conclusion, *Kedma*, the first film of the corpus I consider as Gitai's new Border Trilogy, represents one of the filmmaker's early reflections on Israeli nationalism upon his return to Israel in 1994 after spending more than a decade in Europe. Though the words pronounced by Yanosh in *Kedma*'s final sequence belong to another time and another period in history, they reflect a dimension that seems to haunt Gitai's cinematic world: the mythologization of the present through its roots in history. One may see in Gitai's approach a revisiting of canonical Israeli history in order to revise its historical details and revive them for the present. This dimension, which can be found in the various chapters of Gitai's documentary House Trilogy (1980–2006), enables us to understand that history is being written right in front of us, as we cross borders in a search of a better world that may not necessarily exist.[17]

The Land Promised to Others: *Promised Land*

Of the three border films, *Promised Land* seems to be the most merciless, maybe because its protagonists are all nameless foreign women, or (and this is more probable) because it deals with Eastern European women who have been forced into prostitution in Israel. Their choice to escape poverty in their home country seems to have taken them to more dangerous places they were not aware of. The film opens with a typical orientalist vision of a camel caravan against the background of the Sinai Desert. The sun has not yet appeared, or it has already set, and those sitting on the camels are women, though the viewer cannot see their faces. Soon after, as they sit around a campfire and speak in Russian, whereas all the men surrounding them speak Arabic, the viewer will realize that they do not understand why they are in the desert and expect to move soon to some other destination. As they talk, the Bedouins look at the girls and evaluate their beauty; at the end of their discussion one of them comes, takes one of the women, and rapes her. She does not say anything to the other women, but the looks on their faces reveal their growing fear.

Then a van comes, out of which exit some strong men and a dark-haired woman. The foreign women are auctioned off by Israelis and Bedouins in the middle of the emptiness, thus creating the first split among the foreign women. Later on, two of them will be dressed in traditional Arabic garb and sent against their will to the occupied territories. But the destiny of the others is no better. After being made up and dressed in a provocative way, they are sent into the hold of an amusement ship, which is in fact a floating brothel symbolically named *The Promised Land*. After being initiated into their new job—again, against their will—they are sent to work as sex slaves in a brothel. Upon their arrival, they are stripped, hosed down, and then dressed and made-up to attract customers. They are humiliated, brutalized, and threatened so that their journey, which was supposed to have a specific destination, turns into a mission of survival. Only a terrorist bombing in the area killing some of the women will free those who are still alive.

A close look at the film reveals a similarity between these women's survival efforts and those of *Kedma*'s protagonists. Yet whereas in *Kedma* the protagonists were Holocaust survivors who had experienced the horrors of World War II, *Promised Land*'s heroines are not part of some historical reconstruction but rather a reflection of today's Israel, where the traffic of prostitutes has been prospering for a while.[18] Therefore, though very different from *Kedma*, *Promised Land* is also an openly political film, in which Gitai and his camera attempt to prick Israeli citizens' conscience by revealing the truth behind the curtains in certain Tel Aviv hotels. As opposed to his typical sequence shots, here Gitai moves between these crowded places with a handheld camera, thus providing a sense of disorientation, while in the background women's half naked bodies move in a chaotic way. One may say that the promised land has never been more distant.

Among the many women who are brutalized in this human market, Gitai focuses on two: Diana, who innocently came from Eastern Europe in a search of a better life; and Rose, a tourist who is fascinated by this human traffic and follows the women out of curiosity. Gitai leads us into an unbearable inferno, with poetic breaks such as the moment during which Diana and Rose wait for the pimp to come, exchanging smiles as Rose says a prayer from the Christian Orthodox Church to which they used to belong. After a series of traumatic events, mostly involving sexual exploitation, Diana and Rose are saved thanks to a terrorist bombing that takes place outside the brothel and enables them to flee, running down the road and loudly shouting, "I'm free!" There is a tragic irony in the fact that the prostitutes are freed thanks to a terrorist attack. Without minimizing the traumatic impact of the attack, Gitai juxtaposes two of contemporary Israel's major threats: the international trafficking of women, and terrorism. Although the two protagonists succeed in escaping the catastrophe, the very juxtaposition of such terrible plagues reflects the growing dangers that Israel faces currently.

Almost documentary in its shooting, *Promised Land* is a film about borders: the open geographical borders between Egypt and Israel that do not succeed in preventing human trafficking, and moral borders that, if we are to judge the violent images of these women's brutalization and rape, seem to have been crossed in an irreversible way. The critique here is openly directed at Israel, which at that time did not do anything to prevent this kind of trafficking.[19] Gitai created a political film in which individuality has been erased and the heroines' fates are all similar. Here the border should read in a symbolic way, as the place where wandering and suffering should be stopped (though in the film the opposite happens). This reflects Gitai's intellectual challenge to the audience: as an excellent documentary filmmaker, he knows that "seeing is believing." Showing violence against women is a means to reveal the very existence of the phenomena. Since most violence against women takes place in the domestic sphere, Gitai feels justly that there is some relevance in staging scenes that, by definition, are hidden from the public eye. And he succeeds. The fact that these acts take place on the border or right after crossing it emphasizes the impact of the border as a space of transgression, where ethics disappear and moral constraints are lifted.

Beyond the Border Metaphor: *Free Zone*

Gitai's border film par excellence is *Free Zone*, the last of my proposed new Border Trilogy.[20] *Free Zone* is a road movie taking place exclusively in the occupied territories of the West Bank, situated near the Jordanian and Syrian borders. As in *Promised Land*, here too the protagonists are in search of a promised land. The way to this piece of land where all problems should be resolved is dangerous, and just as in any other road movie, it involves outside dangers and inner reflections about the protagonists' identities and desires. Almost entirely shot in a taxi cab, the film opens with a nine-minute medium-tight close-up shot of a young woman, Rebecca, crying as she sits as a passenger in the car. The camera is immobile, and the only movement is the silhouettes moving in the background as seen from the cab's open window; a close viewing will reveal soldiers, traditionally dressed Arab women, and a man or two walking in this undefined space. On Rebecca's silent face Gitai superimposes Israeli singer Chava Alberstein's song "Had Gadya," the traditional Passover song, which originally was a kind of parable in which one eats or consumes the other and whose lyrics have been updated by Alberstein to emphasize the relevance of this ancient song to the ongoing Israeli-Palestinian conflict.[21] Banned by government radio upon its release in 1989, the track's insistent, lilting rhythm and urgent lyrics recount how a father buys a kid lamb for two pennies; the lamb is eaten by a cat, which is choked by a dog, who's beaten with a stick, and so forth, completing a chain of "natural" brutality that has the singer wondering, "How long will the cycle of violence continue?" The song, which returns in the film's final sequence, emphasizes the absurdity of the ongoing violence in the Middle East. This first sequence ends with the offscreen voice of the female cab driver, who announces to Rebecca that she's going far away and will not be able to take her any further because she has "serious family business there." Rebecca, still crying, implores the driver, Hanna, to take her along, and they finally begin their impossible journey into the wasteland of the occupied territories.

As with the conventional road film, these two characters will come to know each other and find common interests.[22] Through their dialogue the viewer will learn about their pasts and their aims. As opposed to *Promised Land*, where the characters had no specific past, here the past is provided not only through conventional flashbacks but also (and primarily) through cinematic superimpositions in which the viewer experiences, after the fact, events that led to the present situation. In the case of Rebecca, the young Jewish American woman, this involves her Israeli boyfriend's confession about his deeds during his military service. In the superimposed scene, he tells her about a beautiful Palestinian woman he saw during his last military operation in one of the villages of the occupied territories. When the battle ended and he was left in a state of fear and confusion, surrounded by corpses, he again noticed the Palestinian woman, whose face attracted his attention as they entered the village, and he followed her. He asked her to cook him a meal, which she did, and then came to her bed for two consecutive nights. "She did not object," he says in his confession to Rebecca. But Rebecca does not accept the explanation and keeps repeating, "You raped her!" He rejects this interpretation of the situation.

This confession, which causes Rebecca's separation from her Israeli boyfriend, reveals an ethical border crossing; it is only one of many, as the two women's journey will reveal. Another crossing of ethical borders is to be found in Hanna's story. Hanna, the daughter of Holocaust survivors, tells Rebecca that she and her husband have been struggling to make a living for many years. They went to live in Yamit, the Israeli city that was built in Sinai, until Sinai was returned to the Egyptians and they had to leave. They went back to Israel, to the Negev Desert, but there they discovered that they could not make a living at agriculture. This was the moment her husband came up with the brilliant idea of selling armored cars to the Palestinians.

After her husband has been hurt in a Palestinian rocket attack, Hanna has decided to reach the free zone and collect the money owed to her husband. But she cannot reach "the American" who is supposed to pay the debt. Instead they come across Laila, a Palestinian woman who is willing to take them to the debtor. In their attempt to retrieve Hanna's husband's money, they come across intense situations, such as a fire set in the village by Walid, the angry son of Laila, and a long sequence taking place against the ruins of a destroyed village, in which a man named Samir tells Rebecca how he became "the American" as the result of a false promise of the Israeli Army after the 1967 war, a promise that cost him twenty-five years of exile. But all these encounters do not solve anything; they simply emphasize the dead end expressed in the film's song, "Had Gadya." The borders between states and human beings disappear and, for a while, the narrative gives the impression that these women are dwelling in a common space. But the cab is an unstable space, emphasizing the fluidity and evasiveness of the border space.

In conclusion, it seems that the three films that compose my reconstructed Border Trilogy indicate Gitai's pessimistic vision of the future. Men and, particularly, women cross these borders in failed attempts to find a solution to the long-lasting problem of the land of Israel/Palestine. As they cross these borders they become more aware of the traumatic history of both people, a history that imposes a perpetual conflict and turns them into its perpetual victims.

Notes

I would like to thank the present volume's anonymous reviewers for their helpful suggestions.

1 Gloria Anzaldúa, *Borderlands/La Frontera: The New Mestiza* (San Francisco: Aunt Lute Books, 1987), 3.
2 Nancy A. Naples, "Borderlands Studies and Border Theory: Linking Activism and Scholarship for Social Justice," *Sociology Compass* 4, no. 7 (2010): 507.
3 Pablo Vila, "Conclusion: The Limits of American Border Theory," in *Ethnography at the Border*, ed. Pablo Vila (Minneapolis: University of Minnesota Press, 2003), 307.
4 Jean-Michel Frodon, "Borders and Woman," in *Munio Weinraub/Amos Gitai: Architecture and Film in Israel* (Munich: Minerva Editions, 2008), 257, emphasis added.
5 This moment is intellectually reflected in of one his best early documentaries, *Field Diary* (Yoman Sadeh, 1982) in which he travels with his film crew in the occupied territories of the Gaza Strip and the West Bank as tensions mount, leading to the Israeli Army's invasion of Lebanon on June 6, 1982.
6 For further discussion, see Munk (2009).
7 See Hefetz (1996). It should be mentioned that Shabtai's oeuvre focused on the day after the 1977 political upheaval, as a generation of Israelis felt they were no longer relevant to their country. Gitai adapted it to the less specific time frame of the 1990s, and yet that time still diffuses the feeling that the country no longer belongs to its legitimate sons.
8 Gertz, Hermoni, and Munk (2011) analyze the thematic shift brought to the classical Zionist texts in *Kedma*, one of them being Hazaz's story "The Sermon." While the original story was aimed to prompt military activism among the 1948 fighting youth, Gertz, Hermoni, and Munk contend that in the film's present "the text cannot support this meaning any longer. The call to transcend passivity and act within history does not fit the end of the battle in which the diasporic survivor emerged out of their passivity and took action in history—fighting for their new country" (2011, 172).
9 As its website explains, "The Coalition of Women for Peace is [an Israeli-Palestinian] feminist organization against the occupation of Palestine and for a just peace. Founded in November 2000, after the outbreak of the Second Intifada, CWP today is a leading voice in the Israeli peace movement, bringing together women from a wide variety of identities and groups. CWP is committed to ending the occupation and creating a more just society, while enhancing women's inclusion and participation in the public discourse. CWP initiates public campaigns and education and outreach programs, working to develop and integrate a feminist discourse on all social levels of society. Coalition of Women for Peace, "About CWP," http://www.coalitionofwomen.org/about-1/about/?lang=en.
10 Amos Gitai and Annette Michelson, "Filming Israel: A Conversation," *October* 98 (2001): 71.

11 Examples include Chaim Halachmi's *Oded the Wanderer* (Oded HaNoded, 1932), Alexander Ford's *Pioneers* (Sabra, 1933), and Baruch Agadati's *This Is the Land* (Zot Hi Ha'aretz, 1935), among others. See Feldstein (2012).

12 Nurith Gertz, Gal Hermoni, and Yael Munk, "*Kedma* (Amos Gitai): The Birth of Two Nations at War in 1948," in *Film and the Middle East and North Africa: Creative Dissidence*, edited by Josef Gugler (Austin: University of Texas Press, 2011), 172.

13 Charles Tesson, "Le Chemin de Jerusalem," *Cahiers du Cinema* 468 (2002): 27.

14 See Muir (2008).

15 Haim Hazaz, "The Sermon," in *The Sermon and Other Stories* (New Milford, CT: Toby Press, 2005), 223.

16 Gitai and Michelson, 55–57.

17 Produced over twenty-five years, Gitai's documentary House Trilogy revolves around one house in Jerusalem that symbolizes the incommensurability of the Israeli-Palestinian land. The first film, *Home* (Bait, 1980), describes a house in West Jerusalem that was occupied by Palestinians until 1948 and was subsequently home to various Jewish families. The film, which was originally commissioned by Channel One (the only Israeli television station at the time), was censored and never broadcast in Israel. In the second film of the trilogy, *A House in Jerusalem* (Bait BeYerushalaim, 1998), Gitai returns to the same house, almost two decades later, interviews the Jewish families who live there, and talks to the Arab families who used to live in the house. Doing so, Gitai wonders aloud what these people think about the situation that led them to switch houses and, by extrapolation, if there is any chance for coexistence between Arabs and Jews. The third film, *News from Home/News from House* (Hadashot MeHaBait, 2005), closes the trilogy with what are more or less closing remarks. As Gitai himself expressed it at the 2016 Viennale, "I wanted to widen the perimeters of my observation to Diasporas, to those links to the original inhabitants of the house by their family history." Vienna International Film Festival, "News from Home/News from House," http://www.viennale.at/en/films/news-home-news-house.

18 According to the findings released in 2005 by a parliamentary inquiry committee, between three thousand and five thousand women were smuggled into Israel and sold into prostitution in the previous four years. Most of the prostitutes came from China, Moldavia, Russia, Ukraine, and Uzbekistan and were smuggled in through Egypt. In 2007 the Israeli Parliament Committee on the Status of Women reported that in recent years the number of trafficked women had dropped to less than one thousand. This drop can be attributed to Article 377A of the Israeli Penal Code, adopted in 2005 (see note 10).

19 Following the American Victims of Trafficking and Violence Protection Act of 2000, Israel passed a similar law in 2005 known as article 377A in the Israeli Penal Code, which states that "Actions intended to sell or purchase or undertake other types of activities regarding turning over or obtaining a dependent person (trafficking in persons), should be subject to arrest—up to six months, or to restriction of freedom—up to three years, or to imprisonment—up to six years."

20 In an interview with Damon Smith (2007), Gitai reveals his inspiration for this incredible script:

> The story came from a guy who works as a driver in most of my films. He was unemployed and he called me one day and he said, "Amos, I got myself a job." And I said to him, "What is your job?" And he said, "I import these Chevrolet

4×4s to my *mushab*"—a mushab is a kind of cooperative. "I make them armored and then I cross the border to Jordan where I found a Palestinian partner in the eastern part of Jordan in an area called Free Zone. And in that place we sell the cars to security companies that work in Iraq." I said to him, "That sounds like science fiction. Would you mind if I join you on one of these journeys?" So we made the journey together and covered most of the territories you see in the film. We started in Tel Aviv and went along the Jordan Valley. We crossed the border next to the Lake of Galilee, we passed Amman, we saw signs saying Iraq, Syria and Saudi Arabia, and then we reached this very large plateau. It's a very flat desert plateau, and in it were something like two square miles of used cars. These were all these people from all origins buying and selling cars. I had been looking for a while for little vignettes which managed to escape the general schematics and the political correctness that we envision this conflict under. So this served as the basis of the story.

21 "Had Gadya" is a song that is traditionally sung at the end of the Passover seder and symbolizing an historical allegory of the Jewish people's hardships. In 1989, in the middle of the First Intifada, the well-known Israeli singer Chava Alberstein reinterpreted the song—adding some political verses to the original—namely, the last line, "How long will the cycle of violence continue?" Needless to say, these new words immediately provoked a public reaction to ban the song on Israeli radio. See Silverstein (2006).

22 The road movie is a typical American film genre in which the road traveled by the protagonists "provides a ready space for explorations of the tension and crisis of the historical moment during which it is produced" (Cohan and Hark 1997, 2).

12

Filipinos at the Border

Migrant Workers in Transnational Philippine Cinema

JOSÉ B. CAPINO

In his review of Olivia Lamasan's *Sana maulit muli* (Hopefully, once more, 1995), a romantic melodrama set in Manila and San Francisco, the film critic Noel Vera predicted that the subject of migrant labor would be "the great story of Philippine cinema."[1] He was mostly correct. In the ensuing years, labor migration loomed large, not only in the movies but also in Philippine life. The percentage of the Filipino labor force employed abroad crept up to a stunning 10 percent by 2010, representing what the sociologist Rhacel Salazar Parreñas describes as "the widest flow of contemporary migration in the world today." Many of these Filipino migrants are employed as domestic workers in "more than 160 countries."[2] What drives the strong demand for Filipino migrant workers is their command of English, their high level of education, their skills, and their productivity.[3] Equally important, sociologist Robyn Rodriguez writes, "Philippine migrants are uniquely 'flexible' as short-term, contractual, and incredibly mobile workers."[4]

This massive labor flight directly impacts the stories told by Philippine cinema. The figure of the Overseas Filipino Worker (a term coined by the government) began to proliferate in dozens of independent and studio-made melodramas, in stories set in places as different as Hong Kong, Milan, and Saudi Arabia. Since the Philippine government initiated a labor exportation program in the 1970s, such migration narratives have appeared in at least three cycles of melodramatic films, in addition to several important off-cycle releases.[5] The cycles appeared, with some overlaps, in the early to mid-1980s, in the 1990s, and again in the years 2000–2009. These melodramatic cycles operated at the border of cinematic genres, their peculiar transgeneric makeup registering both historical changes in the situation of migrants and developments in Filipino film culture. The 1980s cycle gravitated toward lachrymose romantic and domestic dramas, while horror-inflected films dominated the 1990s cycle. Romance and family melodramas returned in the new millennium, but they were markedly cheerful and showed the influence of romantic comedy. Owing to the subject matter and foreign settings of migrant films, the three cycles additionally incorporated some aspects of cinematic thrillers, films about social problems, and documentaries.

The ubiquitous figure of the Filipino migrant laborer has traveled not only across genres but also crossed the border into other national cinemas, appearing in foreign movies such as Swedish director Lukas Moodysson's *Mammoth* (2009), Wi Ding Ho's Taiwanese comedy *Táibei xingqitian* (Pinoy Sunday, 2009), Anthony Chen's Singaporean melodrama *Ilo Ilo* (2013), and Tomer Heymann's Israeli documentary *Paper Dolls* (2006).

As I have begun to suggest here, melodrama is a useful rubric for understanding much of the Philippine-made films about migrant laborers. The term *melodrama* refers, in critic Linda Williams's words, to "a form of exciting, sensational, and above all, moving story."[6] Melodrama is for Michael Walker "the most important generic root of the American cinema," one that capaciously subsumes a wide variety of cinematic types or genres.[7] Both are true of Filipino cinema as well, modeled as it is after Hollywood and the equally melodramatic theater of Spain, another country that previously colonized the Philippines. Melodramatic narratives feature protagonists beset by formidable external conflicts and moral dilemmas; in Philippine melodramas about migrant laborers, the external conflicts are typically brought about by problems of hospitality and violence in the host country.[8] The social costs of leaving home are emphasized as well, including the alienation of migrants and the delinquency or disaffection of their children. Often in these melodramas the ethical dilemmas arise out of the migrants' responses to their exploitation, their wayward desires, and their divided loyalty to their homeland and their host nations. Because of melodrama's penchant for rudimentary moral instruction, the resolution in these films is often heavy-handed.[9] In such resolution, immigrant workers die, their loved ones condemn their country's inutile diplomacy and the host nation's cruelty, and migrant women turn their backs on foreign lovers to return to the loving embrace of native men and their homeland. At times these stark endings work in contrast to the more subtle treatment of the various issues surrounding labor migration in the rest of the narrative. Somewhere in these narratives one finds characters and incidents that point to more measured and pragmatic explanations of the legal, economic, and personal circumstances behind a migrant's terrible misfortunes. Equally important, one also finds subplots, figures, and scenes that, while peripheral to the narrative, suggest a livable path for overseas workers. This contrast between extreme and subtle rhetoric is partly attributable to melodrama's formal predilections. If tragedies and triumphs dominate their endings, one also finds in melodramas enough stuff for the melancholy reckoning of opportunities that the protagonist may have taken but has instead chosen to forgo. In the melodrama of the overseas migrant worker, those sacrificed possibilities consist of the strategies and openings for prolonging one's stay in the host country against the odds.

There is much to be gained from studying these melodramas about Philippine migrant laborers. First, they represent a corpus of border cinema that is long-lived yet understudied. Second, the stylistic features and industrial practices of Philippine cinema, in addition to the textures of the Filipino experience of labor migration, constitute a particular instantiation of border cinema. No account of border cinema will be complete without discussing the vast spread of Filipino migration, a phenomenon that traverses so many national borders. Like other border cinema films, these melodramas about Philippine migrant laborers contrast what Arjun Appadurai calls the émigré's "fantasies of wanting to move" with the actual rewards and tribulations of living in exile.[10] By dwelling on the experience of the "new proletariat of workers" in the First World, these understudied Philippine instantiations of border cinema provide supplements and counternarratives to more dominant representations of inter-American and transatlantic immigration.[11]

In what follows, my discussion will touch on four issues salient to Philippine films about labor migration: (1) the problem of representing the workings and consequences of a far-reaching labor export policy; (2) the vulnerability of female, queer, and undocumented migrants; (3) the affective dynamics of nationalist identification and immigrant exilic belonging; and (4) the legal predicaments created by inhospitable receiving societies. My illustrations will draw from each cycle of Filipino migrant worker melodramas, from the 1980s to the present. In elucidating the sociohistorical context of these melodramas, I shall also posit their broader significance to the notions of border cinema that the present collection advances.

Miss X: Trafficking in Women's Bodies

Gil Portes's *Miss X* (1980) tells the supposedly true story of a twenty-five-year-old woman who is recruited to work as a chambermaid in Belgium but ends up as a nightclub dancer and prostitute in Amsterdam. The film belongs to a pioneering cluster of melodramas about Filipino migrant workers that were made for independent production companies by directors such as Portes. These films include his *Bukas . . . May pangarap* (Tomorrow's dream, 1984) and Lino Brocka's *Napakasakit, kuya Eddie* (It hurts, brother Eddie, 1986), both about migrant workers illegally recruited to work in the Middle East. These scrappy films exploited the topicality of overseas contract work in the first decade or so after the Philippine government established a labor export policy. The policy, introduced in 1974 at the height of the dictatorship of Ferdinand Marcos, aimed to prop up a weak labor market and sagging dollar reserves.[12] The government used some of the dollars remitted by foreign workers to underwrite widespread corruption, massive public spending, and an export-oriented industrialization policy that depended heavily on importing foreign materials and technology. For a short period, the government even required overseas laborers to send 50 to 80 percent of their income back to the country or lose the privilege of working abroad.[13] The government's schemes to profit from trafficking its citizens across borders also included luring Filipino expatriates to return to the homeland "as tourists and, ultimately, as investors."[14]

Miss X employs the conventions of Hollywood-style crime films and adult melodramas to evocatively represent the conditions and consequences of labor migration. The narrative realistically depicts the immigrant woman's plight while also weaving an allegory of Filipina femininity and nationalism in the wake of labor exportation. Since women in patriarchal societies function as "the symbolic repository of group identity," their bodies are identified with the nation and appropriated as its conspicuous and invisible markers.[15] The heroine of Portes's film thus functions as a stand-in for her fellow overseas Filipinas as well as an image of the mother country.

The female protagonist, Filomena, or Luming, is a single mother who departs her country to support her child and extended family. At the Manila airport she meets an eighteen-year old seafarer named Dave, who is charmed by her provincial innocence and friendliness, but nothing becomes of their brief encounter. One year after this meeting, the two reunite by happenstance in Amsterdam. While strolling in the entertainment district, Dave sees a poster announcing Luming's appearance at the Palace nightclub, in an orientalist disco act titled *Miss X and the Asiatic Duo*. A compatriot later tells Dave that Luming prostitutes herself during warmer months, in one of the city's iconic window brothels. Dave and Luming's unplanned reunion is due in part to the consequence of illegal recruitment: her chambermaid job quickly turned into white slavery, while he never received the work permit for seafaring promised by his recruiter. They both found their way to Amsterdam, known for its leniency toward undocumented workers.

As is often the case in crime films, multiple parties vie for the heroine of *Miss X*. Dave is the first of those parties. He begins a romantic relationship with Luming, hoping to share her life in the diaspora. The feisty woman bluntly tells him that she is unsure of their long-term prospects but wishes to give him a shot anyway. Dave promises to save Luming from a life of prostitution but loses his illegally acquired job as a dockhand due to a crackdown on illegal immigration. She ends up rescuing him instead, feeding and sheltering him by returning to sex work and doing trashy floor shows for older men of different races. In keeping with the film's nationalist allegory, Dave's romantic rival is a foreigner: a Dutch gangster unimaginatively named Hans. He acts as the Filipina's on-and-off lover and also her pimp, controlling and profiting from Luming by booking her at nightclubs and arranging her "dates" with clients. Apart from getting a hefty cut of her earnings, Hans also steals from her purse to feed his out-of-control drug habit, pocketing money she has saved up for her daughter's medication. In a voice-over, Luming explains her reasons for putting up with Hans: he took her in when she was homeless, gave her the means to thrive in Amsterdam, and seemed to have truly loved her until drugs got the better of him.

The third entity vying for Luming's heart and body is not another romantic rival but rather her family, to whom she is also a sexual commodity and a steady source of labor power. This includes her mother and the chronically ill female child she had out of wedlock. Her mother makes contradictory demands in her phone calls and letters, asking Luming to provide money to keep the family afloat while also making her feel guilty for not remaining in the Philippines to tend to her sick child.

Luming's untenable predicament of trying to serve all three parties dramatizes the gendered exploitation of female migrant workers. Parreñas uses the term "force of domesticity" to describe "the persistence of the ideology of women's domesticity, in the labor market, the family, and the migrant community, as well as in migration policies and laws."[16] Like most migrant women, Luming engages in the feminized labor of care and sex work. Her wages support her maternal duties, a series of also feminized obligations. Society measures her worth as a person by how well she provides for her child and her ability to uphold the moral standards deemed appropriate to a Filipina mother and woman. The force of domesticity keeps women like Luming in their "proper" place—that is, slaving for her family and being subservient to men whether at home or abroad. In addition to representing the force of domesticity, Luming's service to Dave and her family indexes her loyalty to the nation. The film initially shows that the Filipinos in her life are the rightful beneficiaries of her affection and the fruits of her efforts. In their constant need for Luming's money and love, Dave and Luming's family resemble the ever-demanding nation-state, with its various schemes to capture the earnings and loyalty of migrant workers.

The narrative of *Miss X* sets up an ideal resolution that is profoundly conservative. It entails turning Luming from a fallen woman into a good wife to Dave, and from an absent mother to her child to one who is physically present. Luming would form (or reconstitute) a proper nuclear family in Amsterdam or—better yet—the Philippines. To Portes's credit, *Miss X* thwarts these familiar and easy terms of resolution in a series of dramatic reversals. Luming's daughter succumbs to an illness, resulting in heartbreak for the heroine but also giving her respite from a heavy financial burden. Although she is loath to admit it, the cost of treating the child's unspecified illness and supporting the extended family had been overwhelming; indeed, so heavy was this burden that Luming instinctively stopped checking in on her family for several weeks. Such bouts of familial disaffection implicitly counter the romanticized narrative of Filipino migrant workers who will do everything for their families. While we could read the death of the child as a moralistic punishment for Luming's fallenness, the tragedy also grants her an unexpected reprieve from the force of domesticity. The child's death creates a new path of self-preservation and happiness for her mother.

The other reversals similarly free Luming from the remaining parties laying claim over her. The narrative casts aside its romantic hero by revealing Dave as ill prepared for a relationship and impurely motivated in his pursuit of Luming. The heroine walks away from him and, acting on her sexual desires, briefly reconnects with Hans. After realizing that the Dutchman is an opportunist and a drug addict, Luming pulls away from him as well. The heroine's decision to rid herself of unworthy men is consistent with the trajectory of her narrative as an immigrant bildungsroman, a tale of her maturation, independence, and modest success in a foreign land. The film highlights Luming's impressive personal growth despite her vulnerability as an undocumented person and her stigmatized occupation as a sex worker. For example, the film portrays her emotional maturity, fine business sense (she reverses a decline in her business), and resistance to the chauvinism of her lovers. The narrative only proceeds toward its tragic climax after demonstrating the strength and resilience of her character.

The explosive finale occurs after Dave visits Luming to make amends and bid her farewell. Hans, whom Luming has recently jilted, barges into the meeting and shoots Dave in a fit of jealousy. The film ends with Luming cradling Dave's body in a pietà-like pose, wailing and also cursing her lot. The cursing hints at Luming's toughness: she is not the typical damsel in distress and does not plead for divine intervention. More important, she does not come running back to the Philippines, thus dispensing with the obligatory homecoming scene that had already become a staple of narratives about Philippine émigrés in film and fiction. The absence of a homecoming hints at a future for Luming in Amsterdam beyond the film's ending. *Miss X*'s bittersweet tale of the migrant woman's bildungsroman might have another chapter that will begin, significantly, with the demise of Luming's most beloved persons from the homeland.

As a work of border cinema, *Miss X* inherits a politically useful ambivalence not only from the genre traditions of melodrama but also from the crime film. In crime films, the depredations and acts of violence suffered by the protagonists often hold a social valence. Such is arguably the case in Portes's film, where sexual exploitation and violence are attributed not only to the work of gangsters but also to the conditions of labor migration. The film links sexual exploitation to the flesh trade in Amsterdam and, more pointedly, to the unbearable conditions of Luming's home and country. Luming occupies two contradictory roles in the crime film repertoire: as the victim of white slavery who falls for one of her captors, and later, when she returns to Hans, as the gangster's moll. As I have noted, the film ends with the suggestion that Luming's newfound resilience will allow her to weather her tragic losses.

The narrative's conclusion is followed by a disclaimer that either pre-empts censorship or placates the censors. Ferdinand Marcos's famously capricious and paranoid censors might have objected to any number of things, including depictions that criticized migrant work (which the state was promoting) or blamed the state for failing to protect its laborers overseas. *Miss X* gives the nation-state the final word by adding the disclaimer. To the "pietà" ending the film superimposes a still image of Luming embracing her daughter, followed by a solarized montage of newspaper headlines that tout the government's success in prosecuting illegal recruiters. The juxtaposition is symptomatic of the state's desire to reconcile sharp contradictions. The family picture validates labor migration—a practice encouraged by the state—by depicting it as a laudable act of familial sacrifice. This idea is then inadvertently undermined by headlines about the menace of illegal recruitment, even as those headlines reassure the public that the Philippine government is already resolving the widespread problem.

The layering of contradictions in the epilogue, and one might say throughout the film itself, is understandable. The issue of labor migration was perhaps even more fraught then—in its originating moments—than it is the present when one-tenth of Filipino workers are overseas migrants. *Miss X* registers such contradictions, occasionally undermining its feminist insights to found a practice of representing the migrant woman's plight in the form of a popular genre film.

Maricris Sioson: Japayuki, a Feminist Critique of Labor Export

In 1988, President Corazon Aquino famously labeled migrant workers from her country as its "bagong bayani" (new heroes and heroines).[17] This statement reflected her government's effort to expand her predecessor Ferdinand Marcos's labor exportation program. Under Aquino, and her successor Fidel V. Ramos, the ranks of migrant laborers swelled. Participation by women in labor migration saw a dramatic increase in the late 1980s and, as Rodriguez notes, "by the early 1990s, it rivaled the migration of Filipino men."[18] The rise in women's out-migration colored public discourse about labor export, strengthening gendered tropes about the special vulnerability of women, the threat posed by absent mothers to the nuclear family, and the national disrepute brought about by the association of Filipinas with "lowly" domestic work and hostessing. In the 1990s, a cycle of biopics and docudramas about labor export reflected national anxieties over the welfare and status of Filipina migrant workers. In a welcome development, the films offered a fuller picture of the migrant's plight; they sharply criticized the Philippine nation-state, in addition to the patriarchy and the societies that host migrant workers. The films leveled such critique by once again hybridizing melodrama with the generic resources of the crime film and—more subtly—the horror film as well. Spanning a half decade, this second cycle of migrant worker films began with films such as Joey Romero's *Maricris Sioson: Japayuki* (The Maricris Sioson story: Japayuki, 1993), a studio-made feature about a Filipina nightclub entertainer who dies under mysterious circumstances in Japan. Following *Japayuki* were three 1995 films about Flor Contemplacion, the Filipina maid hanged in Singapore despite worldwide protests.[19] The cycle ebbed in 1997 with Joel Lamangan's *The Sarah Balabagan Story* (1997), a film about a fourteen-year-old maid sentenced to death in the United Arab Emirates (UAE) for killing the employer who molested her. The UAE pardoned Balabagan, thanks to the assistance of the Philippine government and the European Parliament.[20] The release of the biopic was delayed by government intervention, owing to concerns that the film would lead to a diplomatic fracas with a country that employs numerous Filipino workers.

Regal Films, one of the leading studios in the Philippines, produced *Maricris Sioson: Japayuki*. The term *japayuki* refers to "foreign women, and especially Filipina women, who traveled through both licit and illicit channels to work in hostess bars and perform other forms of sexualized labor."[21] Regal made *Japayuki* a little more than a year after Sioson's death, to cash in on a cause célèbre and ride the bandwagon of so-called massacre films, exploitation movies based on true crime stories. Sioson's case captured the imagination of Filipinos because of sensational claims about the brutality of her demise, the involvement of the Yakuza (an international crime syndicate), and an alleged cover-up by a Japanese hospital and that country's authorities. Fortunately, the Sioson biopic project was assigned to the fine director Joey Romero and to the leftist feminist writer Lualhati Bautista. The filmmakers structured *Japayuki* as a postmortem, opening the film with the repatriation of Maricris Sioson's remains from Fukushima. Hewing closely to published accounts of the incident, Romero depicts

Sioson's body arriving with "bruises, welts and wounds."[22] The corpse's ghastly appearance belies the findings of the Japanese, who have attributed her death to "multiple organ failure and fulminant hepatitis." The sight of the battered corpse upsets Sioson's elder sister Onnie, as does the recruiter's insistence that the family had previously agreed to abstain from having the corpse examined in the Philippines as a condition of its repatriation by the Japanese. Sioson's family and the National Bureau of Investigation defy the supposed agreement and proceed with the autopsy. In contradiction to Japanese reports, the bureau's pathologist blames Sioson's death on a traumatic head injury; he also notes a deep laceration in the decedent's genitals. The movie's fractured narrative returns again and again to Sioson's corpse and the conflicting accounts of her demise, repeatedly posing the rhetorical question of who killed the Filipina entertainer. Much of the narrative unfolds during the more than two weeks when Sioson's corpse is waked, a ritual unnecessarily prolonged to wait for the government's release of its official autopsy results. It is important to note that the film's interest in Sioson's autopsy is not simply a (political) tactic to draw audience sympathy but also a sensationalist ploy to satisfy the lurid interests of the massacre film subgenre and its horrific rendition of true crime stories.

The tale of Sioson's demise is pieced together by a Filipina activist and writer, Cynthia, who is writing a story to draw attention to the precarious situation of Filipina migrant laborers in Japan. In a nod to American crime films and procedurals, Cynthia conducts interviews, visits crime scenes, and supplies voice-over commentary in which she reflexively composes and revises her narrative about Sioson's death. Alvin, a male employee of the government-run Overseas Workers Welfare Administration (OWWA), tags along with her. In a sly criticism of the government and mainstream cinema's obsession with romance, the film shows Alvin as being more interested in courting Cynthia than in investigating Sioson's death. When, for instance, Cynthia grills him about the OWWA's response to the newly released autopsy report indicating a laceration in Sioson's genitals, the bureaucrat exclaims, "I'm not the government! Can we have coffee or something and talk about more pleasant things?"

As in *Miss X*, *Japayuki* identifies both the Filipino family and overseas recruiters as responsible parties in the migrant worker's death. Although Sioson had once dreamed of taking a degree in nursing, the death of her father and the failure of the family business have prevented her from attending college. Bella, another of Sioson's older sisters, sets an "unfortunate" example by working as an entertainer in Japan and boasting about the Japanese husband she met during her stint there. Bella asks Sioson to accompany her to the recruiter's office, showing off her little sister to the sleazy male agent and planting a seed in the young woman's mind. When Sioson eventually decides to try her luck in Japan, the Manila training center for Japan-bound entertainers connives with her to misrepresent her real age in her enrollment records, turning her seventeen years into nineteen. The recruiter also turns a blind eye as Sioson fudges her age in her travel papers. Sioson's family weakly protests her decision to leave for Japan, also citing her age as a concern. In the end all parties knowingly send an underage woman to the Japanese flesh trade.

Apart from criticizing the institutions and individuals mentioned above, the film also indicts the patriarchy in the Philippines and the host country for Sioson's troubles. Before she leaves the country, Sioson discovers that Filipino men—even those close to her—can be misogynistic and violent. Her once sweet boyfriend Dario insists that all "japayukis are *putas*" (prostitutes). He also deflowers her at a cheap motel, crassly insisting that she should give him "first dibs instead of giving it up to a Japanese man."

The film depicts Sioson's Japanese employers, handlers, and some customers maltreating her and her fellow entertainers at every turn. Cynthia points out at the start of the film that thirty-three Filipina entertainers have already died in Japan, and many more are suffering from mental illness, presumably from the pressures of doing sex work. The shady Yakuza-associated men, who help run the club, secretly drug the Filipinas to make them more cooperative to favored customers. The men also order the entertainers to take contraception and pills that would "prevent bad smell down there." Predictably, the men are not averse to beating the women. The worst of the Japanese men is Saito, the owner of the club where Sioson works; his character is based on Keizo Sato, a businessman who operates multiple clubs in Japan and the Philippines.[23] Saito is a gangster figure straight out of a Martin Scorsese film: moody, autocratic, ultraviolent. When Sioson escapes from his club, Saito asks his men to capture and rough her up before he bashes her head and plunges a samurai sword into her vagina. The use of excessive violence, gangster and slasher film clichés, East Asian exoticism, and kitschy production design to malign the Japanese is appropriate to the film's target audience and betrays the film's strong affinity to exploitation cinema. The result is an odd kind of agitprop, one that extends the range of forms and political concerns of border cinemas.

The film's investigation into the Filipina's death eventually points the finger at the Philippine government. Halfway into *Japayuki*, Alvin has an epiphany of sorts and admits to Cynthia that the state bears a great deal of responsibility for the misfortunes of Sioson and other migrant workers. He says, "I work for the government. But sometimes I think it would be better if there were no overseas job opportunities for Filipinos. Their dollar remittances . . . save the government from its debts and obligations to provide jobs for the people. The government got used to overlooking the problem of unemployment. That's why if there were no jobs in Saudi, Japan and elsewhere, the government would be forced to find jobs for Filipinos here instead of making them work as slaves in other countries." Alvin's full-throated critique of the state's labor export policy is followed by an unexpected burst of rainfall, a sign (in Philippine culture) that the heavens approve.

The film ends shortly after the Philippine government accepts the Japanese government's final report about Sioson's death, which reiterates that the Filipina entertainer died of liver disease and not at the hand of underworld characters. The Philippine government's decision to kowtow to Japan puzzlingly disregards the findings of the government's pathologist. While visiting the scene of the crime, Cynthia obtains the testimony of one of Sioson's fellow Filipina entertainers, a woman named Rowena. Rowena's account, which she heroically provides at great risk, serves as the basis of the film's depiction of Sioson's final days, including the circumstances of the latter's death. The film places sound and image in a contrapuntal relationship to underscore the disparity between Cynthia's account and those of the Japanese. The soundtrack carries Saito's testimony about Sioson's death while the images present (and privilege) a contradictory account based on Rowena's narrative.

The film ends with two nearly identical tirades against the Japanese and Philippine governments, launched by Sioson's sister Onnie and by Cynthia. The former, enraged by the news that her government has formally accepted the Japanese report on Sioson's death, insists that the condition of her sister's corpse tells the true story. Cynthia gives an interview to the press and echoes Onnie's point that the woman's body "is the strongest piece of evidence" against the official record. Before the end credits roll, the film offers three images of Sioson's "body" in a montage. First, we see Sioson's tomb in a rural cemetery. Over this image soon appears an image of Sioson, her hair given a halo-like appearance by backlighting, suggesting that she is at peace (and maybe even in heaven). The penultimate image before the end credits is of Sioson, a little out of sorts, performing in a floor show.

The epilogue's juxtaposition of asynchronous images of Sioson's body mimics the fractured temporal structure of the film's plot. The jumping back and forth in time is not insignificant and serves various functions. First, the disordered temporality troubles the neat and confidently told story in the official accounts of Sioson's ordeal. Second, the nonlinear and constantly interrupted narration registers the emotional toll of telling and rehearsing the woman migrant's tragic story. The storytelling proceeds in fits and starts, occasionally breaks down at unbearable moments, and sometimes loses its way altogether. This manner of storytelling refuses to normalize the death and abuse of migrant women such as Sioson; instead, it registers the filmmakers' exasperation and outrage. Third, the narrative's temporal ruptures not only compress the story for practical reasons but also reflexively indicate wide gaps in the official record and lapses in the memory of those involved. The gaps and ruptures show the limits of cinematic and fictional storytelling and index the Philippine government's restricted purview over migrant workers beyond the nation's borders.

One finds the fractured, temporally shifting narration of *Japayuki* in other 1990s films about migrant workers, most notably in Joel Lamangan's *The Flor Contemplacion Story* (1995). Disorderly narration works similarly across this body of films, performing the ethical functions of challenging ostensibly settled accounts and lingering on the emotional flashpoints of Overseas Filipino Worker tragedies. This example of melodramatic storytelling corrects the historical record, fosters empathy for "disposable" workers, and attempts to shock the state and its citizens into reforming or even terminating the labor export program.

As in the case of *Miss X*, Sioson's tragedy calls attention to the dangers of hostessing and sex work. By doing so, Romero's film implicitly stokes paternalistic calls for the state to "curtail and better regulate women's emigration." As Rodriguez points out, one possible effect of such messages is to diminish both the employment choices and social standing of female migrant laborers and would-be migrants.[24] The depiction of female entertainers and sex workers as fallen women is endemic to melodramas, and while they are often exceptionally sympathetic to those characters, the moralizing attitude limits the progressive discourse of films about figures such as Luming and Sioson.

In My Life: Queering the Migrant's Tale

President Joseph Estrada declared the 2000 the "Year of the Overseas Filipino Worker." Estrada, a former movie actor and producer, continued a labor export policy that was by then already a quarter century old. When he was ousted in 2001 by a popular uprising similar to that which ended the Marcos dictatorship, the vice president, an economist and former college professor, took his post. In spite of the stark differences in their politics and style of governance, Estrada's successor Gloria Macapagal-Arroyo followed a similar playbook in exporting Filipino workers. On one occasion, Arroyo described herself as "the CEO of a global Philippine enterprise of 8 million Filipinos who live and work abroad and generate billions of dollars a year in revenue for our country."[25] Her rhetoric baldly characterizes the nation's business as one of trafficking its citizens internationally for profit and development. Rodriguez uses the term "labor brokerage state" to describe the immense bureaucratic apparatus that "mobilizes and deploys labor for export to profit from migrants' remittances."[26] This system, which has grown in complexity since the 1970s, facilitates the large-scale traffic in migrant labor by training workers, appointing diplomats who scour the globe for jobs for Filipino citizens, and providing benefits for migrant workers and their families, among other functions.

In the early 2000s, the third cycle of films indexed various changes in the experiences of migrant laborers and the nation's system of labor brokerage. Public outrage over the 1990s deaths of Contemplacion and Sioson and led to sweeping reforms, including the passage of additional laws to protect migrant workers during their stints abroad.[27] Due in part to such developments, most of the films belonging to this third cycle no longer centered on conflicts over the life and liberty of Filipino migrants. Equally significant, the state's labor brokerage apparatus—an object of criticism in the 1990s cycle—receded or disappeared entirely from view. The social problem at the heart of this new cycle of films shifted to broader issues of assimilation, including the protagonists' immigration status and their claims to social acceptance. Instead of the crime film, the emphasis of this genre cycle turned once more to romance and the bildungsroman. Pioneering filmmakers like Gil Portes, the director of *Miss X,* continued to make lachrymose films about Filipino émigrés in the new millennium, but his work and that of others in the 1990s was less severe than the earlier movies on the subject. The sunnier disposition of this third cycle is due to the rationale and the organization behind the production of many of those films. The media conglomerate ABS-CBN produced about a dozen films about Filipino overseas workers between 1995 and 2011, the bulk of them created in the new millennium. A chief aim of those films was to promote the global expansion of the conglomerate, which began in the 1990s to offer telecommunication and financial services to Filipinos all over the world. Films set in Australia, Dubai, Hong Kong, London, Milan, New York, and San Francisco placed Filipino characters and stories in the same cities and nations where the conglomerate operated. The inevitable travelogue-like aspect of these films also appealed to domestic audiences, including those for whom working abroad was still a pipe dream.

The success of the conglomerate's international operations and the films that promoted them meant that the latter films in the cycle no longer had to function as extended commercials. It is still generally true, however, as Rolando B. Tolentino notes in his critique of these films, that they "glamorize foreign lands and the migrant body's capacity to survive in these lands."[28] That said, such elements do not always read like advertisements for the migrant worker's lifestyle; sometimes they function quite progressively to demonstrate the Filipino workers' extraordinary industriousness and resilience.

An important feature of several films in this cycle is the centering of the migrant's narrative around a male protagonist in addition to a female one, effectively displacing the 1990s cycle's typical figure of the hapless woman migrant. In many cases, the cycle of the early 2000s featured female migrants who were tougher and enjoyed more social advantages than similar characters in the earlier cycles. The arc of these narratives proceeds as a bildungsroman, one that shows the migrant workers reaching a new level of maturity, learning the ways of the world, and finding their place in the cosmopolitan city.

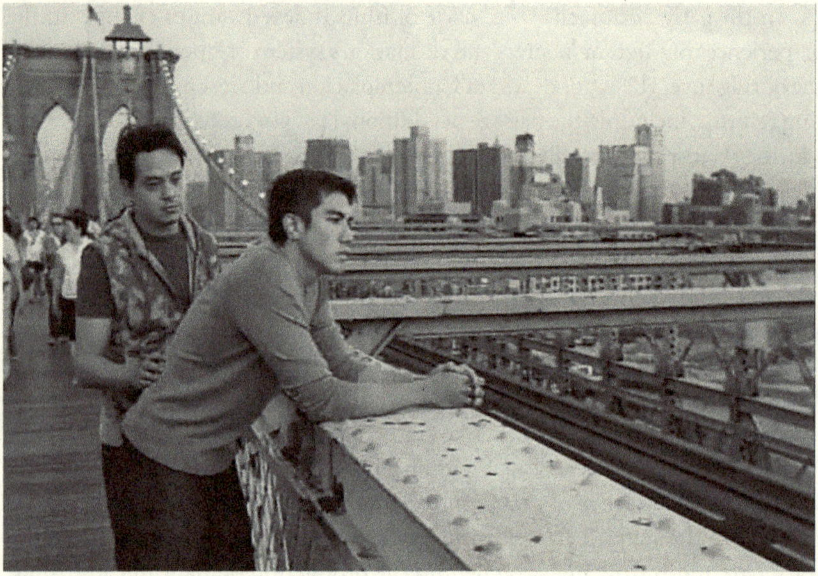

FIG. 12.1 *In My Life* (2009): Two gay Filipino migrants commiserate on the Brooklyn Bridge.

Such is the case in Olivia Lamasan's *In My Life* (2009), a romance and maternal melodrama set in New York. The film's protagonist, a chauffeur and lackey named Noel, finds himself on the cusp of several borders—namely, of gender, class, and national belonging. Noel is masculine, not fully out of the closet, undocumented, and struggling to hold on to his place in the middle class. He is unlike his partner Mark in several respects; the latter is an out gay man, a successful white-collar employee, and a legal immigrant. The disparity in the lovers' social positions is emphasized throughout the film, functioning as a social exposé about undocumented immigrants, a tale of gay affirmation, and a plot device to introduce conflict into an otherwise uneventful romantic coupling (see figure 12.1).

Like most films about migrant laborers, *In My Life* shows the undocumented émigré's lot as a something of a death-in-life existence. Noel is run ragged by his multiple low-paying jobs, the fear of deportation, social ostracism, and feeling the pressure to succeed for the benefit of helping his family. His troubles worsen when Mark's mother comes to visit and stays with them. The feisty and overbearing matriarch, Shirley Templo, is a widow, a retired school librarian, and a physical education teacher. She had remarried, but the relationship fell apart and was annulled (there is no divorce in the Philippines). Her daughter prevailed upon her to sell the family home and use the proceeds so that they may begin new lives abroad. Shirley quit her job and opted to move to the United States, while her daughter and family have emigrated to Australia. Unlike Mark and Noel, Shirley is not technically an immigrant—she is a natural-born U.S. citizen who has spent most of her life in the Philippines. In spite of this privilege, she has a hard time readjusting to American society and entering the U.S. labor market at an advanced age. Like Noel, Shirley must toil in low-paying menial jobs.

In an odd plot turn, Mark implores Shirley to enter into a green card marriage with Noel, who had been previously swindled by a Filipina American who had agreed to marry him so he could obtain legal immigrant status but instead ran away with his money. Noel's only other prospect of securing a green card is to marry an unattractive Filipina American named Pamela, but both he and Mark cannot bear it—and neither can the film's liberal politics, because such a resolution would dissolve the gay couple. Shirley is upset by the pseudo-incestuous nature of her son's proposal but changes her mind after Mark suddenly perishes from a car mishap (this, after recently going into remission from colon cancer). Due to filial piety, Noel and Shirley form an unlikely queer couple to replace the one that previously existed between Noel and Mark.

The crucial significance of these queer couplings is worth examining, even briefly. One of the most progressive elements of films about migrants—and of border cinemas—is their Janus-faced critique of the homeland and the host country. The migrants' critical subject position permits them to see the inhospitable and unlivable aspects of their former and current societies. The unlikely queer triangle that binds Noel to Mark and Mark's mother is symptomatic of various aspects of their lives in the Philippines and the United States. All of them have fled a homeland that has "queered" them because of their nonconformity to Christian morality and recently, in Shirley's case, to the idealized nuclear family. Although the United States is more receptive to cisgender gay couples such as Noel and Mark, it can also be inhospitable, legally and economically, to undocumented persons and the underclass. The queer and queered immigrants in *In My Life* learn to behave defiantly toward their old and new societies after becoming wise to the mechanisms of their abjection. Noel flees the Philippines as an economic migrant. Mark remains in the United States in part to escape his mother's homophobia. When she comes to live with him, he gets his mother to accept his and Noel's sexuality and rid herself of her aversion to homosexuality. He also deftly puts his lover and mother on a path that will end the former's crippling illegality. After Mark's death, Noel and Shirley commit themselves to their unorthodox, morally problematic, and illicit scheme to secure Noel's future. Turning their backs on the Philippine nation-state, the three of them have proceeded to defraud their host nation with impunity and without guilt. Contrary to many immigrant bildungsromans, their American modus vivendi embraces illegality rather than valorizing the wounded attachment (to use Wendy Brown's term) of one who waits helplessly for amnesty or legal reprieve from U.S. immigration law.[29] To keep the green card marriage under wraps, Shirley quietly detaches herself from her white suitor, a deli owner named Elai, for several years, even if it means losing him for good. To be sure, as in most maternal melodramas, Shirley carries the water for the men. The narrative reassigns her maternal responsibilities to her son's lover after Mark's death; in the Philippines and America, her identity revolves around being a mother figure. But in its closing moments, the film mitigates even this stubborn aspect of gender inequality. On the Brooklyn Bridge—significantly, a border setting—Shirley bumps into Elai, who tells her that he misses her and would like to reconnect. She volunteers that she has gotten married but keeps mum about her groom. Then, with a hearty smile and twinkly eyes, she tells him to seek her again after she gets a divorce "in two years." Shirley's openness to Elai's romantic interest is an intimation of her path to liberation from her remaining maternal duties. In two years, her son's lover will have a green card. In two years, she will be that much more emotionally distant from her other children, who forced her to start over abroad. Even if the balding, decrepit Elai may not seem like a good catch, he represents the promise of a renewed love life. Perhaps with his modest wealth, she might also find a gentler way of earning her keep than working menial jobs.

At its most progressive, *In My Life* articulates an exilic feminist, queer, postnational, and transnational consciousness within a work of commercial cinema. Lamasan's film undermines not only the romance of national attachment but also the fantasy of extraordinary success associated with the American dream. The "happily ever after" scenarios promised by the film for both Shirley and Noel are decidedly modest: just a reprieve from the U.S. immigration system and a return to the simple middle-class lives they had in the Philippines.

It is true, as Tolentino suggests of this third cycle of "melodramatic OCW [Overseas Contract Worker] films," that *In My Life* forgoes the stylistic grittiness of the previous cycle of migrant worker films for the unrealistic and slick form of the romantic travelogue.[30] The same may also be said of the absence of the strident political critique that marked the 1990s cycle. Such variations do not necessarily make *In My Life* (or others in the cycle of the early 2000s) inferior, for the politics and form of both émigré films and border cinemas demand persistent recalibration and revaluation if they are to retain their powers of criticism.

Coda: *Transit* and the Problem of Hospitality

Although sociopolitical critique in Philippine cinema reached a watershed in the 1970s and 1980s, during and shortly after the Marcos dictatorship, one finds in some contemporary movies examples of a far more imaginative and nuanced approach. The same can be said of certain films about migrant workers, although I do not wish to imply a narrative of constant progress. Hannah Espia's independently produced family melodrama *Transit* (2013) treats the politics of migration with a density of information and insight that rivals that of documentary cinema. Set in Israel, the film's conflict derives from that country's inhospitable treatment of its foreign workers. This problem of hospitality is evident in new restrictive immigration laws that command the deportation of the children of migrant workers below a certain age. Those restrictions join statutes that bar older children of migrant workers as well as the workers themselves from gaining citizenship in that country.

Transit centers on two Filipino caregivers/housekeepers and their children. The film's narrative—fractured, as in a previous cycle of émigré films—shifts in focalization to dramatize the impact of the law on each of the pivotal characters. Moises is a newcomer whose son Joshua is subject to deportation by the Israeli immigration authorities because he is under five years old and not currently in school. His only chance at remaining in the country where he was born and raised is through legal adoption by his Filipina mother Susan and her new husband, an Israeli. Afraid that even having a relationship with her son could strain her marriage, Susan refuses to take him in. Moises's older sister Janet is a longtime resident of Israel; she has a teenage daughter named Yael who, although fathered by an Israeli and not presently subject to a deportation edict, remains without a path to citizenship. Janet fears it is just a matter of time before the state passes legislation that would also lead to Yael's deportation (see figure 12.2).

The mechanisms of social exclusion in *Transit* highlight the lowly status of Filipino émigrés as disposable workers, hired precisely because they can be easily retrenched from their jobs and expelled at will by their host countries. Janet and Moises's social disadvantage recalls the predicament that Parreñas names as "partial citizenship," referring to "the stunted integration of migrants in receiving nation states, which in the case of women is demonstrated by discriminatory measures that deny them their reproductive rights."[31] Such drastic circumscription of immigrant's rights causes much unnecessary suffering. Apart from being cruel, it is also, as Parreñas notes, especially ironic because the host nation denies "reproductive rights for women, who not only contribute to the economic growth but also perform the reproductive labor of receiving nations."[32] Reproductive labor is, for Parreñas, the activity that sustains a "productive labor force"; it involves "caring, feeding, clothing, teaching, and nurturing individuals so that they may have the faculties and abilities to be productive workers in society."[33] Janet's situation typifies such irony, for her reproductive labor allows a First World woman to enjoy a career and family even as her host country bars her from having children there.

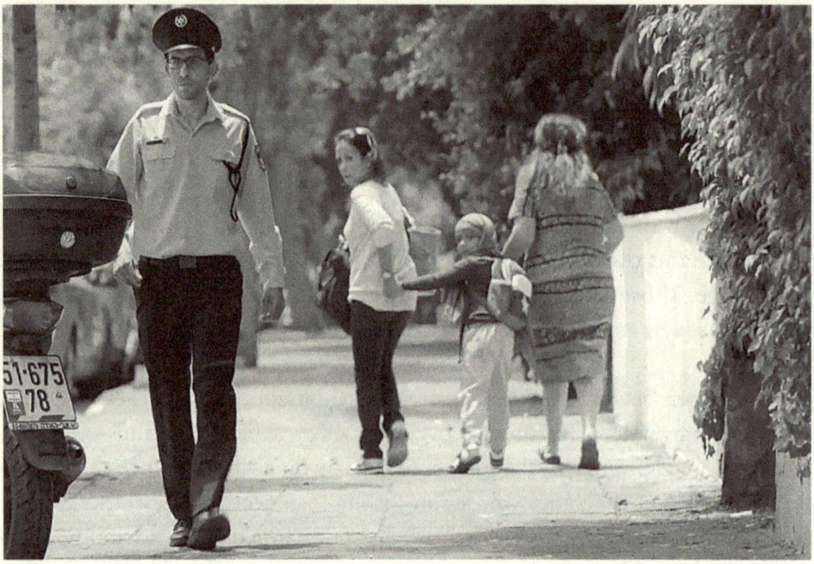

FIG. 12.2 *Transit* (2013): A Filipina caregiver nervously pulls her undocumented nephew away from an Israeli policeman.

Transit repeatedly questions the fairness of Israel's immigration policy, depicting the edict to deport young children as one so cruel that even citizens oppose it. Janet and Moises's employers defy their government by providing assistance or refuge to Joshua. The film also shows Israeli activists gathering petitions to repeal the unjust statutes. The film vivifies the effects of these legal predicaments on Filipinos by using documentary-style handheld shots, harsh lighting, and gritty locations. Moreover, the film uses long takes and almost real-time pacing in scenes that depict Joshua and Moises separately pleading their cases to immigration authorities. The film likewise uses documentary-style techniques in scenes of actual Filipino émigrés and their children gathering outdoors to celebrate special occasions together and to discuss their worries about the immigration system.

As with the other films discussed in this chapter, *Transit* operates at the border of cinematic genres. Apart from drawing on the documentary and social problem film, *Transit* functions as a maternal melodrama with two sets of mother-child dyads. The maternal melodrama, as Williams notes, is animated by the "parental fantasy of possessing the child," a "quest for connection" that is "always tinged with the melancholy of loss."[34] In Espia's film the Israeli state represents the powerful external force that crushes the Filipino parents' fantasy of possessing their children while slaving away in their host country. Janet and Moises function as the suffering parents in the film's maternal melodrama. Moises is emasculated by his restricted legal rights and by the cruel indifference of his child's mother. The film's recourse to the generic structure of the maternal melodrama supercharges the film's politics with primal emotions. The daily prospect of enforced familial separation taxes the parents and children in the film, and the viewers feel the anxiety of impending loss in almost every scene.

Apart from its recourse to the conventions of maternal melodrama, *Transit* also owes a debt to border cinemas from the West, particularly in its representation of the disparate politics of national belonging and cultural identification between émigré or ethnic parents and their children. Such models of implicit multigenerational divisions over the politics of identification and assimilation include Orlando Jiménez and Leon Ichaso's Latino film *El Super* (1979), Damien O'Donnell's British American feature *East Is East* (1999), and Gene Cajayon's Filipino American indie feature *The Debut* (2000). Echoing some of these films, Joshua and Yael respond to their disenfranchisement by asserting not only their Israeli nationality but also their Israeli cultural identity. Joshua goes further by demonstrating in one of the film's dramatic highlights that he is spiritually Jewish, making a last-ditch effort to stop his deportation by passionately reciting to immigration police a long passage from the Torah. The impromptu bar mitzvah impresses some of the police, but not enough to spare the kid from expulsion. This profession of Israeli belonging follows two similar incidents. Earlier in the film, Joshua delights in a visit to the Wailing Wall. He also asks his Filipino father if a person could be born Jewish even if he belongs to a different race. Even after his deportation, Joshua shows his loyalty to Israel by loudly worrying (at the airport) that his "memories of Israel" might "fade away." For her part, Yael proves her Israeliness by emulating the racialized offspring in British and U.S. films who disidentify with their ethnic parents. Similar to Sarah Jane in Douglas Sirk's *Imitation of Life* (1959) and Tariq Khan in *East Is East*, Yael asserts her loyalty to Israel by explicitly disavowing her mother's national identity. She defiantly refuses Janet's tearful interpellation of her as Filipino, countering that she is in fact Israeli.

Demonstrating the steady erosion of Filipino nationalism through the impact of labor migration and, in part, by the earlier cycles of Filipino émigré films I have discussed here, *Transit* concludes with a weak expression of hope about Joshua's new life in the Philippines. Moises comforts his son by telling a fairy tale that uses the clichéd symbol of rainbows to evoke hope, but his words do not provide a satisfying conclusion to their real-life narrative. The film ends with an unresolved complaint about the boy's and Yael's disenfranchisement within the nation of their birth. As the film makes clear, the Israeli-born Filipinos find themselves marginalized or expelled from the same country that benefits from the blood, tears, and caring labor of their émigré parents. This melancholy and defiant concluding note is addressed not primarily at Filipinos but Israelis—and the Global North—more generally. Such a political statement via cinema may be characterized as rhetoric because it is directed at a transnational audience that may or may not be attentive and sympathetic to the plight of migrants and the diaspora. *Transit* thus participates in a kind of cinematic transnationalism or border cinema practice in which a "weaker" nation tries to speak to a more powerful one that may not even be disposed to listen.[35] The gesture is important not only because the message might be eventually received through indirect channels (such as in the responses of global film audiences and critics) but also because it expresses an abiding faith among Third World filmmakers in transnational or border cinema's potential as an instrument of social justice in the world.

The philosopher Alain Badiou values cinema for its unique ability to envision human presence and facilitate a "thinking of the Other."[36] Cinema's imaginative and contemplative work takes the form, he says, of "ethical genres" such as melodrama. Such genres "address humanity in order to offer it a moral mythology."[37] In the films I have described here, the "Other" is the new proletariat class from the Global South, and the "ethical genre" is the melodrama of that class's presence in the First World. The ethical and cultural work of that melodramatic tradition involves conjuring diverse and compelling visions of the Filipino migrant's plight, sparking domestic and international debates about the personal and social costs of exporting workers en masse, and even helping migrant workers and their host societies process the cross-cultural encounters spurred by the inequities of the global system and the doings of the Philippine nation-state. Melodrama enables a versatile and pluralistic discourse about the Filipino émigré, inscribing a wide range of concerns and perspectives about this now ubiquitous figure of the transnational worker. Whether largely progressive or conservative in its politics, the melodrama of Filipino émigrés is always productively ambivalent, keeping unsettled the matter of the émigrés' global deployment. The ambivalent moral mythology on offer in this type of entertainment is one that ethically bears witness to the suffering, exploitation, resilience, and small victories of the workers impelled by dreams and often dire circumstances to traverse borders and live "among strange lands and peoples."[38]

Notes

1 Noel Vera, "I Left My Brain in San Francisco," *Manila Chronicle*, August 12, 1995.
2 Rhacel Salazar Parreñas, *The Force of Domesticity: Filipina Migrants and Globalization* (New York: New York University Press, 2008), 4, 3.
3 Robyn Magalit Rodriguez, *Migrants for Export: How the Philippine State Brokers Labor to the World* (Minneapolis: University of Minnesota Press, 2010), x.
4 Ibid., xii.
5 Parreñas, *The Force of Domesticity*, 5.
6 Linda Williams, "Melodrama Revised," in *Refiguring American Film Genres:*

History and Theory, ed. Nick Browne (Berkeley: University of California Press, 1998), 50.

7 Michael Walker, "Melodrama and American Cinema," *Movie* 29–30 (1982): 2.

8 Peter Brooks, *The Melodramatic Imagination: Balzac, Henry James, Melodrama, and the Mode of Excess* (New Haven, Conn.: Yale University Press, 1995), 157.

9 Daniel Gerould, "The Americanization of Melodrama," in *American Melodrama*, ed. Daniel Gerould (New York: Performing Arts Journal Publications, 1983), 8.

10 Arjun Appadurai, *Modernity at Large: Cultural Dimensions of Globalization* (Minneapolis: University of Minnesota Press, 1996), 34.

11 Parreñas, *The Force of Domesticity*, 7.

12 Rodriguez, *Migrants for Export*, 80.

13 Ibid., 81.

14 Ibid.

15 Deniz Kandiyoti, "Identity and Its Discontents: Women and the Nation," in *Colonial Discourse and Post-Colonial Theory: A Reader*, ed. Patrick Williams and Laura Chrisman (New York: Columbia University Press, 1994), 388.

16 Parreñas, *The Force of Domesticity*, 9.

17 Rodriguez, *Migrants for Export*, 84.

18 Ibid., 97.

19 For more on this famous case, see Anne-Marie Hilsdon, "The Contemplacion Fiasco: The Hanging of a Filipino Domestic Worker in Singapore," in *Human Rights and Gender Politics: Asia-Pacific Perspectives*, ed. Martha Macintyre, Martha Macintyre, Anne-Marie Hilsdon, Vera Mackie, et al. (London: Routledge, 2000), 172–192.

20 Ibid., 179.

21 Lieba Faier, *Intimate Encounters: Filipina Women and the Remaking of Rural Japan* (Berkeley: University of California Press, 2009), 91.

22 Michael Dueñas, "The Maricris Sioson Story: A Dance with Death," *Philippines Free Press*, November 2, 1991.

23 Ibid.

24 Rodriguez, *Migrants for Export*, xxvii.

25 Rodriguez, *Migrants for Export*, 8.

26 Ibid., xv.

27 Ibid., 104–105.

28 Rolando B. Tolentino, "Female Work and Representation in Women's Films," *Philippine Studies* 57, no. 3 (2009): 429.

29 Wendy Brown, *States of Injury : Power and Freedom in Late Modernity* (Princeton N.J.: Princeton University Press, 1995), 49.

30 Tolentino, "Female Work and Representation in Women's Films," 426–427.

31 Rhacel Salazar Parreñas, "Transgressing the Nation-State: The Partial Citizenship and 'Imagined (Global) Community' of Migrant Filipina Domestic Workers," *Signs: Journal of Women in Culture and Society* 26, no. 4 (2001): 1130.

32 Ibid., 1134.

33 Parreñas, *The Force of Domesticity*, 12.

34 Linda Williams, "Film Bodies: Gender, Genre, and Excess," in *Film and Theory: An Anthology*, ed. Toby Miller and Robert Stam (Malden, Mass.: Wiley, 2000), 218.

35 I refer to this practice of transnational cinematic address in José B. Capino, *Dream Factories of a Former Colony: American Fantasies, Philippine Cinema* (Minneapolis: University of Minnesota Press, 2010), 66, 110, 183.

36 Alain Badiou, *Cinema*, translated by Susan Spitzer (Malden, Mass.: Polity, 2013), 8.
37 Ibid., 240.
38 John Durham Peters, "Exile, Nomadism, and Diaspora: The Stakes of Mobility in the Western Canon," in *Home, Exile, Homeland: Film, Media and the Politics of Place*, ed. Hamid Naficy (New York: Routledge, 1999), 39.

Acknowledgments

In many ways, this collection owes its inception to students who have participated in our Border Cinema course at California State University, Fullerton, and the iteration of the course Rebecca A. Sheehan taught at Harvard University. We thank these students for giving us the energy, inspiration, and momentum to endeavor this project. We would also like to thank Frederick Aldama for his enthusiastic support and encouragement, which has made all the difference in bringing these essays to print in a timely fashion. Finally, we thank our contributors for bringing the diverse perspectives, insightful ideas, and hard work that have made this collection such a generative conversation across geographic regions, genres, and aesthetic concerns.

Bibliography

"1980: Castro Announces Mariel Boatlift." History.com, http://www.history.com/this-day-in-history/castro-announces-mariel-boatlift.

Agamben, Giorgio. *State of Exception*. Translated by Kevin Attell. Chicago: University of Chicago Press, 2005.

"Alex Rivera speaking at Platform Summit 2014." *YouTube*, https://www.youtube.com/watch?v=eHPsmfLdiUs.

Andrijasevic, Rutvica. "From Exception to Excess: Detention and Deportations across the Mediterranean Space." In *The Deportation Regime: Sovereignty, Space, and the Freedom of Movement*, edited by Nicholas de Genova and Nathalie Peutz, 147–165. Durham, N.C.: Duke University Press, 2009.

Anzaldúa, Gloria. *Borderlands/La Frontera: The New Mestiza*. San Francisco: Spinsters/Aunt Lute, 1987.

Appadurai, Arjun. *Modernity at Large: Cultural Dimensions of Globalization*. Minneapolis: University of Minnesota Press, 1996.

Arendt, Hannah. *The Human Condition*. Chicago: University of Chicago Press, 1998.

Badiou, Alain. *Cinema*. Translated by Susan Spitzer. Malden, Mass.: Polity, 2013.

Bardenstein, Carol. "Cross/Cast: Passing in Israeli and Palestinian Cinema." In *Palestine, Israel and the Politics of Popular Culture*, edited by Ted Swedenberg and Rebecca Stein. Durham, N.C.: Duke University Press, 2005.

Barrera, Cordelia. "Cyborg Bodies, Strategies of Consciousness, and Ecological Revolution on the US-Mexico Borderlands." *Chicana/Latina Studies: The Journal of Mujeres Activas en Letras y Cambio Social* 14, no. 1 (2014): 28–55.

Beckman, Karen. "Animation on Trial." *Animation: An Interdisciplinary Journal* 6, no. 3 (2011): 259–275.

Benjamin, Walter. *Illuminations*. Translated by Harry Zohn. London: Fontana, 1973.

Berghahn, Daniella, and Claudia Sternberg, eds. *European Cinema in Motion: Migrant and Diasporic Film in Contemporary Europe*. New York: Palgrave Macmillan, 2010.

Bhabha, Homi K. "Signs Taken for Wonders: Questions of Ambivalence and Authority under a Tree outside Delphi, May 1817." *Critical Inquiry* 12, no. 1 (1985): 144–165.

Birri, Fernando. "For Nationalist, Realist, Critical, and Popular Cinema." In *New Latin American Cinema*, vol. 1, *Theories, Practices, and Transcontinental Articulations*, edited by Michael T. Martin, 95–98. Detroit: Wayne State University Press, 1997.

Bizzocchi, Jim. "The Fragmented Frame: The Poetics of the Split-Screen," 2009, http://web.mit.edu/comm-forum/legacy/mit6/papers/Bizzocchi.pdf (accessed on October 3, 2018).

Bolter, Jay, and Richard Grusin. *Remediation: Understanding New Media*. Cambridge, Mass.: MIT Press, 1999.

Bowden, Charles. *Juarez: The Laboratory of Our Future*. New York: Aperture, 1998.

Brooks, Peter. *The Melodramatic Imagination: Balzac, Henry James, Melodrama, and the Mode of Excess*. New Haven, Conn.: Yale University Press, 1995.

Brown, Wendy. *States of Injury: Power and Freedom in Late Modernity*. Princeton, N.J.: Princeton University Press, 1995.

———. *Walled States, Waning Sovereignty*. Brooklyn, N.Y.: Zone, 2010.

Brown, William. "Contemporary Mainstream Cinema Is Good for You: Connections between Surrealism and Today's Digital Blockbuster." *Studies in European Cinema* 6, no. 1 (2009): 17–29.

Butler, Judith. *Precarious Life: The Power of Mourning and Violence*. New York: Verso, 2006.

———. *Frames of War: When Is Life Grievable?* New York: Verso, 2009.

Cacho, Lisa Marie. *Social Death: Racialized Rightlessness and the Criminalization of the Unprotected*. New York: New York University Press, 2012.

Camacho, Alicia Schmidt. *Migrant Imaginaries: Latino Cultural Politics in the U.S.-Mexico Borderlands*. New York: New York University Press, 2008.

Capino, José B. *Dream Factories of a Former Colony: American Fantasies, Philippine Cinema*. Minneapolis: University of Minnesota Press, 2010.

Caquard, Sebastien. "Foreshadowing Contemporary Digital Cartography: A Historical Review of Cinematic Maps in Films." *Cartographic Journal* 46 (2009): 44–55.

Carroll, Amy Sara. "'Accidental Allegories' Meet 'the Performative Documentary': *Boystown*, *Señorita Extraviada*, and the Border-Brothel→Maquiladora Paradigm." *Signs* 31, no. 2 (2006): 357–396.

———. "From *Papapapá* to *Sleep Dealer*: Alex Rivera's Undocumentary Poetics." *Social Identities* 19, nos. 3–4 (2013): 485–500.

Cassano, Franco. *Il pensiero mediterraneo*. Rome: Laterza, 1996.

Castro, Teresa. "Cinema's Mapping Impulse: Questioning Visual Culture." *Cartographic Journal* 46, no. 1(2009): 9–15.

Castro Caycedo, Germán. *El hueco*. Bogotá: Editorial Planeta Colombiana, 1989.

Cepeda, María Elena. *Musical ImagiNation: U.S-Colombian Identity and the Latin Music Boom*. New York: New York University Press, 2010.

Chambers, Iain. *Mediterranean Crossings: The Politics of an Interrupted Modernity*. Durham, N.C.: Duke University Press, 2008.

Chanan, Michael. *Cuban Cinema*. Minneapolis: University of Minnesota Press, 2003.

Chávez, Leo. *The Latino Threat: Constructing Immigrants, Citizens, and the Nation*. Stanford, Calif.: Stanford University Press, 2013.

Chee, Fabio. "Science Fiction and Latino Studies Today . . . and in the Future." In *The Routledge Companion to Latina/o Pop Culture*, edited by Frederick Luis Aldama, 110–119. New York: Routledge, 2016.

Cohan, Steven, and Ina Rae Hark, eds. *The Road Movie Book*. New York: Routledge, 1997.

Conley, Tom. *Cartographic Cinema*. Minneapolis: University of Minnesota Press, 2006.

Cortés-Conde, Florencia. "Telling Identities: Crime Narratives for Local and International Markets in *María, Full of Grace* (Marston, 2004) and *Rosario Tijeras* (Maillé, 2005)." *Studies in Latin American Popular Culture* 29 (2011): 80–101.

Costa, Barbara. "Tom Tykwer's *Run Lola Run* and the Usual Suspects: The Avant-Garde, Popular Culture, and History." In *German Pop Culture: How American Is It?*, edited by Agnes C. Müller, 165–179. Ann Arbor: University of Michigan Press, 2004.

Cubilié, Anne. *Women Witnessing Terror: Testimony and Cultural Politics of Human Rights*. New York: Fordham University Press, 2005.

Debord, Guy. "Report on the Construction of Situations and on the International Situationist Tendency's Conditions of Organization and Action (1957)," translated by Ken Knabb. Situationist International Online, http://www.cddc.vt.edu/sionline/si/report.html.

———. "Two Accounts of the Dérive." In *On the Passage of a Few People through a Rather Brief Moment in Time: The Situationist International 1957–1972*, edited by Elisabeth Sussman, 135–139. Cambridge, Mass.: MIT Press, 1989.

De Certeau, Michel. *The Practice of Everyday Life*. Berkeley: University of California Press, 1984.

De la Moya, Sergio. "Terrorismo de género en la frontera México-EUA: asesinato, mujeres, y justicia en *Señorita Extraviada*." *El ojo que piensa*, August 2003, http://www.elojoquepiensa.cucsh.udg.mx/index.html (accessed on July 11, 2009).

De la Torre, Michelle Rocío Nasser. "*Bellas por naturaleza*: Mapping National Identity on U.S. Colombian Beauty Queens." *Latino Studies* 11, no. 3 (2013): 293–312.

Deleuze, Gilles. *Cinema 1: The Movement-Image*, translated by Hugh Tomlinson and Barbara Habberjam. Minneapolis: University of Minnesota Press, 1986.

———. *Cinema 2: The Time-Image*, translated by Hugh Tomlinson and Barbara Habberjam. Minneapolis: University of Minnesota Press, 1989.

Deleuze, Gilles, and Félix Guattari. *A Thousand Plateaus*, translated by Brian Massumi. London; New York: Continuum, 1988.

Delgadillo, Theresa. *Spiritual Mestizaje: Religion, Gender, Race, and Nation in Contemporary Chicana Narrative*. Durham, N.C.: Duke University Press, 2011.

Derrida, Jacques. "A Self-Unsealing Poetic Text: Poetics and the Politics of Witnessing." In *Revenge of the Aesthetic: The Place of Literature in Theory Today*, edited by Michael P. Clark, 180–207. Berkeley: University of California Press, 2000.

———. *Of Hospitality*, translated by Rachel Bowlby. Stanford, Calif.: Stanford University Press, 2000.

Desai, Jigna. *Beyond Bollywood: The Cultural Politics of South Asian Diasporic Film*. New York: Routledge, 2004.

Doane, Mary Ann. *The Emergence of Cinematic Time: Modernity, Contingency, the Archive*. Cambridge, Mass.: Harvard University Press, 2002.

Dueñas, Michael. "The Maricris Sioson Story: A Dance with Death." *Philippines Free Press*, November 2, 1991.

Eleftheriotis, Dimitris. "*A Touch of Spice*: Mobility and Popularity." In *Greek Cinema: Texts, Histories, Identities*, edited by Lydia Papadimitriou and Yiannis Tzioumakis, 18–36. Bristol, England: Intellect, 2011.

Elsaesser, Thomas. *European Cinema: Face to Face with Hollywood.* Amsterdam: Amsterdam University Press, 2005.

———. "Real Location, Fantasy Space, Performative Place: Double Occupancy and Mutual Interference in European Cinema." In *European Film Theory*, edited by Temenuga Trifona, 47–62. New York: Routledge, 2009.

Engler, Mark. "Science Fiction from Below: Alex Rivera, Director of the New Film Sleep Dealer, Imagines the Future of the Global South." Foreign Policy in Focus, http://fpif.org/science_fiction_from_below/.

Epstein, Jean. "On Certain Characteristics of Photogénie." In *French Film Theory and Criticism: A History/Anthology*, vol. 1, *1907–1929*, edited by Richard Abel, 314–318. Princeton, N.J.: Princeton University Press, 1988.

Faier, Lieba. *Intimate Encounters: Filipina Women and the Remaking of Rural Japan.* Berkeley: University of California Press, 2009.

Fanon, Frantz. *The Wretched of the Earth*, translated by Richard Philcox. New York: Grove Press, 1963.

Farago, Jason. "Iñárritu's 'Carne y Arena' Virtual Reality Simulates a Harrowing Border Trek." *New York Times*, May 17, 2017, https://www.nytimes.com/2017/05/17/arts/design/alejandro-gonzalez-inarritu-carne-y-arena-virtual-reality-cannes.html?_r=0.

Feldstein, Ariel F. *Cinema and Zionism: The Development of a Nation through Film.* Portland, Ore.: Vallentine Mitchell, 2012.

Felman, Shoshana, and Dori Laub. *Testimony: Crises of Witnessing in Literature, Psychoanalysis, and History.* New York: Routledge, 1991.

Flores, Juan. *From Bomba to Hip-Hop: Puerto Rican Culture and Latino Identity.* New York: Columbia University Press, 2000.

Fox, Claire. *The Fence and the River: Culture and Politics at the U.S.-Mexican Border.* Minneapolis: University of Minnesota Press, 1999.

Franco, Jorge. *Paradise Travel*, translated by Katherine Silver. New York: Farrar, Straus and Giroux, 2006.

———. *Paraíso Travel.* Bogotá: Editorial Planeta Colombiana, 2001.

Fregoso, Rosa-Linda. "California Filming: Reimagining the Nation." In *Art/Women/California, 1950–2000: Parallels and Intersections*, edited by Diana Burgess Fuller and Daniela Salvioni, 257–274. Berkeley: University of California Press, 2003.

———, ed. *Feminicidio en América Latina.* México City: Universidad Nacional Autónoma de México/Centro de Investigaciones Interdisciplinarias en Ciencias y Humanidades, 2011.

———. "Introduction: Tracking the Politics of Love." In *Lourdes Portillo:* The Devil Never Sleeps *and Other Films*, edited by Rosa-Linda Fregoso, 1–23. Austin: University of Texas Press, 2001.

———. *meXicana Encounters: The Making of Social Identities on the Borderlands.* Berkeley: University of California Press, 2003.

———. "Sacando los trapos al sol (Airing Dirty Laundry) in Lourdes Portillo's Melodocumentary *The Devil Never Sleeps.*" In *Redirecting the Gaze: Gender, Theory, and Cinema in the Third World*, edited by Diana Robin and Ira Jaffe, 307–330. Albany: State University of New York Press, 1998.

———. "Transforming Terror: Lourdes Portillo's *Señorita Extraviada* (2001)." In *A Companion to Contemporary Documentary Film*, edited by Alisa Lebow and Alexandra Juhasz, 233–251. Hoboken, N.J.: Wiley-Blackwell, 2015.

———. "Voices without Echo: The Global Gendered Apartheid." *Emergences* 10, no. 1 (2000): 137–155.

———. "'We Want Them Alive!': The Politics and Culture of Human Rights." *Social Identities* 12, no. 2 (2006): 109–138.

Fregoso, Rosa-Linda, and Cynthia Bejarano, eds. *Terrorizing Women: Feminicide in the Américas.* Durham, N.C.: Duke University Press, 2010.

Frodon, Jean-Michel. "Borders and Women." In *Munio Weinraub/Amos Gitai: Architecture and Film in Israel*, 256–274. Munich: Minerva Editions, 2008.

Galt, Rosalind. *The New European Cinema: Redrawing the Map.* New York: Columbia University Press, 2006.

Gerould, Daniel. "The Americanization of Melodrama." In *American Melodrama*, edited by Daniel Gerould, 7–29. New York: Performing Arts Journal Publications, 1983.

Gertz, Nurith, Gal Hermoni, and Yael Munk. "*Kedma* (Amos Gitai): The Birth of Two Nations at War in 1948." In *Film and the Middle East and North Africa: Creative Dissidence*, edited by Josef Gugler, 167–176. Austin: University of Texas Press, 2011.

Gertz, Nurith, and Raz Yosef. *Traces of Days to Come: Trauma and Ethics in Contemporary Israeli Cinema.* Tel Aviv: Am Oved, 2017.

———. "Television in a Time of Terror: Trauma and Singular Plurality in the Series *Fauda*," edited by Miri Talmon. London; New York: Routledge, forthcoming.

Gitai, Amos, and Annette Michelson. "Filming Israel: A Conversation." *October* 98 (2001): 47–70.

González, Christopher. "Latino Sci-Fi: Cognition and Narrative Design in Alex Rivera's *Sleep Dealer*." In *Latinos and Narrative Media: Participation and Portrayal*, edited by Frederick Luis Aldama, 211–223. New York: Palgrave Macmillan, 2013.

González Iñárritu, Alejandro. "Alejandro Gonzalez Inarritu's LACMA Speech 'Undocumented Dreamers,'" *Variety*, November 8, 2015, https://variety.com/2015/scene/vpage/alejandro-gonzalez-inarritu-undocumented-dreamers-immigration-lacma-1201636134/.

Goodwin, Matthew. "The Technology of Labor, Migration, and Protest." In *The Routledge Companion to Latina/o Pop Culture*, edited by Frederick Luis Aldama, 120–128. New York: Routledge, 2016.

Grieveson, Lee. "Fighting Films: Race, Morality, and the Governing of Cinema, 1912–1915." In *The Silent Cinema Reader*, edited by Lee Grieveson and Peter Kramer, 169–186. New York: Routledge, 2003.

Gruesz, Kirsten Silva. "The Gulf of Mexico System and the 'Latinness' of New Orleans." *American Literary History* 18, no. 3 (2006): 468–495.

Guerin, Frances, and Roger Hallas. "Introduction." In *The Image and the Witness: Trauma, Memory, and Visual Culture*, edited by Frances Guerin and Roger Hallas, 1–20. London: Wallflower, 2007.

Haney López, Ian. *Dog Whistle Politics: How Coded Racial Appeals Have Reinvented Racism and Wrecked the Middle Class.* New York: Oxford University Press, 2015.

Harford Vargas, Jennifer. "The Undocumented Subjects of el Hueco: Theorizing a Colombian Metaphor for Migration." *Symbolism: An International Annual of Critical Aesthetics* 17 (2017): 31–53.

Hassapopoulou, Marina. "*Babel*: Pushing and Reaffirming Mainstream Cinema's Boundaries." *Jump Cut* 50 (2008), http://www.ejumpcut.org/archive/jc50.2008/Babel/text.html.

———. "Reconfiguring Film Studies through Software Cinema and Procedural Spectatorship." *NECSUS: European Journal of Media Studies* 3, no. 2 (2014), http://www.necsus-ejms.org/reconfiguring-film-studies-software-cinema-procedural-spectatorship/.

Hazaz, Haim, "The Sermon." In *The Sermon and Other Stories*, 219–237. New Milford, CT: Toby Press, 2005.

Hefetz, Fabiana. 1996. "Amos Gitai Dared Touching the Glorious and Almost Sacred 'Memorandum' by Yaakov Shabtai." *Tel-Aviv*, November 29, 1996.

Heredia, Juanita. "South American Latino/a Writers in the United States." In *The Routledge Companion to Latino/a Literature*, edited by Suzanne Bost and Frances R. Aparicio, 436–444. New York: Routledge, 2013.

Herrera, Santiago. "Qué diablos es ficción y qué documental?" *Kinetoscopio* 9 (1998): 45–47.

Hetherington, Kevin. "Spatial textures: place, touch, and praesentia," *Environment and Planning A*, vol. 23 (2003): 1933–1944.

Hillman, Roger. "*Goodbye Lenin* (2003): History in the Subjunctive." *Rethinking History* 10 (2006): 221–237.

Hilsdon, Anne-Marie. "The Contemplacion Fiasco: The Hanging of a Filipino Domestic Worker in Singapore." In *Human Rights and Gender Politics: Asia-Pacific Perspectives*, edited by Martha Macintyre, Anne-Marie Hilsdon, Vera Mackie, and Maila Stivens, 172–192. London: Routledge, 2000.

Hjorth, Larissa, and Sun Sun Lim. "Mobile Intimacy in an Age of Affective Mobile Media." *Feminist Media Studies* 12, no. 4 (2012): 477–484.

Imre, Anikó. *Identity Games: Globalization and the Transformation of Media Cultures in the New Europe.* Cambridge, Mass.: MIT Press, 2009.

Jameson, Fredric. *Postmodernism; or, the Cultural Logic of Late Capitalism.* Durham, N.C.: Duke University Press, 1995.

Kandiyoti, Deniz. "Identity and Its Discontents: Women and the Nation." In *Colonial Discourse and Post-Colonial Theory: A Reader*, edited by Patrick Williams and Laura Chrisman, 376–391. New York: Columbia University Press, 1994.

Kantaris, Geoffrey. "Desreferenciar lo real: Paisajes mediáticos en los documentales de Carlos Marcovich (*¿Quién diablos es Juliette? y Cuatro labios*)." *Revista Iberoamericana* 81, no. 251 (2015): 627–644.

Kemp, Adriana. "Border, Space and National Identity." *Theory and Criticism* 16 (2000): 13–43.

Kempadoo, Kamala. *Sexing the Caribbean: Gender, Race, and Sexual Labor.* New York: Routledge, 2004.

Kinder, Marsha. "Narrative Equivocations between Movies and Games." In *The New Media Book*, edited by Dan Harries, 119–132. London: British Film Institute, 2002.

Klein, Norman M., Rosemary Comella, Andreas Kratky, and Marsha Kinder. *Bleeding Through: Layers of Los Angeles 1920–1986.* DVD-ROM and book. Los Angeles: Annenberg Center for Communication, University of Southern California, 2003.

Kunitz, Stephen J. "The Making and Breaking of Yugoslavia and Its Impact on Health." *American Journal of Public Health* 94, no. 11 (2004): 1894–1904.

Lazzarato, Mauricio. "Immaterial Labor." In *Radical Thought in Italy: A Potential Politics*, edited by Paolo Virno and Michael Hardt, 133–147. Minnesota: University of Minnesota Press, 2006.

Lefebvre, Henri. *The Production of Space*, translated by Donald Nicholson-Smith. New York: Wiley-Blackwell, 1992.

Liz, Mariana. "From Europe with Love: Urban Space and Cinematic Postcards." *Studies in European Cinema* 11, no. 1 (2014): 3–13.

Lomas, Laura. *Translating Empire: José Martí, Migrant Latino Subjects, and American Modernities*. Durham, N.C.: Duke University Press, 2009.

Los Angeles County Museum of Art. "*Carne y Arena*: About the Exhibition," July 2, 2017–July 1, 2018, http://www.lacma.org/carne-y-arena#about-the-exhibition.

Manovich, Lev. *The Language of New Media*. Cambridge, Mass.: MIT Press, 2001.

Manovich, Lev, and Andreas Kratky. *Soft Cinema: Navigating the Database*. Cambridge, Mass.: MIT Press, 2005.

Marc, Franz. "Im Fegefever des Krieges" [In the purgatory of war], *Vossische Zeitung*, December 15, 1914.

———. *Letters from the War*, edited by Klaus Lanheit and Uwe Steffen. Translated by Liselotte Dieckmann. New York: Lang, 1992.

Marcantonio, Carla. "Border-Crossing the Global Imaginary: *The Bubble* and *Babel*." In *Global Melodrama: Nation, Body, and History in Contemporary Film*, 79–109. New York: Palgrave Macmillan, 2015.

Marks, Laura U. *The Skin of the Film: Intercultural Cinema, Embodiment, and the Senses*. Durham, N.C.: Duke University Press, 2000.

Martí, José. "Letter to Manuel Mercado." In *Selected Writings*, trans. Esther Allen, 347. New York: Penguin, 2002.

Martin, Deborah. "Spectatorship, Performance, Resistance: Carlos Marcovich's *¿Quién Diablos Es Juliette? Journal of Latin American Cultural Studies* 15, no. 3 (2006): 341–353.

Mesch, Claudia. "Racing Berlin: The Games of Run Lola Run." *Journal of Media Culture* 3, no. 3 (2000), http://journal.media-culture.org.au/0006/berlin.php.

Mezzadra, Stefano. *Diritto di fuga. Migrazioni, cittadinanza, globalizzazione*. Verona, Italy: Ombre corte, 2001.

Mezzadra, Stefano, and Brett Nielson. *Border as Method, or, the Multiplication of Labor*. Durham, N.C.: Duke University Press, 2013.

Mignolo, Walter. *The Darker Side of Western Modernity: Global Futures, Decolonial Options*. Durham, N.C.: Duke University Press, 2011.

Minich, Julie. "Rehabilitating Neoliberalism: Disability Representation in the Films of Alejandro González Iñárritu and Guillermo Arriaga." *Journal of Popular Culture* 48, no. 5 (2015): 970–989.

Mora, Sergio de la. "Terrorismo de género en la frontera de EUA-México." *Cinémas d'Amérique Latine* 12 (2004): 116–132.

Muir, Dana. "A Land without a People for a People without a Land." *Middle Eastern Quarterly* 15, no. 2 (2008): 55–62.

Munk, Yael. "Déplacement du mythe du *Sabra*: L'adaptation cinématographique de *Pour Inventaire* de Yaakov Shabtai par Amos Gitai." *Yod: Revue des Études Hébraïques et Juives* 14 (2009): 303–317.

Naaman, Dorit. "A Rave against the Occupation? Speaking for the Self and Excluding the Other in Contemporary Israeli Political Cinema." In *Israeli Cinema:*

Identification in Motion, edited by Miri Talmon and Yaron Peleg, 257–275. Austin: University of Texas Press, 2011.

Naficy, Hamid. *An Accented Cinema: Exhilic and Diasporic Filmmaking.* Princeton, N.J.: Princeton University Press, 2001.

Nancy, Jean-Luc. *Being Singular Plural,* translated by Robert Richardson and Anne O'Byrne. Stanford, Calif.: Stanford University Press, 2000.

Naples, Nancy A. "Borderlands Studies and Border Theory: Linking Activism and Scholarship for Social Justice." *Sociology Compass* 4, no. 7 (2010): 505–518.

Nasser, Michelle Rocío. "Tra(n)zando Identidades: Colombian Neighborhoods, Images, and Narratives from Narco-Trafficking to Beauty Queens." PhD diss., Tulane University, 2008.

Ngai, Mae. *Impossible Subjects: Illegal Aliens and the Making of Modern America.* Princeton, N.J.: Princeton University Press, 2004.

Nichols, Bill. *Introduction to Documentary.* Bloomington: Indiana University Press, 2001.

Oboler, Suzanne. "Introduction: *Los que llegarón*: 50 Years of South American Immigration (1950–2000)—An Overview." *Latino Studies* 3, no. 1 (2005): 42–52.

Ochoa Camacho, Ariana. "Living with Drug Lords and Mules in New York: Contrasting Colombian Criminality and Transnational Belonging." In *The Immigrant Other: Lived Experiences in a Transnational World*, edited by Rich Furman, Greg Lamphear, and Douglas Epps, 166–179. New York: Columbia University Press, 2016.

Oliver, Kelly. *Women as Weapons of War.* New York: Columbia University Press, 2007.

Parreñas, Rhacel Salazar. *The Force of Domesticity: Filipina Migrants and Globalization.* New York: New York University Press, 2008).

———. "Transgressing the Nation-State: The Partial Citizenship and 'Imagined (Global) Community' of Migrant Filipina Domestic Workers." *Signs: Journal of Women in Culture and Society* 26, no. 4 (2001): 1129–1154.

Perales, Monica. "On *Borderlands/La Frontera:* Gloria Anzaldúa and Twenty-Five Years of Research on Gender in the Borderlands." *Journal of Women's History* 25, no. 4 (2013): 163–173.

Perna, Vincenzo A. "Selling Cuba by the Sound: Music and Tourism in Cuba in the 1990s. " In *Sun, Sea, and Sound: Music and Tourism in the Circum-Caribbean,* edited by Timothy Rommen and Daniel T. Neely, 44–72. Oxford: Oxford University Press, 2014.

Peters, John Durham. "Exile, Nomadism, and Diaspora: The Stakes of Mobility in the Western Canon." In *Home, Exile, Homeland: Film, Media and the Politics of Place,* edited by Hamid Naficy, 17–41. New York: Routledge, 1999.

Piotrowska, Agnieszka. "Animating the Real: A Case Study." *Animation: An Interdisciplinary Journal* 6, no. 3 (2011): 335–351.

Portillo, Lourdes. "Filming *Señorita Extraviada.*" *Aztlán* 28, no. 2 (2003): 229–234.

Ramírez, Catherine. "Afrofuturism/Chicanafuturism: Fictive Kin." *Aztlán* 33, no. 1 (2008): 185–194.

Renov, Michael, ed. *Theorizing Documentary.* New York: Routledge/American Film Institute, 1993.

Riofrio, John D. "Rio." *Continental Shifts: Migration, Representation, and the Struggle for Justice in Latin(o) America.* Austin: University of Texas Press, 2015.

Roberts, Brian Russell, and Michelle Stephens. "Special Forum: Archipelagic American Studies and the Caribbean." *Journal of Transnational American Studies*, 5, no. 1 (2013): 1–20, https://cloudfront.escholarship.org/dist/prd/content/qt52f2966r/qt52f2966r.pdf?t=ncgsql.

Rodriguez, Robyn Magalit. *Migrants for Export: How the Philippine State Brokers Labor to the World*. Minneapolis: University of Minnesota Press, 2010.

Rosaldo, Renato. "Cultural Citizenship, Inequality, and Multiculturalism." In *Latino Cultural Citizenship: Claiming Identity, Space, and Rights*, edited by William F. Flores and Rina Benmayor, 27–38. Boston: Beacon, 1997.

Rosello, Mireille. "Imagining European Subjects as Chaotic Borders: Cédric Klapisch's *Pot Luck* and *The Russian Dolls*." In *Zoom In, Zoom Out: Crossing Borders in Contemporary European Cinema*, edited by Sandra Barriales-Bouche and Marjorie Attignol Salvodon, 16–33. Newcastle, England: Cambridge Scholars, 2007.

Santa Ana, Otto. *Brown Tide Rising: Metaphors of Latinos in Contemporary American Public Discourse*. Austin: University of Texas Press, 2002.

Saona, Margarita. "Migrant Mothers: The Domestication of Latina Images for the Global Market." *Letras femeninas* 34, no. 1 (2008): 125–145.

Sassen, Saskia. *Guests and Aliens*. New York: New Press, 1999.

Schmitt, Carl. *Political Theology: Four Chapters on the Concept of Political Sovereignty*. Edited and translated by George Schmitt. Chicago: University of Chicago Press, 2005.

Schrieber, Rebecca M. "The Undocumented Everyday: Migrant Rights and Visual Strategies in the Work of Alex Rivera." *Journal of American Studies* 50, no. 2 (2016): 305–327.

Schultermandl, Silvia. "From Drug Mule to Miss America: American Exceptionalism and the Commodification of the "Other" Woman in *María Full of Grace*." *Journal of American Culture* 34, no. 3 (2011): 275–288.

Scott, A.O. "Emotion Needs No Translation." *New York Times*, October 27, 2006, http://www.nytimes.com/2006/10/27/movies/27babe.html.

Shohat, Ella, and Robert Stam. "Introduction." In *Multiculturalism, Postcoloniality, and Transnational Media*, edited by Ella Shohat and Robert Stam, 1–17. New Brunswick, N.J.: Rutgers University Press, 2003.

Sieg, Katrin. *Choreographing the Global in European Cinema and Theater*. New York: Palgrave Macmillan, 2008.

Silverstein, Richard. "'Chad Gadya,' Chava Alberstein Protest against Israeli Militarism," August 10, 2006, https://www.richardsilverstein.com/2006/08/10/chad-gadya-chava-alberstein-protest-against-israeli-militarism/.

Sinka, Margit. "Tom Tykwer's *Lola rennt*: A Blueprint of Millennial Berlin." *Glossen* 11 (June 2000), http://www2.dickinson.edu/glossen/heft11/lola.html.

Smith, Damon. "Cinema in a State of Conflict: Interview with Amos Gitaï." *Senses of Cinema* 42 (2007), http://sensesofcinema.com/2007/cinema-engage/amos-gitai-interview/.

Sobchack, Vivian. *Carnal Thoughts: Embodiment and Moving Image Culture*. Berkeley: University of California Press, 2004.

Soja, Edward. *Thirdspace: Journeys to Los Angeles and Other Real-and-Imagined Places*. Malden, Mass.: Blackwell, 1996.

Sontag, Susan. *On Photography*. London: Penguin, 1977.

———. *Regarding the Pain of Others*. New York: Farrar, Straus and Giroux, 2003.

Speier, Hans. "Magic Geography." *Social Research* 8, no. 3 (1941): 310–330.

Stephens, Michelle, and Brian Russell Roberts. "Archipelagic American Studies and the Caribbean." *The Journal of Transamerican Studies* 5, no. 1 (2013): 1–20.

Stratford, Elaine, Godfrey Baldacchino, Elizabeth McMahon, Carol Farbotko, and Andrew Harwood. "Envisioning the Archipelago." *Island Studies Journal* 6, no. 2 (2011): 113–130.

Suárez, Lucía M. "Consuming Cubanas: *¿Quién diablos es Juliette?*" *Cuban Studies* 42 (2011): 155–171.

Takahashi, Tess. "Experiments in Documentary Animation: Anxious Borders, Speculative Media." *Animation: An Interdisciplinary Journal* 6, no. 3 (2011): 231–245.

Taylor, Diana. *Disappearing Acts: Spectacles of Gender and Nationalism in Argentina's Dirty War.* Durham, N.C.: Duke University Press, 2003.

Tesson, Charles. "Le Chemin de Jerusalem." *Cahiers du Cinema* 568 (2002): 1–30.

Tierney, Dolores. "Alejandro González Iñárritu: Director without Borders." *New Cinemas: Journal of Contemporary Film* 7, no. 2 (2009): 101–117.

Tolentino, Rolando B. "Female Work and Representation in Women's Films." *Philippine Studies* 57, no. 3 (2009): 419–442.

"Tonto corazón." Performer Benny Ibarra, https://www.youtube.com/watch?v=x6kbiqA7ZgY.

Torres-Saillant, Silvio. "Pitfalls of Latino Chronologies: South and Central Americans." *Latino Studies* 5, no. 4 (2007): 489–502.

Trinh, T. Minh-ha. "The Totalizing Quest for Meaning." In *When the Moon Waxes Red: Representation, Gender, and Cultural Politics*, 29–50. New York: Routledge, 1991.

———. *Woman, Native, Other: Writing Postcoloniality and Feminism.* Bloomington: Indiana University Press, 1989.

Vera, Noel. "I Left My Brain in San Francisco." *Manila Chronicle*, August 12, 1995.

Vila, Pablo. "Conclusion: The Limits of American Border Theory." In *Ethnography at the Border*, edited by Pablo Vila, 306–342. Minneapolis: University of Minnesota Press, 2003.

Villaseñor, Maria-Christina. "Lourdes Portillo Interview." *Felix: A Journal of Media Arts and Communication* 2, no. 3: *Risk/Riesgo* (2003): 170–178.

Walker, Michael. "Melodrama and American Cinema." *Movie* 29–30 (1982): 2–38.

Wayne, Mike. *The Politics of Contemporary European Cinema: Histories, Borders, Diasporas.* Chicago: University of Chicago Press, 2002.

Weizman, Eyal. *Hollow Land: Israel's Architecture of Occupation*. London; New York: Verso, 2007.

Whitfield, Esther. *Cuban Currency.* Minneapolis: University of Minnesota Press, 2008.

Williams, Linda. "Film Bodies: Gender, Genre, and Excess." In *Film and Theory: An Anthology*, ed. Toby Miller and Robert Stam, 207–221. Malden, Mass.: Blackwell, 2000.

———. "Melodrama Revised." In *Refiguring American Film Genres: History and Theory*, edited by Nick Browne, 42–88. Berkeley: University of California Press, 1998.

Zanger, Anat. "Women, Border, and Camera: Israeli Feminine Framing of War." *Feminist Media Studies* 5, no. 3 (2005): 341–357.

———. *Place, Memory and Myth in Contemporary Israeli Cinema*. London; Portland, Ore.: Vallentine Mitchell, 2012.

Zeitchik, Steven. "In 'Birdman,' Alejandro G. Iñárritu Takes His Doubts and Lets Them Fly." *Los Angeles Times*, October 10, 2014, http://www.latimes.com/entertainment/movies/la-et-mn-ca-birdman-inarritu-20141012-story.html.

Zurbano, Roberto. ""For Blacks in Cuba, the Revolution Hasn't Begun." *The New York Times*, March 23, 2013, http://www.nytimes.com/2013/03/24/opinion/sunday/for-blacks-in-cuba-the-revolution-hasnt-begun.html.

Filmography and Videography

Amélie. Directed by Jean-Pierre Jeunet. France/Germany, 2001.
American Refugees. Web series. Seattle University, 2003–.
Amores perros/Love's a bitch. Directed by Alejandro González Iñárritu. United States, 2000.
Babel. Directed by Alejandro González Iñárritu. United States, 2006.
The Battle of Chile. Directed by Patricio Guzman. Chile, 1975, 1976, 1979.
Boreg/Self Made. Directed by Shira Geffen. Israel, 2014.
The Bridge. TV series, FX. United States, 2013–2014.
Corpus: A Home Movie about Selena. Directed by Lourdes Portillo. United States, 1998.
Daughters of the Dust. Directed by Julie Dash. United States, 1992.
Deus e o diabo na terra do sol/Black God, White Devil. Directed by Glauber Rocha. Brazil, 1964.
The Devil Never Sleeps. Directed by Lourdes Portillo. United States, 1995.
Dyketactics. Directed by Barbara Hammer. United States, 1974.
Eden. Directed by Amos Gitai. France/Israel/Italy, 2001.
Eurotrip. Directed by Jeff Schaffer, Alec Berg, and David Mandel. Czech Republic and United States, 2004.
Ezor Hofshi/Free Zone. Directed by Amos Gitai. Belgium/France/Israel/Spain, 2005.
Frontline. "Mapping the Black Sites." TV episode, PBS. United States, n.d.
Fuocoammare/Fire at Sea. Directed by Gianfranco Rosi. Italy, 2016.
Gömd/Hidden. Directed by Hanna Heilborn and David Aronowitsch with Mats Johansson. Sweden, 2002.
Ha'aretz Hamuvtachat/Promised Land. Directed by Amos Gitai. France/Israel, 2004.
History and Memory. Directed by Rea Tajiri. United States, 1991.
Im Juli/In July. Directed by Fatih Akin. Germany/Turkey, 2000.
In My Life. Directed by Olivia Lamasan. Philippines, 2009.
Itnatkut/Disengagement. Directed by Amos Gitai. France/Germany/Israel/Italy, 2007.
It's Like That. Directed by Southern Ladies Animation Group. Australia, 2005
Kedma. Directed by Amos Gitai. France/Israel/Italy, 2002.

Killer.berlin.doc. Directed by Tina Ellerkamp and Jörg Heitmann. Germany, 1999.

Kippur. Directed by Amos Gitai. France/Israel, 2000.

La hora de los hornos/The Hour of the Furnaces. Directed by Fernando Solanas and Octavio Getino. Argentina, 1968.

Las Madres: The Mothers of the Plaza de Mayo. Directed by Lourdes Portillo. Argentina, 1985.

L'auberge espagnole/The Spanish Apartment. Directed by Cédric Klapisch. France/Spain, 2002.

Lola rennt/Run Lola Run. Directed by Tom Tykwer. Germany, 1998.

Madeni mesec/Honeymoons. Directed by Goran Paskaljevic. Albania/Serbia, 2009.

Maquilopolis. Directed by Vicki Funari and Sergio de la Torre. Mexico/United States, 2006.

Maria Full of Grace. Directed by Joshua Marston. Colombia/Ecuador/United States, 2004.

Maricris Sioson: Japayuki/The Maricris Sioson Story: Japayuki. Directed by Joey Romero. Philippines, 1993.

Mavet Be-Beer Sheva/Death in the Terminal. Directed by Tali Shemesh and Assaf Sudry. Israel, 2016.

Measures of Distance. Directed by Mona Hatoum. England, 1988.

Me'Ever Laharim Vehagvaot/Beyond Mountains and Hills. Directed by Eran Kolirin. Israel, 2015.

Miss X. Directed by Gil Portes. Philippines, 1980.

Nadia Shem Zmani/AKA Nadia. Directed by Tova Asher. Israel, 2015.

Narco Cultura. Directed by Shaul Schwarz. Mexico/United States, 2013.

Paraíso Travel/Paradise Travel. Directed by Simón Brand. Colombia/United States, 2008.

Politiki Kouzina/A Touch of Spice. Directed by Tassos Boulmetis. Greece/Turkey, 2003.

¿Quién diablos es Juliette?/Who the Hell Is Juliette? Directed by Carlos Marcovich. Mexico, 1997.

Rabin, HaYom Aahron/Rabin, the Last Day. Directed by Amos Gitai. France/Israel, 2015.

Reassemblage. Directed by Trinh T. Minh-ha. Senegal, 1982.

Running for Freedom. Directed by Agniezka Piotrowska. United States, 2003–2004.

Sana Maulit Muli/Hopefully, Once More. Directed by Olivia Lamasan. Philippines, 1995.

Seeking Refuge. TV miniseries, BBC. England, 2012.

Señorita extraviada/Missing Young Woman. Directed by Lourdes Portillo. Mexico, 2002.

Sharaf. Directed by Hanna Heilborn and David Aronowitsch. Sweden, 2013.

Shoah. Directed by Claude Lanzmann. France, 1982.

Slaves. Directed by Hanna Heilborn and David Aronowitsch. Sweden, 2008.

Sleep Dealer. Directed by Alex Rivera. Mexico/United States, 2008.

Stranger Comes to Town. Directed by Jacqueline Goss. United States, 2006.

Transit. Directed by Hannah Espia. Israel/Philippines/Thailand, 2013.

21 Grams. Directed by Alejandro González Iñárritu. United States, 2003.

Walz im Bashir/Waltz with Bashir. Directed by Ari Folman. France/Germany/Israel/United States, 2008.

Notes on Contributors

MONICA HANNA is an associate professor of Chicana and Chicano studies at California State University, Fullerton, specializing in U.S. Latina/o literary and cultural studies. She is coeditor (with Jennifer Harford Vargas and José David Saldívar) of *Junot Díaz and the Decolonial Imagination*. Her work has appeared in *American Literature*, *Callaloo*, *Metamorphoses*, *Quaderni del '900*, and *Latino/a Literature in the Classroom*.

REBECCA A. SHEEHAN is an associate professor of cinema and television arts at California State University, Fullerton. Beyond topics in border cinema, she works at the intersections of avant-garde cinema and film philosophy and the interface of the sculptural arts and cinema. Her work has appeared in *Screening the Past*, *Screen*, the *Journal of Modern Literature*, *Discourse*, *Interdisciplinary 19*, and in various edited collections. She is the author of *American Avant-Garde Cinema and the Ethics of the In-Between*.

FREDERICK LUIS ALDAMA is Arts and Humanities Distinguished Professor of English, Spanish, and Portuguese as well as University Distinguished Scholar at Ohio State University. He is the editor and author of twenty-one books, including *The Cinema of Robert Rodriguez*.

JOSÉ B. CAPINO is an associate professor of English and cinema and media studies at the University of Illinois, Urbana-Champaign. He is the author of *Dream Factories of a Former Colony: American Fantasies, Philippine Cinema*, winner of the 2012 Cultural Studies Book Award from the Association for Asian American Studies. His essays on film have appeared in *Film Comment*, *Cinema Journal*, *Jump Cut*, and *Animation Journal*.

ROSA-LINDA FREGOSO is a professor of Latin American and Latino studies at the University of California, Santa Cruz. Her publications cover issues of human rights, feminicide, gender and racial violence, media and visual arts, and cultural politics in the Américas. Her publications include *Terrorizing Women: Feminicide in the Américas* (coedited with Cynthia Bejarano), *meXicana Encounters: The Making of Social Identities on the Borderlands*, and *The Bronze Screen: Chicana and Chicano Film Culture*.

NURITH GERTZ is a professor emerita of Hebrew literature and film at the Open University of Israel and full professor in the Department of Culture Creation and Production at Sapir Academic College. She has served as head of the Cinema Studies Program in the Department of Film and Television at Tel Aviv University and headed the Department of Culture Creation and Production at Sapir Academic College. She won the Brenner Prize for Literature in 2009 for her book *Unrepentant*, which was also nominated for the Sapir Prize for Literature. Among her recent books are *Captive of a Dream: National Myths in Israeli Culture*; *Holocaust Survivors, Aliens and Others in Israeli Cinema* (in Hebrew); *Palestinian Cinema: Landscape, Trauma and Memory* (coauthored with George Khleifi); and *An Ocean between Us*.

JENNIFER HARFORD VARGAS is an associate professor of English at Bryn Mawr College. She is the author of *Forms of Dictatorship: Power, Narrative and Authoritarianism in the Latina/o Novel* and coeditor (with Monica Hanna and José David Saldívar) of *Junot Díaz and the Decolonial Imagination*. Her articles have appeared in such journals as *MELUS* and *Callaloo*, as well as the collections *Latina/o Literature in the Classroom: 21st Century Approaches to Teaching* and *Colonialism, Modernity, and the Study of Literature: A View from India*.

MARINA HASSAPOPOULOU is a visiting assistant professor of cinema studies at New York University. Her academic interests include digital media and participatory culture, interactive cinema, transnational cinema, European cinema, digital humanities, and hybrid pedagogy. She has published in journals including *Jump Cut*, *NECSUS: European Journal of Media Studies*, *Alphaville*, the *Journal of Media Arts and Practice*, the *Journal of Interactive Technology and Pedagogy*, the *Journal of the Hellenic Diaspora*, and *Screening the Past* on topics such as digital spectatorship, experimental and Hollywood cinema, fan studies, representations of Hellenism in U.S. media, and experimental pedagogy. She has also authored a chapter on transmedia storytelling and expanded television for the anthology *Writing and the Digital Generation: Essays on New Media Rhetoric*. She is currently working on her book *Interactive Cinema: An Alternative History of Moving Images*, which focuses on participatory experiments in the history of cinema and develops new theoretical frameworks for understanding spectatorship in the digital age. In addition, she is working on a web-based interactive historiographical project on European history through youth-oriented cinema.

ELENA LAHR-VIVAZ is an assistant professor in the Department of Spanish and Portuguese Studies at Rutgers University–Newark, where she specializes in Latin American literature and film. Her first book is *Mexican Melodrama: Film and Nation from the Golden Age to the New Wave*, and she has published articles in the *Journal of American Studies*, *Revista de Estudios Hispánicos*, and *Revista Canadiense de Estudios Hispánicos*. She is at work on her next book-length project, on the negotiation of space and identity in the transnational Cuban archipelago.

YAEL MUNK is a senior lecturer in film at the Open University of Israel. She has published two books in Hebrew: *Exiled in Their Borders: Israeli Cinema between Two Intifada* and, in collaboration with Nurith Gertz, *Looking Back: A Revised History of Israeli Cinema 1948–1990*. Munk's research is concerned with Israeli and Palestinian cinemas, Holocaust studies, criticism of colonialism, postcolonial theory, women's documentary, and gender studies in general.

ANITA PINZI is a researcher whose interests and publications deal with issues of translingualism, postcolonialism, postcommunism, and theory of the body. Her publications include "The Translingual Poetic Subject," in *Shifting and Shaping a National Identity*, and "Corpi-Cerniera," in *Il confine liquido*. She is currently translating into English the poetry collection *Il poema dell'esilio* by Albanian poet Gëzim Hajdari, and a collection of essays on the strategies of politicization of migrant bodies. She teaches philosophy at H. Lavity Stoutt Community College in the British Virgin Islands.

ANAT ZANGER is an associate professor in the Department of Film and Television and chair of the master of arts program in film studies at Tel Aviv University. Her areas of research include Israeli cinema, seriality and repetitions in the media, mythology, collective memory, intertextuality, and space and landscape. She is author of *Film Remakes as Ritual and Disguises* and *Place, Memory and Myth in Contemporary Israeli Cinema*. Her project on Israeli space and cinema has received a grant from the Israeli Science Foundation, as has her recent project on Jerusalem. She is coeditor (with Boaz Hagin, Sandra Meiri, and Raz Yosef) of *Just Images: Ethics and the Cinematic*.

Index